THE NOVELS OF
THE HARLEM RENAISSANCE

Amritjit Singh

THE

THE   HARLEM

TWELVE   BLACK

NOVELS

OF

RENAISSANCE

WRITERS   1923-1933

Cop. a

The Pennsylvania State University Press
University Park and London

Publication of this book has been assisted by
The Ford Foundation Ethnic Studies Program

Library of Congress Cataloging in Publication Data

Singh, Amritjit.
  The novels of the Harlem renaissance.

  Bibliography: p. 153.
  Includes index.
  1. American fiction—Afro-American authors—
History and criticism.   2. American fiction—
20th century—History and criticism.   3. Afro
-Americans in literature.   I. Title.
PS374.N4S5   813'.03   75-27170
ISBN 0-271-01208-0

Printed in the United States of America

PREFACE

This study is based primarily on twenty-one novels published between 1923 and 1933 by twelve black writers of the Harlem Renaissance—Arna Bontemps, Countee Cullen, W.E.B. DuBois, Jessie Redmon Fauset, Rudolph Fisher, Langston Hughes, Nella Larsen, Claude McKay, George S. Schuyler, Wallace Thurman, Jean Toomer, and Walter F. White. It focuses on the intraracial issues of self-definition, class, caste, and color in the works of these writers, using an integrated approach that simultaneously evaluates aesthetic and sociocultural impulses. Organizing the study around a few key themes transfers the emphasis from a discussion of individual authors to a cohesive commentary on the central values suggested by their works as a whole.

Chapter 1 describes and analyzes at length the social, political, and cultural forces at work in the black scene of the twenties, providing the backdrop against which Alain Locke, Charles S. Johnson, and others tried to develop a conscious movement of the black American arts. It also suggests reasons for the failure of the Harlem Renaissance writers to form a literary movement or develop a shared aesthetic and critical outlook on matters relating race to art and literature. In chapters 2 through 5, works are grouped according to thematic affinities; their sequence within each chapter is determined by ideational content. The book discussed last in each chapter culminates the discussion of the selected theme. My analysis of self-definition in chapter 2 confirms that the Afro-American's cultural roots lie overwhelmingly within the range of his American experience. Chapter 3 reveals the class conflicts and distrusts that are deeply embedded in black life. Chapter 4 travels part of the way along the long road traversed by black Americans in their continuing confrontation with American color caste. Chapter 5 underscores the international implications of an intraracial issue that is still moderately important in Afro-America.

The twenty-one novels selected for this study reveal the variety and richness of black writing during the Harlem Renaissance years. I have not included any of the white novelists of the twenties who dealt with black characters and themes. Also absent is Zora Neale Hurston, who, although an active member of the Renaissance, did not publish her first novel until 1934. I have concentrated on novels that attempt to realize the major issues of black American experience as seen and understood by their creators during the twenties. My work barely touches on the possible relationship between the Harlem Renaissance and what Robert Spiller has described as the "Second American Renaissance." I do not presume to have written a definitive history of the Harlem Renaissance in my opening chapter nor have I offered a final judgment on the writers discussed in the others. What follows, then, is only a step toward a general literary study of the Harlem Renaissance.

Although I am responsible for the interpretations in this book, I would be failing in my duty if I did not acknowledge the help and support I received from many individuals, especially the following: Louis J. Budd, Bhim S. Dahiya, Charles T. Davis, Ralph W. Ellison, Michel Fabre, Lee Finkle, Addison Gayle, Jr., William M. Gibson, Jean Blackwell Hutson, Ernest Kaiser, Chris W. Kentera, Akshey Kumar, Edward Margolies, John M. Pickering, J. Saunders Redding, Carole Schwager, James W. Tuttleton, and Jean Fagan Yellin. A very special vote of thanks is due Hale Woodruff for the dust jacket illustration and Marjorie Pavesich and Vern Wagner for their many valuable editing suggestions.

I am deeply indebted to my wife and son, Premjit and Samir Punit, for bearing with me during the difficult days of my research and writing.

Amritjit Singh

CONTENTS

To Darji and Bibiji
my proud parents

"WHEN THE NEGRO WAS IN VOGUE"

THE HARLEM RENAISSANCE AND BLACK AMERICA IN THE TWENTIES

"as Harlem goes, so goes all black America"

Harold Cruse,
The Crisis of the Negro Intellectual

The 1920s in American history were marked by a sociocultural awakening among Afro-Americans. More blacks participated in the arts than ever before, and their number increased steadily throughout the decade. This florescence of creative activity extended to many areas—music, poetry, drama, fiction. In literature, the few Negro novels published between 1905 and 1923 were presented mainly by small firms unable to give their authors a national hearing. However, in the succeeding decade, over two dozen novels by blacks appeared, and most of them were issued by major American publishers.[1]

The needs of this new black self-expression were served by magazines and journals, black as well as white. The twenties gave rise to all-black literary quarterlies and "little magazines," some of rather short duration, such as *Fire, Harlem, Stylus, Quill,* and *Black Opals.* The National Association for the Advancement of Colored People (NAACP) and the National Urban League both published powerful journals, *The Crisis* and *Opportunity* respectively, which encouraged young black writers. *The Messenger,* published by A. Philip Randolph and Chandler Owen, also made stimulating literary contributions from time to time. In addition, the leading journals in America published articles, short stories, poems, and reviews from black writers.

By the middle of the decade, many people had become conscious of this literary upsurge and tried to direct and influence its orientation. Alain Locke, describing himself later as a "midwife" to the younger generation of black writers of the twenties, propounded the concept of a Negro renaissance and tried to develop a movement of black American arts. In March 1925, he edited a special Harlem issue of *Survey Graphic*, which he expanded later that year into an anthology entitled *The New Negro*. This anthology contained the recent work of young black writers and called for continued attempts at racial self-expression within a culturally pluralistic American context. Many black writers answered Locke's call by offering accounts of all strata of black life, from Philadelphia's blue-vein "society" Negroes to Harlem's common folk, including streetwalkers and criminals.

Locke's anthology also initiated a debate on black writing that caused endless controversy in the twenties and continues vigorously today. The term "New Negro," though not original with Locke, caught on in black circles even more than his concept of cultural pluralism. New Negro societies sprang up in several large cities and it became fashionable to declare oneself a member of the New Negro coterie.[2] The fresh interest in the Negro evinced by white writers such as Carl Van Vechten led journals other than *Survey Graphic* to devote entire issues to the Negro. In October 1926, *Palms* featured a "Negro Number" edited by Countee Cullen.[3] Both *The Crisis* and *Opportunity* awarded annual prizes in sponsored literary contests. In 1926, the publishers Albert and Charles Boni offered a $1,000 cash prize in addition to royalties for the best novel about black life written by a Negro. In June of that year, *Publishers' Weekly* noted the increasing contributions to the literary scene by the "colored race."[4]

Some scholars and critics have questioned the use of the term "renaissance" to describe the creative activity of blacks in the twenties. They think the term is misapplied because they see no evidence of an earlier Afro-American tradition. The use of the term renaissance is justified by the intense interest of Afro-American writers in coming to terms with the peculiar racial situation in the United States and in exploring their emotional and historical links with Africa and the American South. This interest is prefigured in the work of the nineteenth-century black writers Frederick Douglass, David Walker, William Wells Brown, Martin R. Delany, and Frances E.W. Harper;[5] it culminates in the poetry, fiction, and essays of Paul Laurence Dunbar, James Weldon Johnson, Charles W. Chesnutt, Sutton E. Griggs, and W.E.B. DuBois in the 1890s. The range of black writing in the twenties, best indicated by *The New Negro*, is also reflected in the fine work done by *The Crisis* and *Opportunity* throughout the period with the active participation of intellectuals such as W.E.B. DuBois, Charles S. Johnson, Sterling Brown, and James Weldon Johnson.

These arguments notwithstanding, critics have failed, so far, to evolve a uniform terminology in discussing the black writers of the twenties. It is generally agreed that the phenomenon referred to as the Negro, Black, or Harlem Renaissance appeared on the American scene during the closing years of World War I, was publicly recognized by men such as Alain Locke and Charles S. Johnson in 1924 or 1925, and had begun declining about the time of the stock market crash in 1929. But the critics John Hope Franklin and Sterling Brown prefer to see the Renaissance as an ongoing movement of black arts since the end of World War I.[6] Robert Bone employs the term "Negro Renaissance" for the nationwide upsurge in black writing during the twenties, describing the young black writers centered in Harlem as the Harlem School. Bone contrasts the Harlem School with the so-called Old Guard, but the Renaissance writers' shared impulses and contradictions render these categories critically confusing rather than helpful.[7] Sterling Brown sums up his refusal to call the New Negro phenomenon of the twenties the "Harlem Renaissance" or even a "renaissance":

> I have hesitated to use the term Negro Renaissance for several reasons: one is that the five or six years generally allotted are short for the life-span of any "renaissance." The New Negro is not to me a group of writers centered in Harlem during the second half of the twenties. Most of the writers were not Harlemites; much of the best writing was not about Harlem, which was the show-window, the cashier's till but no more Negro America than New York is America. The New Negro has temporal roots in the past and spatial roots elsewhere in America, and the term has validity, it seems to me, only when considered to be a continuing tradition.[8]

This literary florescence reverberated throughout the country; it was not confined to Harlem. And although short-lived, it was in some sense a renaissance.

For many reasons, to be discussed later, Harlem has continued to be associated with the New Negro movement. Many socioeconomic and cultural factors made Harlem unique among the all-black communities that developed in Northern cities as a result of the massive urban migration around the time of World War I. The term Harlem Renaissance reflects an awareness of the complexity of the sociocultural forces at work in the New Negro movement and gives Harlem credit for its contributions.

It is also necessary to document and understand the contributions made by other urban centers to this renaissance. Lawrence Rubin has, for example, written about the significance of Washington, D.C.: "With its complexities and contrasts, Washington, like all Negro communities, contained the tensions and excitements necessary for the production of both significant art and contributing artists." He outlines the associations of Renaissance figures, such as Alain Locke, Jean Toomer, Jessie Fauset, Rudolph Fisher, and Zora Neale Hurston, with Howard University and Washington, D.C.[9] In addition, Dean Kelly Miller, sociologist E. Franklin Frazier, historian Dr. Carter G. Woodson, and poet-critic Sterling Brown helped create and promote the New Negro consciousness. Other poets or writers connected to Washington, D.C., include Gwendolyn Bennett, Lewis Alexander, Waring Cuney, Montgomery Gregory, and Willis Richardson. Many of these writers met at the poet Georgia Douglas Johnson's home to exchange ideas.

Black communities in many cities experienced similar literary and dramatic activity. In Los Angeles, Wallace Thurman had tried to organize a literary group before he came to New York in 1925. Writing, dramatic, and art groups existed in Chicago and Indianapolis, and "little theater" groups in Cleveland and New Haven. Many Negro painters and sculptors exhibited their works in Rochester, Nashville, Chicago, and San Diego. In Boston, Eugene Gordon, Dorothy West, and others established a literary group and published a magazine called *The Quill*. Philadelphia produced three distinguished "New Negroes"—Alain Locke, Jessie Fauset, and Ethel Waters—and a Philadelphia group published *Black Opals*.[10] Langston Hughes had heard of Duke Ellington, Bessie Smith, Paul Robeson, and Bert Williams before he left the Midwest at age nineteen, and his native Kansas could claim Aaron Douglas and George Walker as its major contributors to the Negro Renaissance.

Recognizing the national scope of the Renaissance is important, but the issue of nomenclature need not become entangled with chauvinistic pleas favoring one city or another. It is impossible to ignore the polemical tone of Lawrence Rubin's otherwise valuable essay on the role of Washington, D.C., in fostering the Negro Renaissance. One simple, if not critically sound, way out of the controversy is to recognize and accept, even if reluctantly, that in the 1970s, the term "Harlem Renaissance" is firmly established in the minds of the reading public as a descriptive label for the emergence of arts among black Americans all over America in the twenties. One indication of this is the "Harlem Renaissance Revisited" issue, in November 1970, of the journal *Black World* edited by Hoyt Fuller. The issue included articles by Arna Bontemps, Dorothy West, John Oliver Killens, John A. Williams, George E. Kent, C.L.R. James, and John Henrik Clarke on the work of black writers of the twenties and early thirties. Since then, the publication of two full-length books, *Harlem Renaissance* (1971) by Nathan Irvin Huggins and *Harlem Renaissance Remembered* (1972) edited by the late Arna Bontemps, has further contributed to the critical currency of the term. These two books are concerned with a nationwide phenomenon and include discussions of writers that may or may not belong in the Harlem School as defined by Bone. The term "Harlem Renaissance" has become acceptable and legitimate through the passage of time. One can find parallel examples of this process in the naming of America after Amerigo Vespucci, described uncharitably by Emerson as "a pickle dealer who managed in this lying world to supplant Columbus and to baptize half the earth with his own dishonest name," or in the naming of natives of the American continent after India.

The philosophical and spiritual relationship between the Renaissance of the twenties and black writing of the 1890s has been explored by Arna Bontemps. He lived during the Renaissance and has written persuasively on the chronology of events leading to it;[11] he associates writers such as Paul Laurence Dunbar, Charles W. Chesnutt, W.E.B. DuBois, and James Weldon Johnson with the 1890s and regards Booker T. Washington as the most prominent leader of the period. Victor F. Calverton, who encouraged many black writers in his *Modern Quarterly* and edited the pioneering *Anthology of American Negro Literature* in 1929, seems to support Bontemps' view that the upsurge of black creativity in the twenties was an assertion and expansion, after a relatively long silence, of the mood that prevailed briefly toward the end of the nineteenth century. Calverton, however, sees the postwar New Negro movement not so much as a revival, but rather as "the hastening of an old birth which had formerly been retarded in its growth and evolution."[12]

The most significant link between the two periods was W.E.B. DuBois.[13] DuBois, sponsoring the Pan-African Congress in 1897, asserted that the black American could best further his cause by rejecting a servile imitation of Anglo-Saxon culture. And writing in the August 1897 issue of *Atlantic Monthly*, he expressed, in his now famous words, the paradox and ambivalence of the Negro's existence in America: "It is a peculiar sensation, this double-consciousness, this sense of always looking at one's self through the eyes of others, of measuring one's soul by the tape of a world that looks on in amused contempt and pity. One ever feels his two-ness—an American, a Negro—two souls, two thoughts, two unreconciled strivings; two warring ideals in one dark body, whose dogged strength alone keeps it from being torn asunder." In 1903, he crystallized his seminal concept of "double-consciousness" in *Souls of Black Folk*[14] and averred that "the problem of the twentieth century is the problem of the color line."[15] DuBois' book was read by many young writers of the Renaissance during their formative years. Claude McKay spoke for his contemporaries with his response to *Souls of Black Folk*: "The book shook me like an earthquake."[16] DuBois' prophetic statements, however, were not fully appreciated until certain other social and political changes forced black Americans to find "a bond in their common grievances and a language through which to express them."[17]

World War I became a major factor in the Afro-American's new awareness of himself and his relationship to American democratic ideals. War-born opportunities brought blacks to Northern cities in great numbers, accelerating the population shift generally known as the Great Urban Migration. During the war, black troops marched and fought alongside white Americans to make the world "safe for democracy." The Negro's experiences abroad revealed the discrepancies between the promise of freedom and his own status in American life; and he was led to hope that democracy would also be won at home. After the Armistice in 1918, the blacks became embittered and defiant to find the whites more than ever determined to keep the Negro in his place. As John Hope Franklin points out, it was not the timorous, docile Negro of the past who said, "The next time white folks pick on colored folks, something is going to drop—dead white folks."[18] The threat posed to legalized white supremacy in the South by returning soldiers and the hostility aroused in the North by a rapidly expanding black population resulted in nationwide expressions of racial animosity. During the "bloody summer" of 1919, race riots erupted in more than twenty-five cities across the nation. Blacks fought back bitterly and audaciously. It was in reaction to these riots that Claude McKay wrote his now famous poem, "If We Must Die," published in *The Liberator*. And in an editorial entitled "Returning Soldiers" in *The Crisis*, DuBois declared:

Under similar circumstances we would fight again. But, by the

God of Heaven, we are cowards and jackasses if, now that the war is over, we do not marshal every ounce of our brain and brawn to fight a sterner, longer, more unbending battle against the forces of hell in our own land.[19]

Meanwhile, the urban migration continued. Stimulated by the promise of industrial jobs in the North in the wake of the cessation of European migration, hundreds of thousands of Southern blacks were pouring into Northern cities. By one estimate, over 500,000 lower-class blacks migrated north between 1910 and 1920, and during the twenties another 800,000 blacks abandoned the South, many of them Negro ministers and professionals who followed their clients. In addition, there were migrants from the Midwest, the West, and the West Indies.[20]

The political and economic implications of this change can be understood best in the light of what went on in black America in the two decades preceding World War I. Booker T. Washington had been the acknowledged leader and spokesman of black Americans for many years. Since Washington did not agitate for social and political equality, he had the approval and confidence of the white industrialists and politicians both in the North and the South. His "Tuskegee Machine" exercised unprecedented control over federal appointments for blacks and funds for black colleges. Washington's accommodationist policy, however, had won very little for Negro citizens. In the last sixteen years of the nineteenth century, there had been more than 2,500 lynchings and they continued at a shocking rate into the twentieth century. Before the outbreak of World War I, the number for the century soared to more than 1,100, many of them taking place in the Midwest.[21] Between 1916 and 1921, the Ku Klux Klan grew from an obscure society in Atlanta to a nationwide secret organization with a membership of over half a million.[22] In 1924, the journalist Stanley Frost accurately described the Klan as "the most vigorous, active and effective force in American life, outside business."[23] More than anything else, the urban migration shook the foundation of Washington's philosophy and confirmed the inadequacy of his program for industrial education that would have tied the black to an antiquated, preindustrial Southern economy. Washington failed to anticipate the predominantly urban role the Afro-American would soon acquire.

The black sharecroppers and farm laborers saw in their move to the cities "a new vision of opportunity, of social and economic freedom."[24] In the Northern cities, they hoped to escape the poverty of Southern agriculture and the violence of racial bigotry. The urban migration also meant being crowded into segregated neighborhoods where the blacks could feel their powers as they never had before.[25] They developed a new self-respect and racial consciousness. Segregation stimulated the growth of a black middle class whose main function was to provide services for the black community that did not interest the white businessman. Such services included barber shops, funeral parlors, restaurants, shoe repair shops, beauty shops, and grocery stores, but some Negroes also successfully ran employment and real estate agencies.

The shift to Northern urban centers had its unpalatable side too. First, white hostility threatened the very existence of black neighborhoods. The overcrowding in black communities led to disease and delinquency. Racketeers and profiteers exploited the new migrants, who were for the most part ignorant of the city's ways. Euphoria Blake in Wallace Thurman's *Infants of the Spring* tells how she moved from the South full of ideas about race uplift, but ended up exploiting her fellow migrants by being an intermediary betwen jobseekers and employers, between landlords and potential tenants. In addition, intraracial and interregional conflicts arose when blacks of different backgrounds were thrown together into areas only ten to twenty blocks long in most cities.[26]

In many ways, Harlem was just another of the new black neighborhoods in Northern cities; it shared their advantages as well as problems. But Harlem differed in that it developed from a white, upper-middle-class suburb, and not from the continued decline of an already poor white area, as was usually the case.[27] In 1925, in an article written for Locke's anthology, *The New Negro*, James Weldon Johnson comments:

> Harlem is not merely a Negro colony or community, it is a city within a city, the greatest Negro city in the world. It is not a slum or a fringe, it is located in the heart of Manhattan and occupies one of the most beautiful and healthful sections of the city. It is not a "quarter" of dilapidated tenements, but is made up of new-law apartments and handsome dwellings, with well-paved and well-lighted streets. It has its own churches, social and civic centers, shops, theaters and other places of amusement. And it contains more Negroes to the square mile than any other spot on earth.[28]

No wonder Harlem became "a symbol of elegance and distinction, not derogation."[29] Since the promise of a better future seemed more tangible in Harlem, it attracted more migrants, intensifying the process of urbanization in a cosmopolitan setting. The community grew from 14,000 blacks in 1914 to 175,000 by 1925 and more than 200,000 by the beginning of the Depression.[30] Negroes came from all parts of the United States, West Indies, and even Africa, and their interaction led to the growth of a highly race-conscious, sophisticated black community—something unprecedented in American history. Black writers, painters, and actors from all over the country experienced the magnetic pull of Harlem as the new cultural capital of black America. "In Harlem," wrote Alain Locke in the special Harlem issue of *Survey Graphic*, which he edited in March 1925, "Negro life is seizing upon its first chances for group expression and self-determination." The black's new aspirations and continued frustrations instilled among the common folk a fiery brand of racial chauvinism; it also led to an assertion of black pride by a broad-based middle-class Negro leadership. Because of the diversity of its population, Harlem also became an ideal testing ground for clashing racial and political points of view. What Roi Ottley said about Harlem in 1943 had perhaps even greater validity for the twenties: "It is the fountainhead of mass movements. From it flows the progressive vitality of Black life. . . . To grasp the inner meanings of life in Black America, one must put his finger on the pulse of Harlem."[31]

The new militancy of the Harlem Negro reflected itself in many ways during the period.[32] In 1910, a group of white radicals and black leaders had met in New York to form the NAACP, which pledged itself to work for the abolition of all forced segregation, equal education for black and white children, the complete enfranchisement of the Negro, and the enforcement of the Fourteenth and Fifteenth Amendments. Its organ, *The Crisis: A Record of Darker Races*, edited by W.E.B. DuBois, became an important outlet for black grievances as well as hopes. The first issue of *The Crisis*, published in November 1910, sold 1,000 copies rapidly and by 1918 the circulation figures reached 100,000 per month. The following year, the National Urban League was organized in New York, and "it undertook to open new opportunities for Negroes in industry and to assist newly arrived Negroes in their problems of adjustment in the urban centers." *Opportunity, A Journal of Negro Life* began publication in January 1923 as the expanded organ of the League under the enterprising editorship of Charles S. Johnson. On 28 June 1917, some 10,000 Harlem citizens carrying placards marched down Fifth Avenue in a Silent Parade led by the NAACP to protest the massacre of blacks in East St. Louis. A. Philip Randolph organized the all-black Brotherhood of Sleeping Car Porters and Maids. Although the Brotherhood was not fully recognized as a bargaining agency until 1937, it won the endorsement of the American Federation of Labor, the NAACP, and the National Urban League during the twenties and played a valuable role in the wage agreements of 1926 and 1929 with the Pullman Company. The NAACP launched a nationwide campaign to promote federal antilynching legislation. In 1919, the House of Representatives passed an antilynching bill, but the Southern senators managed to prevent a vote on the measure in the Senate. In Harlem, as elsewhere in Northern cities, numerous small leftist groups were active among the black masses, even though their impact was very limited.

But the most significant Harlem-related mass movement in the twenties was the "Back to Africa" movement of Marcus Garvey. A Jamaican by birth, Garvey came to Harlem in 1916, and, unlike any leader black America had seen before, he had the ability and charisma to "convince masses of ordinary black men and women of the notion of their collective potential."[33] Garvey's ideas were not new, but he used his demagogic techniques effectively on his growing audiences. Garvey's success was a measure of the black American's mounting frustration over his efforts to achieve self-respect and dignity as an American citizen. In 1917, after a few abortive attempts to catch the public eye, Garvey won a tremendous response at a huge meeting at Bethel AME Church and established the New York division of the Universal Negro Improvement Association (UNIA). Through his newspaper, *Negro World*, and his many followers, Garvey reached hundreds of thousands of Negroes in America and abroad. The 1920 convention of UNIA attracted delegates from many different parts of the world, including Brazil, Colombia, Central America, and even Africa.[34]

The essence of Garvey's message was that black was superior to white and that the destiny of the Negro race lay in Africa, not America. Garvey won a large following estimated anywhere between half a million and six million.[35] Although Garvey's followers did not all desire to exchange their present lot, however difficult, for an unknown future in Africa, they found in UNIA a much-needed outlet for race pride and self-assertion. Garvey's movement constituted a promise to provide what most black folk had always cherished—an opportunity to work and achieve on a par with others. Garvey attempted to build black pride and self-help through emphasis on the great history and future of Africa, and a program of black capitalistic enterprise that took its cue, through Emmett Scott and others, from Booker T. Washington's philosophy and economic programs, and anticipated the work and ideas of Elijah Muhammad and his Nation of Ismal. Through his exaltation of blackness, Garvey gained followers among the demoralized blacks in urban ghettos all over the country.

However, the middle-class Negro leadership of organizations such as the NAACP, the Urban League, and the Brotherhood of Sleeping Car Porters was not prepared for the belligerent, separatist philosophy of Marcus Garvey. Almost all the black leaders of the period, including W.E.B. DuBois, James Weldon Johnson, Walter White, and A. Philip Randolph, were reformers rather than radicals; they saw Garvey as a threat to their influence on both blacks and whites and to the Negro's civil rights cause in the United States. They did not share Garvey's professed mystique of blackness, but found race pride a useful tool in the fight to obtain greater opportunities for black American citizens. Many Negro leaders, however, recognized that Garvey's sway over the masses represented something much deeper than a mere desire to migrate to Africa. In 1925, Charles S. Johnson admitted that Garvey had shown "the clairvoyance to place himself at the head of a docile sector of a whole population, which, in different degrees, has been expressing an indefinite restlessness and broadening of spirit."[36] Randolph had helped Garvey in his early efforts to gain public attention and DuBois praised him for his sincerity and eloquence but felt that Garvey had "absolutely no business sense, no *flair* for organization."[37] Writing in the August 1923 issue of *Opportunity*, Charles S. Johnson recognized Garveyism as an expression of the urge for racial self-determination, but characterized Garvey's methods as "injudicious and bunglesome" and his program as "absurdly visionary and impossible."

Garvey continued to attack individual black American leaders and their ideas with a ferocious invective that finally brought angry responses from DuBois and others. Garvey refused to answer charges by DuBois and Randolph about the poor handling of business and management details relating to his many auxiliary organizations, such as Universal African Legion, Black Cross Nurses, the Universal African Motor Corps, and the Black Eagle Flying Corps. Since neither Garvey nor any of his followers knew anything about ships, they squandered hundreds of thousands of dollars when they purchased run-down ships at exorbitant prices for Garvey's Black Star Line. His efforts to colonize Africa were doomed to failure from the beginning because of a general lack of technical and business skills among his followers and Garvey's own ignorance of the geopolitical situation of the African continent.

Although he had never been to Africa, Garvey assumed the title of Provisional President of Africa in 1920 and bestowed similar ranks and titles on his close associates. The colorful parades of the African Legion, the uniforms for its rank and file, and other paraphernalia of a royal hierarchy had great appeal for the masses. Claude McKay, writing in the April 1922 issue of *The Liberator*, denounced his fellow Jamaican as "bourgeois-obsolete." McKay was amazed at Garvey's intolerance and ignorance and saw him as a direct descendant of the "imperial traditions of nineteenth-century England." Almost forty years later, Richard B. Moore, another black Marxist of West Indian background, confirmed McKay's judgment by relating Garvey's failure to his "Napoleonic urge for personal power and empire."[38] Garvey's significance, however, was far greater than his unsuccessful ventures indicate. Henry Lincoln Johnson, a black attorney who represented one of Garvey's codefendants at their trial for mail fraud in 1923, had said: "If every Negro could have put every dime, every penny into the sea, and if he got in exchange the knowledge that he was somebody, that he meant something in the world, he would gladly do it. . . . The Black Star Line was a loss in money but it was a gain in soul."[39]

In many ways, the New Negro movement of the twenties was the educated, middle-class black's response to the same changes that magnetically drew the unlettered and lower-class Negroes to Garvey's ideas and programs. In keeping with the political thinking of organizations such as NAACP and the Urban League, the black culture enthusiasts advocated race pride and racial expression, without developing a mystique of blackness based on African roots. Instead, they emphasized race differences with the definite objective of achieving racial cooperation and harmony in a culturally pluralistic American society. That the Garvey movement and the New Negro phenomenon failed to interact in any meaningful way indicates the extent of class cleavage in the black society of the twenties.

The term New Negro was not new to Afro-Americans in the twenties.[40] It had been used earlier with similar definitions and meanings, and its first use may have been that of the *Cleveland Gazette* in 1895 to describe a group of blacks who had just secured a New York civil rights law. In 1900, Booker T. Washington published a collection of essays entitled *A New Negro for a New Century*, and in 1916, William Pickens used the term in his book, *The New Negro*.[41] Alain Locke's contribution in the twenties was to establish a relationship between the sociocultural and political import of the term and the literature of the period. In the special Harlem number of *Survey Graphic*, which he revised and published as his anthology, *The New Negro*, in 1925, and in his numerous magazine reviews and articles, Locke described and interpreted the changes on the Afro-American scene and pointed out their relevance to the work of many young black writers and artists, such as Jean Toomer, Langston Hughes, Aaron Douglas, Rudolph Fisher, Countee Cullen, and Claude McKay.

In the social and political contexts, there were others who wrote about the New Negro. In the August 1920 issue of *The Messenger*, W.A. Domingo writes that the New Negro "cannot be lulled into a false sense of security with political spoils and patronage." He would insist on "absolute and unequivocal *social equality*." The New Negroes stressed and sometimes glorified certain characteristics of the race they believed to be uniquely Negro. Although their long-term goals were assimilationist, they recognized the value of racial institutions within the segregated community.[42] To them, Harlem, with its churches, theaters, restaurants, and night clubs, typified the vitality and diversity of black life. Neither desiring an all-black nation in North America nor looking forward to an all-black republic in Africa, they extended the use of institutions such as the black press beyond their social and cultural roles in order to deal with political and economic issues of national importance.

The Harlem Renaissance was thus a logical extension in the areas of art, music, and literature of the New Negro's racial, cultural, and political thinking. Arna Bontemps traced the origins of the Renaissance to the year 1917, when Claude McKay published a poem entitled "Harlem Dancer" in an obscure magazine. "In that same year, James Weldon Johnson collected poems he had been writing in a small volume called *Fifty Years and Other Poems*, but none of these verses had the sock of Claude McKay's poetry or of Johnson's own later poems. A serious dramatic presentation with a black cast appeared for the first time on Broadway in that same year."[43] Soon after, many black artists and musicians, including Roland Hayes, Duke Ellington, Louis Armstrong, Bessie Smith, Jelly Roll Morton, W.C. Handy, and Aaron Douglas, came to public attention.

By 1920 the "coon" shows of Tom Fletcher, Ernest Hogan, George Walker and Bert Williams had given way to the musical revues and plays at the Apollo, Lafayette, and Lincoln theaters in New York.[44] Already, talented black actors and musicians— Josephine Baker, Charles Gilpin, Paul Robeson, Frank Wilson, Florence Mills, Irvin Miller, Noble Sissle and Eubie Blake—were giving spectacular performances in plays and musicals by both black and white dramatists. The great success in 1921 of *Shuffle Along*, produced by Flourney Miller and Aubrey Lyles, was followed by the moderate success of many black musicals. In Washington, D.C., Montgomery Gregory organized and directed the Howard Players between 1919 and 1924, and in Harlem, W.E.B. DuBois founded the Krigwa Little Theater Group in 1923. In 1925, Garland Anderson's *Appearances* became the first full-length play by an Afro-American produced on Broadway. It was followed in 1929 by *Harlem*, a collaboration between Wallace Thurman and William Jordan Rapp.[45] In 1927, Alain Locke and Montgomery Gregory collected twenty one-act plays by white and black playwrights. The collection was entitled *Plays of Negro Life: A Source Book of Native American Drama*, and in the introduction Locke quoted Eugene O'Neill's forecast that "the possibilities are limitless and to a dramatist open up new and intriguing opportunities: the gifts the Negro can and will bring to our native drama are invaluable ones."[46] In 1930, Willis Richardson edited *Plays and Pageants from the Life of the Negro* (Washington, D.C.: Associated Publishers), twelve nondialect works by black authors.

Many young painters and sculptors traveled abroad and moved away from the academic realism and modified impressionism associated with Henry Tanner. Locke's *The New Negro* was the first book to present a number of drawings and paintings indicating the new trends in Afro-American art. As Judith Wragg Chase points out, by the midtwenties, the first group-conscious school of Afro-American art was practicing a combination of realism, Americanism, and cultural racialism.[47] Freed from the timid conformity of earlier generations, black American artists experimented in a variety of styles and attempted a more objective and effective self-portrayal. Among the younger artists who achieved striking pictures of black life and characters were Aaron Douglas, Richard Barthé, Hale Woodruff, James A. Porter, Lois Mailou Jones, Archibald Motley, Malvin Gray Johnson, and Palmer Hayden.

In literature, the first stage of the Harlem Renaissance culminated in the events that led to the publication of *The New Negro* in December 1925. The first of these events was a dinner at the Civic Club on 21 March 1924, for a group called the "Writers' Guild." Charles Johnson describes the dinner in a letter to Ethel Ray (later secretary to Johnson in his *Opportunity* office):

> You could have been of enormous assistance to me this past week when I was arranging for the "debut" of the younger Negro writers. It was a most unusual affair—a dinner meeting

at the Civic Club at which all of the younger Negro writers—Cullen, Walter White, Walrond, Jessie Fauset, Gwendolyn Bennett, Alain Locke, M. Gregory, met and chatted with the passing generation—Dubois, Jas. Weldon Johnson, Georgia Douglas Johnson, etc. and with the literary personages of the city: Carl Van Doren, editor of the *Century*, Frederick Allen of *Harper's*, Walter Bartlett of *Scribner's*, Devere Allen of the *World Tomorrow*, Freda Kirchwey of the *Nation*, Paul Kellogg of the *Survey*, Horace Liveright of Boni, Liveright Publishers, etc.—about 100 guests and tremendously impressive speaking. I'll have an account of it in the magazine. It would have given you a first hand introduction to the "last worders" in literature. But principally it served to stimulate a market for the new stuff which these young writers are turning out. The first definite reaction came in the form of an offer of one magazine to devote an entire issue to the similar subjects as treated by representatives of the group. A big plug was bitten off. Now it's a question of living up to the reputation. Yes, I should have added, a stream of manuscripts has started into my office from other aspirants.[48]

Most of the prominent writers of the Renaissance were present at this dinner. (However, Langston Hughes, Claude McKay, and Jean Toomer were out of the country at the time.) Paul Kellogg, the editor of *Survey Graphic*, was also present; he invited Alain Locke to be the guest editor of a special issue devoted to Harlem.[49] Locke accepted the invitation and the March 1925 issue of the *Survey* was entitled "Harlem, the Mecca of the New Negro"; it became "the single most notable achievement of the journal in these years."[50] Two printings totaling 42,000 copies were sold, a record unsurpassed by the *Survey* until World War II. Even before the issue came out, Albert and Charles Boni expressed interest in publishing it later in book form and *The New Negro* was printed in a deluxe edition in December 1925.

In the words of Locke, *The New Negro* was put together "to document the New Negro culturally and socially,—to register the transformations of the inner and outer life of the Negro in America that have so significantly taken place in the last few years." He emphasized the need for and value of the Negro's self-portraiture, and he declared, "so far as he is culturally articulate, we shall let the Negro speak for himself." In a prophetic tone, Locke spoke of the New Negro in a national and international scope; he compared the New Negro movement with the "nascent movements of folk expression and self-determination" that were taking place "in India, in China, in Egypt, Ireland, Russia, Bohemia, Palestine and Mexico."[51]

Locke, the first person to call the black arts movement of the twenties a renaissance, also became its major interpreter. He presented his views in four different essays included in his anthology, *The New Negro*, and continued to write review articles for *Opportunity* until 1945.[52] With one or two exceptions, Locke chose pieces for *The New Negro* that illustrated his own philosophy. *The New Negro* contained a broad range of material—short stories, poems, one play, and many essays on aesthetic, historical, and sociological subjects. In addition, it contained illustrations by the young black artist Aaron Douglas and the Austrian artist Winold Reiss. To borrow the words of Robert Hayden, "sophisticated and urbane, race conscious without being chauvinistic— there were several white contributors, for instance—it [*The New Negro*] presented facets of Negro life and thought that stimulated the imagination and challenged traditional prejudices."[53]

Locke contended that a spirit of cultural nationalism, based on pride in the Negro's own traditions and folk arts, had led to a desire for self-determination and to "an unusual burst of creative expression." He compared the black's cultural reawakening to national movements in Ireland, Czechoslovakia, and Yugoslavia, but also saw the New Negro movement as parallel with and at the same time part of America's struggle to throw off European cultural hegemony and to develop its own literature, art, and music. Locke felt that the New Negro spirit embraced the masses as much as it did the Renaissance leaders and writers. "It is the rank and file who are leading, and the leaders who are following. A transformed and transforming psychology permeates the masses." He saw hope for the sharecroppers and plantation workers in their move to the urban setting; he placed great value on the cosmopolitan black communities in the North where blacks from diverse backgrounds could discover one another. He thought Harlem was a perfect example of this change, because Harlem was a point of contact for diverse groups with special motives, "so what began in terms of segregation becomes more and more, as its elements mix and react, the laboratory of a great race-welding."[54]

Locke's philosophy of cultural pluralism is similar to the thinking of his white contemporaries Waldo Frank, V.F. Calverton, Randolph Bourne, and Van Wyck Brooks.[55] Locke recognized that "the conditions that are molding a New Negro are [also] molding a new American attitude." To him, the racialism of the Negro was "no limitation or reservation with respect to American life, it is only a constructive effort to build the obstructions in the stream of his progress into an efficient dam of social energy and power." The choice for Locke, and for the white literary radicals, was "not between one way for the Negro and another way for the rest, but between American institutions frustrated on the one hand and American ideals progressively fulfilled and realized on the other."

Locke's optimism in *The New Negro* reflects the idealism of the American progressive reformers. Locke underplays the negative forces operating on the Negro and stresses the few hopeful signs on the horizon. He believed that the Old Negro had already become more of a myth than a man—the Negro who had for long been a formula rather than a human being—"a something to be argued about, condemned or defended . . . a social bogey or a social burden." At the same time, Locke saw the New Negro nourishing his racial roots and responding keenly to his responsibilities as a participant in the American experience. He defined as the creed of his own generation its belief in "the efficacy of collective effort, in race co-operation." He added:

> In this new group psychology we note the lapse of sentimental appeal, then the development of a more positive self-respect and self-reliance; the repudiation of social dependence, and then the gradual recovery from hypersensitiveness and "touchy" nerves, the repudiation of the double standard of judgment with its special philanthropic allowances and then the sturdier desire for objective and scientific appraisal; and finally the rise from social disillusionment of race pride, from the sense of social debt to the responsibilities of social contribution, and offsetting the necessary working and commonsense acceptance of restricted conditions, the belief in ultimate esteem and recognition.

The New Negro movement had no formal organization and its orientation "was more aesthetic and philosophical . . . than political."[56] Of course, Locke never made high political claims for his philosophy of cultural pluralism. He made sure not to assign Harlem the political significance that places like Dublin and Prague had for cultural movements in New Ireland and New Czechoslovakia. And although he welcomed a scientific exposition of the Negro race by objective sociologists and anthropologists, he did not think more knowledge necessarily meant better treatment for blacks. He also observed that the New Negro was only a "forced radical"—a social protestant rather than a genuine radical, as he put it. Notwithstanding the basic soundness of his views on racial self-expression in a culturally pluralistic society, his contention that such self-expression "must lead to considerable further betterment of race relationships" is politically naive. Like the black political leaders of the period, Locke seems to have believed that the American system would ultimately work for the Negro, but he refused to take cognizance of the disagreeable political leverage the system recognized. Such an approach implied a relatively complete dependence of any black hopes for political change or reform upon white men of influence and their good intentions.[57]

Strictly in terms of art and literature, however, Locke's views on racial self-expression by black Americans offered a valuable perspective for young black writers. In Locke's pluralistic view, there was no conflict between being "American" and being "Negro," but rather an opportunity to enrich both through cultural reciprocity.[58] In a way, Locke was reinterpreting DuBois' "double consciousness" concept for aesthetic and cultural uses, and it seems there was enough room in Locke's view for many different kinds of talents to exist and thrive together. For *The New Negro*, he deliberately chose poems and short stories that illustrated his views about the use of folk culture and about "realism." Locke used the term "realism" rather loosely. He gives some indication of his meaning in an article written on French-African literature in 1924. In this article, Locke praised René Maran's novel *Batouala* for "its candor, its ruthlessness, and its humane but unemotional human portraiture." He also valued *Batouala* because it rejected "that decadent cult of the primitive which is the pastime of the sophisticated." Locke's realism has been defined negatively to include "works which were *not* in the genteel tradition, *not* melodramatic, sentimental, romantic or didactic; works in which the characters and situations were *not* idealized or sentimentalized, or viciously stereotyped. He also meant works which were *not* written in the Oscar Wilde manner of decadent sophistication."[59]

Locke was, therefore, suggesting a well-balanced and flexible approach for the black writer to transform the richness and diversity, the intensity and anguish of the black American experience into the stuff of art and literature. He had little sympathy for the didactic and propagandistic literature that DuBois called for, nor did he want to inhibit the artistic depiction of the Negro by confining it to a particular class, group, or region. Alain Locke did not see any direct connection between the black American's "self-expression" and the African arts that had inspired and influenced the work of many European painters and sculptors. According to Locke, the most important lesson the black artist could derive from African art was "not cultural inspiration or technical innovations, but the lesson of a classic background, the lesson of discipline, of style, of technical control."[60] At the same time, Locke emphasized the American identity of the young black writers by suggesting that "race for them is but an idiom of experience, a sort of added enriching adventure and discipline." He hoped in time to develop a Negro school of art and literature, with its own distinctive idiom and subject matter, that would parallel the growth of other "regional" and "local color" schools in American literature.[61] To Locke, all such developments were a welcome indication of America's ethnic and regional diversity.

Locke's view of Afro-American artistic expression did not have a tremendous impact, even though Locke did more than write reviews and magazine articles to get his views across to the younger Renaissance poets and novelists. Most of the writers included in *The New Negro* were Locke's protégés, "men he knew personally, whose work he had encouraged, criticized, applauded, promoted and sometimes supported financially."[62] Among the younger writers who received special encouragement from Alain Locke are Jean Toomer, Countee Cullen, Langston Hughes, and Rudolph Fisher.

Locke, however, was not alone in his encouragement of black writers. James Weldon Johnson was of great help to a number of young writers, especially Langston Hughes and Claude McKay. Johnson consistently praised and defended Hughes' blues-based poetry, and his sympathetic understanding of McKay's position on class issues sustained McKay through continual wrangles with black American leaders and critics.[63] Although Walter White did not always succeed, he made genuine efforts to help in the publication of works by writers as diverse as Jean Toomer, Nella Larsen, Claude McKay, Countee Cullen, and Georgia Douglas Johnson. Carl Van Vechten was also instrumental in finding publishers for Renaissance writers. Victor F. Calverton, the literary radical, offered personal assistance to many black writers and encouraged them in his magazine, *The Modern Quarterly*.[64]

If anyone matched the enthusiasm and vigor of Alain Locke in promoting the concept of a renaissance in the twenties, it was the sociologist Charles S. Johnson, who was later to be the first black president of Fisk University.[65] Johnson did not, however, share Locke's optimistic vision of cultural pluralism. Under the influence of Robert E. Park, Johnson saw the Afro-American as a marginal person, who, although rent by the conflict between two cultures, could stand apart and objectively view each. For him, the black's move from folk culture to industrial culture was an inevitable and painful process. Johnson was the first editor of *Opportunity*, and, for the five years he was editor, he stressed the need for the black American to advantageously understand and absorb this change from rural South to urban North. Although *Opportunity* placed more emphasis on creative writing than DuBois' *The Crisis*, it was equally interested in examining migration, education, housing, health, and employment as they affected the daily lives of black Americans. As a pragmatist, Johnson offered incentives to young authors through *Opportunity* literary contests, and encouraged contacts between the black writers and the white publishing world. His objective was, to use his own words, "to stimulate and encourage creative literary effort among Negroes . . . to encourage the reading of literature both by Negro authors and about Negro life . . . to bring these writers into contact with the general world of letters . . . to stimulate and foster a type of writing by Negroes which shakes itself free of deliberate propaganda and protest."[66] In 1927, Johnson edited *Ebony and Topaz*, which in many ways was a companion volume to Locke's *The New Negro*. He intended *Ebony and Topaz* as an indication of the black writer's increasing maturity and independence in portraying black life.

It is difficult today to account for all the factors that prevented the growth of a black American school of literature. Harlem Renaissance writing is marked by racialism, but the writers reflect the spirit of the times in their refusal to join causes or movements. "Individuality is what we should strive for. Let each seek his own salvation," says Raymond Taylor, the alter ego of Wallace Thurman in *Infants of the Spring*.[67] As a creative writer, Zora Neale Hurston was interested not in social problems, but in the problems of individuals, black or white. Alain Locke's idea of a black literary movement had political implications, but he did not base it on a rigid social or political ideology. Locke's views were opposed by W.E.B. DuBois, Benjamin Brawley, and Allison Davis, who contended that black writers had a responsibility to defend and uplift the race by portraying educated, middle-class Negroes. Claude McKay, acutely conscious of his position as a black man in Western civilization, asserted his artistic independence while alternating between Marxist and nationalistic ideologies.[68] Wallace Thurman, lost in the world of contemporary bohemia, would not compromise with the high artistic standards he set for himself and others. There were, however, many black writers of the period who—independently or under Locke's influence—resolved their dilemmas of conflicting racial and artistic loyalties in ways resembling Locke's approach. Among these writers are Langston Hughes, Jean Toomer, Rudolph Fisher, Eric Walrond, Sterling Brown, Arna Bontemps, and Zora Neale Hurston.

It is necessary to look outside Harlem and black America for the major explanation of the Harlem Renaissance writers' failure to develop into a cohesive group or movement. In discussing white interest in the Negro, Huggins argues that "the black-white relationship has been symbiotic, [and that] blacks have been essential to white identity (and whites to blacks)."[69] In American history, this black-white symbiosis has resulted in the black being called on to uphold a new stereotype. In the twenties, both in Europe and America, interest in the Negro came to be focused around the cult of the primitive. It had become fashionable in the Jazz Age to defy prohibition and to find joy and abandon in exotic music and dance. In such an atmosphere "the Negro had obvious uses: he represented the unspoiled child of nature, the noble savage— carefree, spontaneous and sexually uninhibited."[70] A popular misinterpretation of Freudian theory contributed to the promotion of primitivism. Freud was seen as exalting instinct over intellect in a revolt against the Puritan spirit. In his *Civilization and its Discontents*, Freud had contended that civilization is based upon renunciation of "powerful instinctual urgencies," and the privation of instinctual gratification demanded by the cultural ideal was a major source of neurosis. No wonder, then, that popularized Freudianism became "the rationalization of sex primitivism," and gave the "cult of the primitive . . . an extraordinary foothold on this continent."[71]

The Negro fad of the twenties encompassed a new Euro-American interest in jazz, African art, and sculpture and a return to the values of a preindustrial society.[72] But in the popular version of the fad the black was simply an uninhibited and unmechanized soul. Paul Morand, the French journalist, expressed gratitude for the Harlem black's contribution toward shattering "the mechanical rhythm of America."[73] With revealing imagery, he compares blacks on the subway, "clinging with long hooking hands to the leather straps, and chewing their gum," with "the great apes of Equitorial Africa."[74] Young black girls playing on the streets with "an animal swiftness, a warlike zest . . . savage and triumphant," suggested to him "black virgins of some African revolution of the future." Morand was sure that if the policeman, the symbol of white civilization, were to vanish from the street corner in Harlem, this "miniature Africa" would immediately revert to a semi-savage state like Haiti, "given to voodoo and rhetorical despotism."[75]

White American writers had already portrayed the black as a person possessing an instinctive simplicity and abandon that contrasted to the fretful and mechanized existence of the white man. In "Melanctha" (1909), Gertrude Stein suggested that instinctive love is best and most satisfying.[76] In 1914, Vachel Lindsay wrote *The Congo: A Study of the Negro Race*. The titles for the three sections of Lindsay's poem reveal his attitude to his subject— "Their Basic Savagery," "Their Irrepressible High Spirits," and "The Hope of their Religion." Lindsay was followed by several white writers, including Eugene O'Neill, E.E. Cummings, and Sherwood Anderson, who saw the Negro's primitivism as a bulwark against increasing standardization. The South was experiencing a Southern Renaissance, which, like the Harlem Renaissance, was notable for its attempted objectivity and detachment.[77] The region's intellectual interest in the Negro was centered at the University of North Carolina, which was considered to be the most progressive school in the South during the postwar years. The Southern writers and scholars who wrote about the Negro during the period include Julia Peterkin, T.S. Stribling, DuBose Heyward, Paul and Elizabeth Lay Green, Frank Graham, Howard Odum, Edward Sheldon, and Frederich Koch. The works of these writers differed from the better-known primitivistic treatments of the Negro, but they contributed to the growing stereotype by concentrating on black common folk, their dialect, and on picturesque aspects of black life.

Carl Van Vechten's *Nigger Heaven* (1926) was the most influential novel, by a white writer, in establishing the image of the Negro as primitive. The book ran into several editions and sold over 100,000 copies; it initiated an unprecedented nationwide interest in the Negro and clearly demonstrated the commercial value of books written about the Negro. And although primitivism had different and wider uses for some black writers—especially Claude McKay—many of the Renaissance writers ignored the challenge of Locke's pluralistic vision under the bandwagon effect of Carl Van Vechten's *Nigger Heaven*.

Described by a contemporary as an "archeologist of the exotic," Carl Van Vechten was interested in the Negro long before he published *Nigger Heaven*. Born and brought up in Cedar Rapids, Iowa, he came to New York in 1906 after studying at the University of Chicago and a short stint as journalist for the *Chicago Amer-*

ican. He was among the first to take jazz seriously as an art form; and he became interested in the Negro by way of jazz and Gertrude Stein. In 1913 he saw a Negro vaudeville show, *Darktown Follies*. "How the darkies danced, sang, and cavorted," Van Vechten recalled later in his *In The Garrett*. "Real nigger stuff this, done with spontaneity and joy in the doing." By this time, he was promoting interracial gatherings by entertaining blacks at his home. During the early twenties, he came to know many black writers and leaders such as Walter White, James Weldon Johnson, Countee Cullen, Langston Hughes, Zora Neale Hurston, Rudolph Fisher, and Eric Walrond. Soon he was a regular visitor in Harlem, and, according to Ethel Waters, came to know more about New York's black belt than any other white person with the exception of the captain of Harlem's police station.[78]

Even before publishing his own book, Van Vechten was influential as a friend and advisor to black writers. The older and more established blacks, Walter White, Alain Locke, Charles S. Johnson, Jessie Fauset, James Weldon Johnson, and W.E.B. DuBois, provided invaluable guidance and encouragement to young black writers, but Carl Van Vechten was their major contact with white journals and white publishers. He also was responsible for many contacts between the white and black artists. Although Van Vechten was not the only initiator or promoter of the Negro fad among New York's white intellectuals, he gave the movement impetus and direction. Through his interracial parties and gatherings in Harlem and in the Village, he made it smart to be interracial. Ethel Waters recalled meeting Eugene O'Neill, Sinclair Lewis, Dorothy Thompson, Alfred Knopf, George Jean Nathan, Alexander Woollcott, Heyward Broun, Cole Porter, Noel Coward, and Somerset Maugham at the Van Vechten apartment.[79] Paul Robeson's singing at an interracial gathering at Van Vechten's place led directly to his first New York concert. Van Vechten was instrumental in getting Langston Hughes' first two volumes of poetry, *The Weary Blues* (1926) and *Fine Clothes to a Jew* (1927), accepted for publication by Alfred Knopf. Through Van Vechten again, Hughes found his way to the pages of *Vanity Fair*. He also persuaded Alfred Knopf to publish James Weldon Johnson, Nella Larsen, Rudolph Fisher, and Chester Himes.

Although a detailed analysis of *Nigger Heaven* may not be pertinent here, an evaluation of the influence of Van Vechten and his book on the milieu and literary careers of the Harlem Renaissance writers is. *Nigger Heaven* is the story of Mary Love, a prim and pretty Harlem librarian, who falls in love with Byron Karson, a struggling young writer. Byron, a recent graduate of the University of Pennsylvania, has been told that he has promise, which he interprets to mean: "pretty good for a colored man." Like Ray in Claude McKay's *Home to Harlem*, Mary Love cannot take sex and love lightly. Randolph Pettijohn, the numbers king, desires her and offers her marriage. "Ah ain't got no education lak you, but Ah got money, plenty of et, an' Ah got love," he tells her. Byron meanwhile fails to find a job compatible with his level of education and refuses to accept a menial job. The exotic and primitive aspects of Harlem life surround Byron's orgiastic affair with Lasca Sartoris, "a gorgeous brown Messalina of Seventh Avenue." Lasca, however, deserts Byron for Pettijohn. Byron avenges himself by impulsively firing two bullets into the prostrate body of Pettijohn, who has already been killed by Scarlet Creeper. At the end, Byron surrenders helplessly to the police.

The unsettling effect of *Nigger Heaven* is best seen in the controversy its publication caused among early reviewers. Many white reviewers questioned its literary value. The *New Republic* thought the book was more successful as a traveler's guide to Harlem than as a novel,[80] and the unimpressed *Independent* called it dull and disappointing in its attempt "to prove that cultivated Negroes talk French and understand the scores of Opera."[81] However, V.F. Calverton praised *Nigger Heaven* for its straightforward presentation of Negro life,[82] and the *New York Times* critic, in a wholly favorable review, concluded that it was a study of the "plight of Colored intellectuals."[83]

For the black reviewers Eric Walrond and Langston Hughes, the book was truthful and objective; Hughes described it as "the first real passionately throbbing novel of contemporary Negro life."[84] But the balance weighed heavily in favor of the book's black detractors. Offended by the title, many simply refused to read the book, and those who read it found the contents distasteful. Allison Davis accused Van Vechten of having "warped Negro life into a fantastic barbarism,"[85] while J.A. Rogers suggested that "Van Vechten Heaven" would be a better title for the book, since Harlem seemed to provide "release of soul" for Van Vechten and others, who were satiated by the meager pleasures offered by the "Nordic" world.[86] According to DuBois, the *Police Gazette* was likely to furnish material of a better quality than *Nigger Heaven*, which was "neither truthful nor artistic. . . . It is a caricature. It is worse than untruth because it is a mass of half-truths"; it is "ludicrously out of focus and undeniably misleading" in trying to express all racial traits in the cabaret life of Harlem, when the overwhelming majority of blacks had never been to cabarets. "The average colored man in Harlem," DuBois added, "is an everyday laborer, attending church, lodge and movie and is as conservative and as conventional as ordinary working folk elsewhere."[87]

The specter of *Nigger Heaven* lurks behind almost all reviews written after 1926. Benjamin Brawley, Allison Davis, and W.E.B. DuBois asserted that some younger black writers and many white writers were misguided by *Nigger Heaven*, and they argued that the emphasis on the exotic and the primitive, the sensual and the bawdy in the depiction of the Negro was detrimental to the black's political future in the United States.

The fad of primitivism cannot be blamed entirely on Van Vechten or on the group of whites who wrote about the Negro in the twenties, but it is reasonable to conclude that the publication of *Nigger Heaven* made many black writers keenly aware of the commercial possibilities of the primitivistic formula, and made it more difficult for the Harlem Renaissance to develop into a black literary movement. The unusual success of *Nigger Heaven* and later of McKay's *Home to Harlem* clearly indicated an eagerness for works exalting the exotic, the sensual, and the primitive. This interest had "no minor effect on certain members of the Harlem *literati* whose work was just what the Jazz Age ordered." Thus, black writers who were willing to describe the exotic scene "had no trouble finding sponsors, publishers and immediate popularity."[88] In his autobiography, *The Big Sea*, Langston Hughes recalled the pessimistic judgment of Wallace Thurman, who thought that the Negro vogue had made the Harlem Renaissance writers "too conscious of ourselves, had flattered and spoiled us and had provided too many easy opportunities for some of us to drink gin and more gin."[89]

It is anybody's guess today as to what might have happened if *Nigger Heaven* had not appeared with a bang at a time when the Harlem Renaissance was just struggling to become a conscious movement. However, the book seems to have had a crippling effect on the self-expression of many black writers by either making it easier to gain success riding the bandwagon of primitivism, or by making it difficult to publish novels that did not fit the profile of the commercial success formula adopted by most publishers for black writers. In 1932, Jessie Fauset complained of the hard time she had publishing four novels depicting middle-class blacks; the publishers explained: "white readers just don't expect Negroes to be like this."[90] Arna Bontemps' first novel, *God Sends Sunday*, had "autobiographical overtones" and was "about a sensitive black boy in a nostalgic setting."[91] Bontemps' publisher, who hoped to find a market for the book even after the stock market crash, forced Bontemps to rewrite it in the sensual-primitive mode. Langston Hughes sums up the Negro writer's difficulties with publishers:

> Here are our problems: In the first place, Negro books are considered by editors and publishers as exotic. Negro material is placed, like Chinese material or Bali material or East Indian material, into a certain classification. Magazine editors will tell you, "We can use but so many Negro stories a year." (That "so many" meaning very few.) Publishers will say, "We already have one Negro novel on our list this fall."
>
> The market for Negro writers, then, is definitely limited as long as we write about ourselves. And the more truthfully we write about ourselves, the more limited our market becomes. Those novels about Negroes that sell best, by Negroes or whites, those novels that make the best seller lists and receive the leading prizes, are almost always books that make our black ghettos in the big cities seem very happy places indeed, and our plantations in the deep South idyllic in their pastoral loveliness. . . . When we cease to be exotic, we cease to sell.[92]

The publishing obstacle is only a step away from the issue of the audience, because publishers' criteria reflect audience taste. As Countee Cullen said in 1926, "Publishers, in general, are caterers, not martyrs and philanthropists."[93] There is no doubt that most black writers of the twenties were writing for a primarily white audience and that—with few exceptions—major publishers' interest in their work was determined by its salability. The situation between black writers and white audiences was complicated by a growing black middle class which had a great urge and need to applaud the work of young black writers, but this applause depended on the satisfaction of certain aesthetic criteria. Some of these criteria are reflected in reviews by Allison Davis, Benjamin Brawley, and W.E.B. DuBois. Objecting to the unrestrained depiction of lower-class subjects, these critics identified with middle-class values by praising Jessie Fauset and Nella Larsen, often for the wrong reasons. Among the Harlem Renaissance writers, Langston Hughes responded to attacks on him and others by the "bourgeois-uplift" critics of the DuBois-Brawley school. Hughes asserted his artistic independence of both whites and blacks, especially in his now famous article "The Negro Artist and the Racial Mountain." Middle-class values and hypersensitivity, said Hughes, led to one criticism of his work: "White people will gain a bad impression of Negroes from my poems." To Hughes, this "implies that a Negro artist should create largely for . . . the approval of white people." Hughes sought to choose his own subjects and audience, concluding that "there are plenty of propagandists for the Negro, but too few artists." He also defended many of his colleagues on similar grounds. He found Rudolph Fisher's stories beautiful "although he deals with common folks. . . . It seems absurd to say that they are not elevating to the race." Toomer, he went on, was "an artist to be proud of," as were, in different ways, Cullen, Thurman, and Zora Hurston.[94]

James Weldon Johnson and Sterling Brown also wrote persuasively on the subject. Johnson saw the black author caught between white stereotypes and black taboos. White audiences viewed the black either as "a simple, indolent, docile, improvident peasant; a singing, dancing, laughing, weeping child" or else as "an impulsive, irrational, passionate savage, reluctantly wearing a thin coat of culture." The taboos of black America, on the other hand, tended to "discourage in Negro authors the production of everything but *nice* literature."[95] In 1930, Sterling Brown declared that the bourgeois attitudes toward the artistic delineation of black life amounted to the "death-warrant of literature." According to Brown, the criticism of black readers is vitiated by at least four fallacies:

> We look upon Negro books regardless of the author's intention, as representative of all Negroes, i.e., as sociological documents.
>
> We insist that Negro books must be idealistic, optimistic tracts for race advertisement.
>
> We are afraid of truthtelling, of satire.
>
> We criticize from the point of view of bourgeois America, of racial apologists.[96]

The controversy over how the black should be portrayed in literature existed long before Hughes, Johnson, and Brown wrote on the subject, but the publication of Locke's *The New Negro* and Van Vechten's *Nigger Heaven* split it into at least two factions, with some individual writers and critics managing to maintain their integrity in the battle that continued throughout the twenties in both black and white journals.

W.E.B. DuBois set the stage for the controversy over the depiction

of the Negro in literature around the issue of art versus propaganda. DuBois was steeped in the nineteenth-century genteel
view of literature, and in his review of *The New Negro*, he attacked Locke's basic approach—that of fostering uninhibited self-
expression and realism instead of promoting art for race uplift. He
noted that *The New Negro* expressed "better than any book that
has been published in the last ten years the present state of
thought and culture among American Negroes," but charged that
Locke's insistence on Beauty rather than Propaganda is likely "to
turn the Negro Renaissance into decadence."[97] In February 1926,
DuBois followed his review of *The New Negro* by sending out a
questionnaire for a symposium in *The Crisis* entitled "The Negro
in Art—How shall he be Portrayed?" He objected to the concept
of artistic freedom because, he said, "the net result of American
literature to date [has been] to picture the twelve million black
Americans as prostitutes, thieves and fools and . . . such 'freedom'
in art is miserably unfair."[98]

The results of the *Crisis* symposium on "The Negro in Art" are
interesting as much for what they reveal about the aesthetic
criteria of black (and white) critics of the Harlem Renaissance as
for the light they throw indirectly on the continuing debate over
Black Aesthetic today. DuBois anticipated the controversy over
Nigger Heaven by raising, as the last and most important of his
questions for the symposium, the issue of the young black writers
succumbing to the temptation of following "the popular trend in
portraying Negro character in the underworld rather than seeking
to paint the truth about themselves and their own social class."
Here are the six questions that preceded this:

1. When the artist, black or white, portrays Negro characters,
   is he under any obligations or limitations as to the sort of
   character he will portray?
2. Can any author be criticized for painting the worst or the
   best characters of a group?
3. Can publishers be criticized for refusing to handle novels
   that portray Negroes of education and accomplishment, on
   the ground that these characters are no different from white
   folk and therefore not interesting?
4. What are Negroes to do when they are continually painted
   at their worst and judged by the public as they are painted?
5. Does the situation of the educated Negro in America with
   its pathos, humiliation and tragedy call for artistic treatment
   at least as sincere and sympathetic as "Porgy" received?
6. Is not the continual portrayal of the sordid, foolish and

criminal among Negroes convincing the world that this and this alone is really and essentially Negroid, and preventing white artists from knowing any other types and preventing black artists from daring to paint them?

The didactic tone of DuBois' questions is unmistakable; here as well as in the book reviews he wrote for *The Crisis*, DuBois demonstrates his limitations as a literary critic. DuBois' perceptive sociopolitical writings are impressive, but his literary criticism is outmoded and reveals his inability to break free of the limitations imposed by his New England Puritan background.

DuBois published excerpts from answers to his questions in various issues of *The Crisis* between March and November 1926. The respondents to DuBois' symposium included the well-known white and black figures H.L. Mencken, Carl Van Vechten, DuBose Heyward, Mary White Ovington, Joel E. Spingarn, Sinclair Lewis, Sherwood Anderson, Vachel Lindsay, Julia Peterkin, Langston Hughes, Countee Cullen, Charles W. Chesnutt, Walter White, Jessie Redmon Fauset, Benjamin Brawley, and Georgia Douglas Johnson. However, Rudolph Fisher, Wallace Thurman, Claude McKay, Sterling Brown, Alain Locke, and Arna Bontemps were conspicuously absent from the list.

According to Clare B. Crane, DuBois must have been disappointed in the answers he received.[99] Only Countee Cullen, Benjamin Brawley, and Jessie Fauset agreed with DuBois that writers were not completely free agents in choosing how to represent black life. Charles W. Chesnutt spoke for most when he declared: "The realm of art is almost the only territory in which the mind is free, and of all the arts that of creative fiction is the freest. . . . I see no possible reason why a colored writer should not have the same freedom. We want no color line in literature."[100] In response to the second question, most answered that a writer could portray the best and/or the worst, so long as his portrait is reasonably accurate. Many respondents, including Countee Cullen, Vachel Lindsay, and DuBose Heyward, recognized that publishers are more concerned with the salability of a book than with its moral tenor or class orientation, but hoped that publishers would encourage writers who wanted to portray the potential drama in the lives of educated Negroes. Some suggested, in response to the fourth question, that the black novelist should get even by depicting the white man at his worst. (But this was easier said than done and easier done than published.) Mencken said that if he found the white man extremely ridiculous, "to a Negro, he must be a hilarious spectacle, indeed."[101] Nobody denied the potential drama in the "pathos, humiliation and tragedy" of the educated black in the United States, but many respondents warned against giving in to propaganda in attempting a literary portrayal of the subject. Walter White found it necessary to recognize that every "honest craftsman . . . can only pour his knowledge and experience, real or imagined, through the alembic of his own mind and let the creations of his subjective or objective self stand or fall by whatever literary standards are current at a time."[102] The sixth question apparently had wide-ranging racial implications in American society. DuBois felt, not unjustifiably perhaps, that the racist elements of American society would use the slightest scrap of evidence to support what they already believed—the inferiority of the Negro. In answering this question, Robert T. Kerlin anticipated Richard Wright's naturalistic fiction by suggesting that the black artist should depict the "sordid," the "foolish," and the "criminal" Negro in relation to "the environment and the conditions—of white creation, of course—which have made him what he is." And he added, "Let the black artist not hesitate to show what white civilization is doing to both races."[103]

The last question on the list received its most provocative answer from Carl Van Vechten: "The squalor of Negro life, the vice of Negro life, offer a wealth of novel, exotic, picturesque material to the artist. On the other hand, there is very little difference if any between the life of a wealthy or cultured Negro and that of a white man of the same class. The question is: Are Negro writers going to write about this exotic material while it is still fresh or will they continue to make a free gift of it to white authors who will exploit it until not a drop of vitality remains?"[104] Van Vechten's *Nigger Heaven*, published a few months later, signaled black writers to take up the challenge of exploiting the exotic material that lay close to their lives or face the threat of preemption. DuBose Heyward reflected on the broader implications of the question when he said: "I think the young colored writer in America need not be afraid to portray any aspect of his racial life. . . . I feel convinced that he alone will produce the ultimate and authentic record of his own people. . . . A real subjective literature must spring from the race itself."[105] Charles W. Chesnutt, speaking from his long experience as a writer, attacked the propagandistic tenor of DuBois' question and asserted the primacy of aesthetic criteria in the writing and reading of literature:

> I think there is little danger of young colored writers writing too much about Negro characters in the underworld, so long as they do it well. Some successful authors have specialized in

crook stories, and some crooks are mighty interesting people
. . . there is no formula for these things, and the discerning
writer will make his own rules. . . . The colored writer, generally speaking, has not yet passed the point of thinking of himself first as a Negro, burdened with the responsibility of defending and uplifting his race. Such a frame of mind, however
praiseworthy from a moral standpoint, is bad for art. Tell your
story, and if it is on a vital subject, well told, with an outcome
that commends itself to right-thinking people, it will, if interesting, be an effective brief for whatever cause it incidentally
may postulate. . . . But the really epical race novel, in which
love and hatred, high endeavor, success and failure, sheer
comedy and stark tragedy are mingled, is yet to be written,
and let us hope that a man of Negro blood may write it.[106]

Although Alain Locke and Charles Johnson failed in their efforts
to create a black literary movement in the twenties, the Harlem
Renaissance writers did interact through mutual contact, correspondence, and by reviewing each other's books in different journals. This extended the critical perspective on their work and also
revealed some common ground on issues that interested them
deeply. W.E.B. DuBois and Sterling Brown ran literary columns in
The Crisis and Opportunity respectively, and Countee Cullen wrote
columns for these journals for a while. In addition, Rudolph Fisher,
Wallace Thurman, George Schuyler, Jessie Fauset, and Walter
White reviewed books by their colleagues and wrote articles about
the Negro as author and subject of literature.

There is remarkably little evidence of the influence of the Harlem Renaissance on later Afro-American writing. But the Renaissance did initiate discussion of many artistic and cultural concerns
of the Afro-American that were to cause heated controversy, especially in the sixties and the seventies. Important among these are
the treatment of black themes and characters by white writers and
the aesthetic criteria by which to appreciate and evaluate black
writing. John A. Williams, the novelist, has written: "For me . . .
the real meaning of the Harlem Renaissance was that it gave us an
example, and having had that example, we do not need to make
the same mistakes its members made."[107] From the passing comments that Richard Wright and Ralph Ellison have made, it appears that they learned from the mistakes of their Renaissance
predecessors, especially in being aware of the dangers inherent in
gearing their artistic impulses to the needs and demands of a
primarily white audience.[108] John Oliver Killens has emphasized
the need for young black critics and authors today to understand

both the achievements and the failings of the Harlem Renaissance because "a people ignorant of their history are condemned to repeat it."[109]

The Afro-American writers have learned more from the Renaissance's failings than from its achievements, but as early as the late 1920s black authors in the West Indies and Africa received positive inspiration from the spirit and individual works of the New Negro movement. Léopold Sédar Senghor of Senegal and Aimé Césaire of Martinique had read the Renaissance poetry and fiction in translation while still students at the Sorbonne.[110] Under its influence, these two poets developed their concept of Negritude, which, according to them, expresses the unifying essence of black experience and culture throughout the world.[111] These and other African intellectuals such as Sembene Ousmane and Ousmane Soce, who have articulated African nationalism, drew their inspiration from Claude McKay's *Banjo*.[112] The South African writer Peter Abrahams has written in his autobiography, *Tell Freedom*, about how, as a teenager at the Bantu Men's Social Center in Johannesburg, he discovered the Harlem Renaissance writers. There he read for the first time works by Claude McKay, Langston Hughes, Georgia Douglas Johnson, Countee Cullen, and W.E.B. DuBois. He recorded his impressions years later: "I read every one of the books on the shelf marked *American Negro Literature*. I became a nationalist, a color nationalist through the writings of men and women who lived in a world away from me. To them I owe a great debt for crystallizing my vague yearnings to write and for showing me that the long dream was attainable."[113]

Many Harlem Renaissance writers who led active lives past the twenties talked and wrote about the period, but Wallace Thurman provided the only detailed contemporary account of the movement. *Infants of the Spring* was published in 1932 toward the end of the Renaissance, a little before Thurman's untimely death; the book is a thinly veiled and largely undramatized fictional treatment of the black Renaissance writers. Thurman, who did not arrive in Harlem until 1925, soon became one of its most promising black writers. Dorothy West, the black novelist, tells how this brilliant, bohemian writer allowed himself to be surrounded by "a queer assortment of the 'lost generation' of Blacks and Whites. They clung to him like leeches, and although he saw them clearly and could evaluate them in a half-dozen brutal words, he chose to allow them to waste the valuable hours of his ripening maturity."[114] In *Infants of the Spring*, Thurman sees his problems with a stark clarity and also brilliantly satirizes Renaissance writers. As the only document from the period that attempted self-evaluation, *Infants of the Spring* deserves a close look for its value in indicating the aesthetic and critical milieu of the Harlem Renaissance.

The center of activity in Thurman's *Infants of the Spring* is the Niggeratti Manor,[115] a house turned into a commune for the black artists by Euphoria Blake, a black businesswoman who believes that only with money and with art can Negroes purchase their complete freedom. Raymond Taylor, Wallace Thurman's alter ego and spokesman in the book, lives in the Manor along with Paul Arbian, a bright, bohemian black writer who ardently admires Oscar Wilde; Eustace Savoy, an actor and singer who wants to sing Schubert downtown, but would not have anything to do with spirituals; and Pelham Gaylord, "a natural born menial," who is too happy to be of service to other artists to know he himself is not one. In addition, there is a self-professed actress who lives on the third floor with her two young daughters, and the Pig-woman, a mysterious witchlike woman who lived in the building before Euphoria Blake took it over. Thurman exposes the lack of direction or vitality among Harlem writers of the twenties by depicting the goings-on at the Manor. The major activity at the Manor is gin-drinking. Raymond Taylor, the soberest and perhaps the ablest of the Manor's resident artists, informs his white friend, Stephen Jorgenson, when the latter first arrives in Harlem, that he could not do without Harlem gin, "a valuable and ubiquitous commodity." The Manor is frequented by all kinds of people, including Aline and Janet, who fight with each other over Jorgenson's sexual attentions; Barbara, "a white girl who lives off Negro men's infatuation for a white skin"; Samuel Carter, a Negrotarian, a white do-gooder of Puritan background, who is making a career of Negroes; Bull, "a burly Negro," who satisfies his hate for white males by sleeping with white females; Lucille, an office secretary who likes Raymond but prefers Bull because he is "at least a man, and knows how to get what he wants."[116] The Manor artists are always without money. In order to replenish the diminishing groceries, they arrange a donation party.

Infants of the Spring presents mediocre artists lost in a web of frivolity and recalcitrance without purpose or privacy, unable to achieve anything worthwhile. Paul Arbian is caught in the swirl of the bohemian mood of his white contemporaries, but "has never recovered from the shock of realizing that no matter how bizarre a personality he may develop, he will still be a Negro, subject to snubs from certain ignorant people" (p. 59). Raymond, who is much more at ease with his racial heritage than either Eustace or

Paul, realizes that his "modicum of talent" was not enough to create great literature (p. 145). Moreover, he can hardly find time to realize his limited potential, surrounded as he is by unproductive relationships.

Although there are many comments on the Negro Renaissance scattered through the pages of *Infants of the Spring*, Thurman provides his most elaborate satire on himself and his colleagues by describing a party of Harlem *literati*, arranged at the initiative of Dr. Parkes, a literary version of Alain Locke.[117] Dr. Parkes is introduced earlier at the donation party as a self-styled "guardian angel to the current set of younger Negro artists" (p. 180). A few days later, Dr. Parkes and Samuel Carter come back to warn Ray against the reputation of drunkenness and decadence that the Manor is gaining in the Negro press. Dr. Parkes advises Raymond soberly: "You can't create to the best of your ability, being constantly surrounded by a group of parasites and drunken nonentities. They sap your energy" (p. 220). At the meeting of the artists, Dr. Parkes unsuccessfully tries to coerce a crowd of conflicting personalities into forming a literary salon. Wallace Thurman's ability in satirical portraiture comes through in *Infants of the Spring* even better than it did in his earlier novel, *The Blacker the Berry*.

The first one to arrive at the gathering is Sweetie May Carr (Zora Neale Hurston), "a short story writer, more noted for her ribald wit and personal effervescence than for any actual literary work" (p. 229). Sweetie May enjoys living up to the whites' notion of what a "darky" should be, but "it seldom occurred to any of her patrons that she did it with tongue in cheek" (p. 229). This is what Sweetie May says about the Negro Renaissance:

> Being a Negro writer these days is a racket and I'm going to make the most of it while it lasts. . . . I don't know a tinker's damn about art. I care less about it. . . . About twice a year I manage to sell a story. It is acclaimed. I am a genius in the making. Thank God for this Negro literary renaissance! Long may it flourish! (P. 230)

Tony Crews (Langston Hughes) walks into the meeting, "smiling and self-effacing, a mischievous boy, grateful for the chance to slip away from the backwoods college he attended" (p. 231). De Witt Clinton (Countee Cullen) is another artist, "a much touted romantic figure," whom Raymond imagines in his creative moment as sitting with his "eyes on the page of Keats, fingers on typewriter, mind frantically conjuring African scenes. And there would of course be a Bible nearby" (p. 236). Others present at the salon meeting include Carl Denny (Aaron Douglas), Cedric Williams (Eric Walrond), and Manfred Trout (Rudolph Fisher). "Small, dapper, with sensitive features, graying hair," Dr. Parkes smiles benevolently at his brood and tries to bring the meeting to order (p. 233). He reminds all of them that the future of the race depends on them: "Because of your concerted storming up Parnassus, new vistas will be spread open to the entire race. The Negro in the south will no more know peonage, Jim Crowism, or loss of the ballot, and the Negro everywhere in America will know complete freedom and equality" (p. 234). Parkes recommends that the black writers should go back to their "racial roots" and cultivate "a healthy paganism based on African traditions"[118] (p. 235).

During the discussion that ensues, Paul questions the value of African heritage: "I'm not an African. I'm an American and a perfect product of the melting pot" (p. 238). Cedric Williams and Raymond Taylor stress individuality. To Raymond, "a wholesale flight back to Africa or a wholesale allegiance to Communism or a wholesale adherence to an antiquated and for the most part ridiculous propagandistic program are equally futile and unintelligent" (p. 240). But a pandemonium follows; Sweetie May and Cedric Williams end up cursing each other, Cedric stalking angrily out of the room. Soon thereafter the first and last salon of Harlem Renaissance writers comes abruptly to an end.

The fate of the literary salon only prefigures the fate of Niggeratti Manor. Euphoria Blake tires of losing profits and not seeing creative results from the Manor artists; she decides to turn the house into a dormitory for young Negro working girls between the ages of eighteen and thirty. Pelham Gaylord, seduced by the actress's young, sexually precocious daughter, ends up in jail on charges of rape. Eustace never recovers from the unsuccessful audition for a concert downtown and spends his remaining years drinking afternoon tea and singing Schubert's songs in a quavering, tired voice. The deliberately bizarre suicide of "Paul the debonair, Paul the poseur, Paul the irresponsible" is relieved only dimly by the vague hope that Raymond will finish his first novel with love and support from Lucille (p. 280).

All this is reinforced in the book by Raymond's analysis of his own failures and his comments on the New Negro art movement. Like Countee Cullen's Constancia Brandon, Ray claims he is not the least bit self-conscious about his race. "I rather love myself as I am and am quite certain that I have as much chance to make good as anyone else, regardless of my color" (p. 61). He recognizes the Negro Renaissance as a national phenomenon, but feels that "nothing or at least very little [is] being done to substantiate the current fad, to make it the foundation for something truly epochal" (p. 221). He is disgusted at attempts to romanticize Harlem and its Negroes. "Harlem has become a state of mind. . . . There are a quarter million Negroes here, and it is fashionable to take notice of a bare thousand . . . the cabaret entertainers, the actors, the musicians, the artists. . . . The rest are ignored." He does not expect to become a great writer nor does he think "the Negro race can produce one now any more than can America" (p. 221). And this is how he judges his generation of black writers: "I know of only one Negro who has the elements of greatness, and that's Jean Toomer. The rest of us are merely journeymen, planting seed for someone else to harvest. We all get sidetracked sooner or later. The older ones become warped by propaganda. We younger ones are mired in decadence. . . . We're a curiosity . . . to ourselves" (p. 221).

Although it is not necessary to fully agree with Thurman's cripplingly self-conscious judgment on individual writers, including himself, *Infants of the Spring* represents a coming-of-age of the Harlem Renaissance *literati*. It demonstrates the ability of the movement to evaluate and possibly modify its direction. Unfortunately, there was little opportunity for Thurman's criticisms to be absorbed. Two years earlier, the stock market had crashed, and white America's ability to sustain and enjoy the Negro fad had been severely hampered. Perhaps, as Ralph Ellison has pointed out, the black writer of the twenties "had wanted to be fashionable and this insured, even more effectively than the approaching Depression, the failure of the 'New Negro' movement."[119] Black writers had "climbed aboard the bandwagon" of exoticism and decadence signaled by *Nigger Heaven* and enjoyed the era when the Negro was in vogue. By the midthirties, exotic and genteel novels were no longer popular with the publishers and were attacked by a new breed of black writers and critics.[120] In early 1934, Eugene Saxton, who had handled McKay's work at Harper & Brothers, bluntly informed him that his popularity had been part of a passing fad.[121] In 1940, Langston Hughes spoke for many when he said, "I had a swell time while it [the Negro Renaissance] lasted. But I thought it wouldn't last long. . . . For how could a large number of people be crazy about Negroes forever?"[122]

It is unfair to evaluate the Harlem Renaissance by the hindsight judgments of Langston Hughes and Claude McKay, or the aesthetic criteria of the DuBois-Brawley school, or the theoretical constructs of Alain Locke, or even the detailed satire on its members and aims by Wallace Thurman. Intense intellectual and artistic activity created fruitful controversy over basic issues relating to art and its appreciation. The racial matrix of artistic expression received serious critical attention and some of the latter-day Afro-American concepts—such as Black Aesthetic—were prefigured in discussions of Harlem Renaissance artists. This is important, even though the attitudes of most Renaissance writers in these matters were characterized by ambivalence and tension, and they did not as a group develop common approaches, and many individual artists failed to resolve their conflicting impulses about race and art while others found only tentative solutions.

Two articles, along with the correspondence that followed from the two authors, contain the aesthetic and critical criteria that underlay black writing in the twenties. These are "The Negro-Art Hokum" and "The Negro Artist and the Racial Mountain," written by George S. Schuyler and Langston Hughes, respectively, for two consecutive issues of *Nation* in June 1926.[123] The exchange between Schuyler and Hughes also confirms that a class bias was consciously or unconsciously at the root of most controversies among Renaissance writers and critics. Schuyler postulates that Negro art is simply an African phenomenon: "to suggest the possibility of any such development among the ten million colored people in this republic is self-evident foolishness." Spirituals, blues, jazz, and the Charleston are not racial expression, but "contributions of a caste in a certain section of the country." Otherwise, in literature, painting, sculpture, and drama, the American Negro has hardly produced anything racially distinctive, because "the Afro-American is merely a lampblacked Anglo-Saxon." He attributes the fad of racial differences to "a few writers with a paucity of themes [who] have seized upon imbecilities of the Negro rustics and clowns and palmed them off as authentic and characteristic Aframerican behavior."

With his uncompromising realism and keen observation, Schuyler notes the danger that any concept of racial difference will be used by Negrophobes and racists to prove the Negro's inferiority: "On this baseless premise, so flattering to the white mob, that the blackamoor is inferior and fundamentally different, is erected the postulate that he must needs be peculiar; and when he attempts to portray life through the medium of art, it must of necessity be a peculiar art." He responded to Hughes' defense of racial art by asserting that black masses in America were no different from the white masses and that both watched "the lazy world go round" and had "their nip of gin on Saturday nights."

Langston Hughes, in turn, noticed the taint of self-hatred in

Schuyler's view of black art and culture. In his response to Schuyler's letter, Hughes wrote: "The very fact that Negroes do straighten their hair and try to forget their racial background makes them different from white people. If they were exactly like the dominant class they would not have to try so hard to imitate them." In his essay, he projected a culturally pluralistic view of black art that placed special emphasis on the integrity of the artist. He indicated that for most blacks and black artists, "the word white comes to be unconsciously a symbol of all the virtues. It holds for the children beauty, morality and money."

For Hughes, the whole issue of racial expression converged on the issue of class within the black group. The "low-down folks," Hughes said, "furnish a wealth of colorful, distinctive material for any artist because they still hold their own individuality in the face of American standardizations. And perhaps these common people will give to the world its truly great Negro artist, the one who is not afraid to be himself." Hughes refrained from using the black American's atavistic or African heritage as a point of departure from his white counterpart. He saw enough themes in the lives of black and white Americans to "furnish a black artist with a lifetime of creative work. To these the Negro artist can give his racial individuality, his heritage of rhythm and warmth, and his incongruous humor that, so often, as in the Blues, becomes ironic laughter mixed with tears." In direct response to Schuyler's charge that "Negro propaganda art, even when glorifying the 'primitiveness' of the American Negro masses is hardly more than a protest against a feeling of inferiority," Hughes contended that "until America has completely absorbed the Negro and until segregation and racial self-consciousness have entirely disappeared, the true work of art from the Negro artist is bound, if it have any color and distinctiveness at all, to reflect his racial background and his racial environment."

As a black artist, Hughes welcomed a growing middle-class black audience for his work, but regarded it as a potential threat to his artistic integrity. "The Negro artist works against the undertow of sharp criticism and misunderstanding from his own group and unintentional bribes from the whites." Using his own poems and Jean Toomer's Cane as examples of the kind of racial expression he approved and cherished, Hughes asserted his independence of both whites and blacks in what came to be known later as the literary manifesto of younger Renaissance writers:

We younger Negro artists who create now intend to express our individual dark-skinned selves without fear or shame. If white people are pleased we are glad. If they are not, it doesn't matter. We know we are beautiful. And ugly too. The tom-tom cries and the tom-tom laughs. If colored people are pleased we are glad. If they are not, their displeasure doesn't matter either. We build our temples for tomorrow, strong as we know how, and we stand on top of the mountain, free within ourselves.

Langston Hughes' clear and resonant voice expresses the highest artistic ideals and achievements of the Harlem Renaissance.

RACE AND SEX

APPROACHES TO SELF-DEFINITION

"Negroes are never so beautiful and magical as when they do that gorgeous sublimation of the primitive African sex feeling."

Claude McKay, Banjo

"And behold he is not so vastly different from any other American, just distinctive . . . he is a dark American who wears his joy and rue as does the white American."

Jessie R. Fauset,
The Chinaberry Tree

One of the ongoing concerns of the black writer in America has been to define the black's situation in American society. Richard Wright, Ralph Ellison, and James Baldwin reflect the whole spectrum of their sociocultural and political beliefs primarily through their treatment of Afro-American identity. The variety and maturity of contemporary black thinking on the subject is an outgrowth of the pioneering work of Harlem Renaissance writers.

The Renaissance novelists' interest in Afro-American identity manifests itself in the use of race and sex to develop or dramatize the messages of their works. Racial protest is part of every Renaissance novel, but Jessie Fauset makes a special effort to integrate it into her four novels of black middle-class life. Emma Lou Morgan's loveless career in *The Blacker the Berry* is seen by Wallace

Thurman to result from her desire to be white. In *One Way to Heaven*, Countee Cullen introduces a note of permanence into the love of the con man, Sam Lucas, and his young paramour, Mattie, that offsets the sterile and bizarre conversations of upper-class blacks in the novel's subplot. In mixing love and politics in their novels *Fire in the Flint* and *Dark Princess*, respectively, Walter White and W.E.B. DuBois were as close in their artistic objectives as they were sometimes apart in their political views. In *Not Without Laughter*, Langston Hughes portrays both the growing awareness of sex and love in the life of an adolescent boy and the hassles and humiliations suffered by poor blacks in their daily lives. In *Quicksand*, Nella Larsen bares the innermost feelings of a woman haunted by a self-image that derives from her acceptance of the larger society's view of miscegenation.

Two patterns emerge from these treatments and both are consciously directed at giving positive portrayals of black life. On one side are McKay, Toomer, and Bontemps, who attempt to bring out the instinctive joy and abandon in the life of the black, and his ability to withstand commercialism and mechanization in a decade when the fear of standardization was almost obsessive in both Europe and America. These writers celebrated the life-styles of poor black folk in the plantations of Georgia or the West Indies, and in the growing black communities in urban centers such as New York, Washington, D.C., and Chicago. On the other side were writers and race leaders who thought that the Negro's best chance for greater civil rights lay in their presenting him as an American, distinguished from white only by skin color. Fauset reflects this approach in her four novels, published between 1924 and 1933. Since only the black bourgeoisie showed any interest or success in imitating the values and manners of the white middle class, the case for the black American's shared Americanness had to be made by depicting middle-class black Americans living quietly in small communities all over the country.

Claude McKay emphasized the distinctiveness of black experience through a treatment of the "lowly" black's situation. As a reflection of the Euro-American fad of black primitivism and antimaterialism[1] (outlined in chapter 1), McKay's work is especially significant because he searched for new, positive definitions of black life. McKay not only wanted to make a dent in the inhibitions and taboos that had constrained earlier black writers and middle-class blacks in general, but also hoped to define the black experience in the West in terms of the Negro's African roots.

The joy and abandon with which McKay's black characters sing, dance, eat, love, and sleep represent the uninterrupted stream of values and attitudes their ancestors brought from Africa and which have helped them cope with torturous lives in the West. In spite of or perhaps because of his grueling menial jobs, McKay's black man has the urge and capacity to give himself to music and dancing, drinking and gambling, sex and love with a passion startling to most white men. The black, for McKay, is a vagabond who takes life as it comes. With healthy and humane instincts, he struggles to remain unmechanized despite constant pressure from the evil civilization that surrounds him.

McKay employs sexual metaphors to capture the black's never-ending vagabondage.[2] The black's ability to enjoy sex without the inhibitions of a Puritan background is evidence for the romance of black life in general. In *Home to Harlem*, Harlem is an all-black city of "primitive joy," of "liquor-rich laughter, banana-rich laughter," where blacks of all possible skin-shades abandon themselves to "pure voluptuous jazzing." At Madame Suarez's buffet-flat, black men and women are seen as "gorgeous animals swaying . . . through the dance, punctuating it with marks of warm physical excitement"[3] (p. 108). Animal images describe the dancing, the sexual overtures and actions, and the fights of men and women over partners. In the sweet, chocolate Harlem, couples dance to the blues, "thick as maggots in a vat of sweet liquor and as wriggling" (p. 14). When the owner of the Biltmore closes the cabaret for the night because of a fight between two men, the "jazzers" stand and talk resentfully in the street, "like dogs flicked apart by a whipcord" (p. 34). Zeddy is compared in different contexts to a bear, an ape, and a gorilla. Rose reclines against Jake "like a lean lazy leopard" when they meet for the first time at the Congo. Later, loving Jake more than ever for hitting her, Rose "moves down on him like a panther, swinging her hips in wonderful, rhythmical motion" (p. 118). At Gin-Head Susy's party, a jungle atmosphere pervades the room and "like some shameless wild animals hungry for raw meat, the females savagely searched the eyes of the males" (p. 68).

In contrasting black sensuality with white passionlessness, McKay indicates the white man's envy: "A colored couple dawdled by, their arms fondly caressing each other's hips. A white man forking a bit of ground stopped and stared expressively after them" (pp. 279-80). The Harlem cabarets are flooded with "white pleasure-seekers from downtown" who are incapable of seeing beyond the "simple, childish grin" that hides "depths of profundity" in the African soul (pp. 337-38).

All ... should be hand

In *Home to Harlem*, McKay moves from the strengths of black sexuality to the distinctive quality of black life and culture through his characterization of Jake. Unashamed of the coarseness of his life and unfettered by middle-class values, Jake refuses to become Rose's "sweet man": "I've never been a sweetman yet. Never lived off no womens and never will. I always works" (p. 20). Later, he decides to quit her rather than demean himself in satisfying her urge for the "knocks." He shuffles away from the "hideous" Miss Curdy before she succeeds in her sexual designs on him. Jake shows the same coolness of judgment and fierce independence in other situations as well. As an early reviewer observed, "Jake does not hate white people, he merely sees them realistically."[4] He would not scab against any fellow worker, black or white, but he holds no illusions about the friendliness of white unions for blacks. When a white worker invites him to sign up in his union, his candid response is: "I ain't no white folks' nigger and I ain't no poah white's fool" (p. 45). Thus, his no-nonsense attitude toward sex and women extends to work too; unlike Agatha, Ray's girl friend, he entertains no romantic notions about his job as a railroad waiter. Jake, in fact, is endowed with a spirit that he looks for in others, men and women. He misses in Rose "the charm and verve, the infectious joy" of the maroon-brown girl, Felice, whom he had met on the first evening after his return to Harlem. Rose has no spirit at all, "that strange elusive something that he felt in himself, sometimes here, sometimes there" (p. 41).

Yet Jake is only a part of the whole. Blues, ragtime songs, and jazzy dancing at the cabarets and speakeasies as well as brutal violence exhibited in fights over petty jealousies create the *Home to Harlem* world. Early readers, especially the middle-class Negro intelligentsia, reacted sharply against the book. The reviewer in *The Tattler* (16 March 1928) was amused that McKay had "out-niggered Mr. Van Vechten. His women keep more men, his men drink more liquor, he spends more time in the cabaret and has more fights and bawdy house brawls." George W. Jacobs, a black New Yorker writing in *The Pittsburgh Courier* (7 April 1928), accused McKay of subverting his artistic powers to the demands of a white reading public and chastized him for depicting the black as "constitutionally unmoral and hyper-sexual" and for endorsing "the current fallacy that a Negro ceases to be a 'real' Negro when he becomes an intellectual." W.E.B. DuBois, in his combined review of *Home to Harlem* and Nella Larsen's *Quicksand* (*The Crisis*, June 1928), praised Larsen's novel as "a fine, thoughtful and courageous piece of work" and found McKay's novel nauseating. McKay, DuBois added, has "used every art and emphasis to paint drunkenness, fighting, lascivious sexual promiscuity and utter absence of restraint in as bold and as bright colors as he can."

More recently, Wayne Cooper and Michael B. Stoff have observed that McKay's view of black folk was influenced considerably by the cult of the Negro as a natural and expressive primitive, uninhibited by the evil forces of modern civilization.[5] In responding to the charge of primitivism in his writings, McKay placed an interesting emphasis on the possibilities of discrete African and Afro-American literatures. Writing in *The Herald Tribune Books* (6 March 1932), under the title, "A Negro to His Critics," Claude McKay noted wryly that many white critics had approached his work as if he "were a primitive and altogether a stranger to civilization. *Perhaps I myself unconsciously gave that impression*" [emphasis mine]. He went on: "I am conscious of my new world birthright as of my African origins, being aware of the one and its significance in my development as I feel the other emotionally." He rejected the suggestion that he should "make a trip to Africa and then write about Negro life in its pure state." To this, he countered a concept familiar to us from its recurrence in the 1960s:

> Negroid Africa will produce in time its own modern poets and artists peculiar to its soil. The Aframerican may gain spiritual benefits by returning *in spirit* to his African origins, but as an artist he will remain a unique product of Western civilization with something of himself to give that will be very different from anything that may come out of a purely African community.

However, by the time McKay wrote this rejoinder to his critics, he had already published *Banjo*, which, although a continued exploration of the issues raised in *Home to Harlem*, definitely shows greater depth and maturity. McKay seems to have written the *Herald Tribune* piece as a conciliatory gesture toward the black reviewers and journalists, who, according to McKay, "often do not distinguish between the task of propaganda and the work of art." In defending himself, he once again asserts his artistic integrity and urges the "artistic exploitation" by younger black poets and novelists of

> the homely things—of Mandy's wash-tub, Aunt Jemima's white folks, Miss Ann's old clothes for work-and-wages, George's yessah-boss, dining-car and Pullman services, barber and shoe-shine shop, chittling and corn pone joints—all the lowly things that go to the formation of the Aframerican soil in

which the best, the most pretentious of Aframerican society still has its roots.

McKay leaves no doubt here and in *Banjo* of his class sympathies. Unlike Jessie Fauset, McKay did not see much future in an uncritical black identification with the values and predilections of the white middle class. At this stage of his career, McKay also perhaps felt that the black leaders, with their strong middle-class orientation, were contributing to the neglect of the richness and variety of what he calls "the background, the fundamental rhythm of Aframerican life." As a creative writer, McKay sympathized with his contemporaries Jean Toomer, Langston Hughes, Sterling Brown, and Zora Neale Hurston, who were making genuine efforts to exploit the rich and original sources available to them in Afro-American folklore—the picturesque black slang, the blues, ragtime, and spirituals. In his *Songs of Jamaica* (1911) and *Constab Ballads* (1912), McKay had written in dialect verse of "the loves and hates . . . the work and play" of the Jamaican peasants—verse which had earned him a reputation as the native Robert Burns. In *Home to Harlem*, by his own statement, he had attempted something "very similar to what I had done for Jamaica in verse."[6]
Many white critics, however, read in McKay's work only a confirmation of what they already knew about the blacks from the widely held social and literary stereotypes. *Home to Harlem* was an instant success and aggressively met the growing interest in the Negro, whetted two years earlier by the appearance of *Nigger Heaven*. It became the first best seller by a black writer. Printed originally in February 1928, it went through five printings in less than two months and sold more than 50,000 copies within a year. In censuring McKay for wasting his energy to prove what white people already thought—that blacks were "buffoons, thugs and rotters anyway"—the Negro reviewer in *The Chicago Defender* (17 March 1928) did not do justice to McKay's intentions as a writer, yet accurately assessed the book's impact on the white reading public. John R. Chamberlain, reviewing for the *New York Times* (11 March 1928), described *Home to Harlem* as "the real stuff, the low-down on Harlem, the dope from the inside." Some reviewers treated the book as a social document, revealing many unsuspected things about black life. However, at least two early reviewers, white Burton Rascoe in *The Bookman* (April 1928) and black Aubrey Bowser in the New York *Amsterdam News* (21 March 1928), discovered some of the book's distinctive qualities. Both praised its characterization, its spontaneous use of dialect, and its poetic descriptions. "He makes no case, he pleads no cause, he

asks no extenuation, and he does not explain his idiomatic phrases," added Burton Rascoe. For Aubrey Bowser the plotless novel harmonized with the vagabondish hero; though *Nigger Heaven* had been "dirt for dirt's sake," *Home to Harlem* was "dirt for art's sake."

In retrospect, we can take McKay's word that *Home to Harlem* was not written to exploit the market created by *Nigger Heaven*. (No doubt, however, publishers intended to do so.) In his autobiography, McKay also discounts any likelihood of Van Vechten's influence; McKay had developed his novel from a story by the same title that he had submitted for the *Opportunity* literary contest in 1925. He said he did not see *Nigger Heaven* until the late spring of 1927. "And by that time I had nearly completed *Home to Harlem*."[7]

Home to Harlem must be read as part of McKay's continuing creative effort to discern public issues in his intensely felt experiences.[8] McKay could not separate his personal problems as a black man from his fascination with the opposition between primitivism and civilization. Critics have seen his three published novels as a thematically connected trilogy raising and attempting to resolve problems that engaged McKay's attention as an individual, social thinker, and artist throughout his career.[9]

In *Banjo*, McKay continues his concern with the vagabond spirit through the central character Lincoln Agrippa Daily, nicknamed Banjo. Like Jake, Banjo is a rollicking roustabout. Recently discharged from the Canadian army and intensely desiring to be on the move, he manages to get himself deported to his favorite port, Marseilles. "It was Banjo's way to take every new place and every new thing for the first time in a hot crazy-drunk manner. He was the type who was never sober, even when he was not drinking" (p. 13). Once again, McKay explores and dramatizes primitivism through his protagonist's sexuality. Banjo takes to women as naturally as Jake and would not allow any female to "cackle ovah" him. When Latnah, the Arab woman who dresses his wound and gives him "a pillow for his head" in her attic room, tries to nag him over money, his response is quite Jake-like: "No woman nevah ride me yet and you ain't gwine to ride me, neither" (p. 26). Unlike Jake, however, who misses the "elusive something" in Rose, Banjo takes "all women as one—as they come—roughly, carelessly, easily" (p. 170). That difference is, however, explained by McKay in terms of the novel's changed setting from Harlem to the waterfront of Marseilles. When Ray teases the metamorphosed

Banjo about his having reduced himself to "a poor slave nigger in coal for *une putaine blanche*," Banjo replies: "I ain't back home where I could find a honey-sweet mamma, so I just had to take what was ready and willing" (p. 234).

Home to Harlem develops under the shadow of Jake's character from the beginning, but in *Banjo*, McKay's spokesman, Ray, becomes the dominant voice at the outset of the second part of the three-part novel. In *Home to Harlem*, Ray, even as a secondary character, opens a pandora's box of unresolved and complex race-related issues, and McKay refuses to settle for simple answers or facile generalizations. As a character, Ray fumbles in trying to express himself. He is still too delicate and sensitive to be a vagabond; he does not gamble or drink, nor can he "pick up love easily on the street" as Jake does. Yet he cannot help feeling that "he was a savage, even though a sensitive one" (pp. 226-27). He wants to become a writer, but can find no use for words he has already acquired. He reads Dostoevsky, D.H. Lawrence, Sherwood Anderson, and James Joyce, but it is not clear what fascinates him in these writers. He realizes that blacks do not need the education provided by whites but fails to suggest viable alternatives. He loves Harlem for "its composite voice, the fruitiness of its laughter, the trailing rhythm of its 'blues,'" but hates it for "its brutality, gang rowdyism, promiscuous thickness" (p. 267).

In *Banjo*, McKay has untangled some of his vague and confused thinking about the black's relationship to the oppositions between "instinct" and "intellect," "primitiveness" and "civilization." McKay's locale, the cosmopolitan port of Marseilles, provides him the freedom to explore some of his "racial" ideas in a context that embraces almost all nations of the world—yellow, brown, black, and white.

The Quartier Reserve on the Marseilles beach, or the Ditch, as the beachboys call it with rough affection, is McKay's major symbol in a book that depends heavily on atmosphere, rather than characterization or plot. *Banjo* opens by depicting the Ditch as a microcosm where all human colors and shades come together in a continual celebrating and contesting of their instinct to live. It is a place where love is easy and cheap and where Western civilization's Protestant ethic, personified ironically in the black preacher Sister Geter, fails to distract the beachboys from the "foamy fascination" of the Mediterranean. To Ray, the Ditch is not an exotic thing; he sees it as an ongoing opera enhanced in its color by an intermittent "volley of bullets tearing down some dark alley." He finds the Ditch "as strikingly natural as the high-heeled fancy shoes and the pretty frocks of popeline de soie and crêpe Marocain and all the voluptuous soft feminine stuff parading there in the mud and slime and refuse" (p. 174). Even though the Ditch has both white and black panhandlers, it comes to be identified— especially toward the end of the book—with the black's capacity to create, to improvise, to live, to love and laugh, and to be a human being even in a hostile environment. Living in and around the Ditch, Banjo views his life existentially: "I'm just a right-there, right-there baby, yestidy and today and tomorrow and forevah. All right-there right-here for me now" (p. 33). Banjo and his friends—Malty, Bugsy, Ginger, Dengel, Goosey, Latnah—are "the bums . . . the vagabond lovers of life," whose spirit, along with the Ditch, embodies a serious challenge to civilization.

In *Banjo*, McKay achieves what Conroy has called "a formless form," and it accurately reflects the spirit of a vagabond life-style. But Conroy[10] and Nathan Huggins[11] have failed to see that with the Ditch as the nerve center of the book's activity, *Banjo* develops into an extended metaphor by which McKay suggests positive meanings and life-styles based on the black's cultural roots. These new meanings and life-styles, McKay hoped, would supplant the "gray respectability" he attacks bitterly at many places in the book. To read *Banjo* as McKay's attempt to romanticize escape and irresponsibility is to take the book superficially. By placing Ray, an educated black aspiring to be a writer, in the position of a disciple to a jazzman whose life is as "unrestrained, free-spirited, and vibrantly alive"[12] as the songs he sings, McKay attempts to develop a view of life that is wide in its human sympathies and free of artificial constraints. After he returns from Paris to become a coal man in Marseilles, Banjo expresses his distilled experience of life: "Life is a rectangular affair and the only thing to do is to take it nacheral" (p. 234).

Although the beachbums generally "knew very little about governments and cared less," *Banjo* is easily the most political novel of the Harlem Renaissance. Both in their dealings and the rap sessions, Banjo and Ray reflect a political consciousness that is neither.raceless nor racist, but sharply ethnic and racial—a sensibility that rejoices in human variety without fear or prejudice. The *Banjo* world is rich in its ethnic and national diversity, but (we have to take Ray's word for it) it is under the imminent threat of standardization. McKay faced the difficult task of delineating many characters with varied ethnic backgrounds without falling into the trap of cultural stereotyping. Except for the Asian characters and the African "bush boys," his sins in group stereotyping are few indeed. McKay creates this unbiased picture partly by having characters from most groups talk about the commonplace images they have of other groups, and also by highlighting the humorous side of intergroup behavior. The ethnic variety is effectively summed up by Banjo with a kinetic image: "Oh, Lawdy! Life is a game a skin; black skin, white skin, sweet skin and all skin and selling one another is living it" (p. 232).

Banjo continues and expands the theme of primitiveness found in *Home to Harlem*, but the emphasis shifts. *Banjo* does not contain the proliferation of animal images that characterizes *Home to Harlem*. Instead, Ray talks about the British and American propaganda against the black during the war that focused on "the sexuality of Negroes—that strange, big bug forever buzzing in the imagination of white people" (p. 146). He rejects the common white notion that blacks are oversexed. "What he inferred was that white people had developed sex complexes that Negroes had not" (p. 252). Banjo and Ray, like Jake and Ray in *Home to Harlem*, experience similar conflicts in reacting to Western civilization; but they represent different ways of rebelling against it.[13] Jake's and Banjo's "gut-level" or instinctual responses are given an intellectual interpretation by Ray in both the books. In *Banjo*, both Banjo and Ray, in spite of their racial integrity and in contrast to "race men" like Bugsy and Goosey, project a humanity that encompasses both black and white. Banjo's camaraderie not only includes black bums but also his white colleagues in the Ditch, and Ray endorses Banjo's giving five francs to a starving white boy despite Bugsy's opposition. At a later point in the book, Ray derides the inability of black leaders and journalists to laugh at themselves, describing as "niggerism" their oversensitiveness to Negro jokes. As Malty puts it, "Can't the race stand a joke?"

But more than anything else, *Banjo* marks McKay's point of departure from the white writers interested in black primitiveness. McKay undoubtedly shared the concerns that his contemporaries on either side of the Atlantic had about crude commercialism and increasing standardization. But the primitive black with his rural and preindustrial wisdom is not seen by McKay simply as a bulwark against the fall of civilization. Instead, McKay grants Ray "the almost superhuman, almost impossible" task of being a colored human being in a white world, as well as the task of being a black intellectual. In a white civilization the black cannot "function normally like his white brother"; he cannot respond spontaneously to common human emotions such as pain, joy, anger, and sorrow. "Only within the confines of his own world of color could he be his own self." It is for the latter reason that Ray pronounces the United States (or "United Snakes" as Goosey labels it) the best place for the black in the Western world. Despite the open hostility of the South and the "friendly contempt" of the North, black Americans have the freedom to develop "their own group life" within a racially segregated society. Both in *Home to Harlem* and in *Banjo*, McKay assaults the self-hatred and hypocrisy of the "race talk" of those who actually desire assimilation into the white world. Ray hates the French hypocrisy that invites him to sit in a restaurant only to suffer the waiter's condescension and prefers the curtailed freedom of segregated institutions in the United States. "If we can't eat downtown we can eat better in Harlem," he says (*Home to Harlem*, p. 298).

Two united terrors, "business and prejudice," stalk the black man all over the world: "Prejudices like the stock market— curtailed, diminishing, increasing, changing chameleon-like, according to place and time, like the color of the white man's soul, controlled by the exigencies of the white man's business" (*Banjo*, p. 193). McKay had no illusions about the European white's moral superiority over the white American; in fact, he underscores the strange contradictions of the American racial situation by having a liberal Southern white stand up for Ray when the latter is man-handled by a French policeman. Racial problems frequently engage Ray's mind, but the problem "of the highest importance was the problem of the individual," from which some try to escape by "joining movements" (p. 272). Here again, Ray feels he has "more individual liberty *under the law* in the Puritan-ridden Anglo-Saxon countries than in the land of "Liberté, Egalité, et Fraternité" (p. 263). At one point, Ray even suggests voluntary isolation as a way "of growing big and strong, for individuals as well as races" (p. 196).

But the problem of the black individual in *Banjo* and *Home to Harlem* becomes inextricably entangled in the Manichean opposition between "instinct" and "intellect." Although in *Banjo* McKay does suggest a possible resolution of what Michael Stoff calls the "structural dualism" inherent in the book's two protagonists,[14] McKay fails once again to piece together Ray's existence satisfactorily. But thorny issues regarding the black's existence in a world dominated by white colonialism—issues such as the black's self-hatred and relationship with other nonwhites—are raised. Again, McKay's views on education reflect a maturity of which there was little hint in *Home to Harlem*. Ray comes to see the black as a challenge, rather than as a problem, to Western civilization; the universal objective of education is teaching "something of real decency in dealing with all kinds and classes of people" (p. 272). In a scathing denunciation of the Afro-American racial renaissance of the 1920s, McKay emphasizes the importance of the common man in any movement for cultural or political resurgence, and admonishes the black American leaders to study the examples of Ireland, Russia, and India (under Gandhi). Addressing a Martinique student who does not believe in "going back to savagery," Ray says:

> Getting down to our native roots and building up from our own people is not savagery. It is culture. . . . You get a white man's education and learn to despise your own people. . . . Then when you come to maturity you realize with a shock that you don't and can't belong to the white race. . . . You are a lost crowd, you educated Negroes, and you will only find yourself in the roots of your own people. (Pp. 200-201)

McKay is not blind to the advantages of "group life" for blacks in the United States, but he rates as poor the black child's chances for a proper education:

> A Chinese or Indian child could learn the stock virtues without being spiritually harmed by them, because he possessed his own native code from which he could draw, compare, accept and reject while learning. But the Negro child was a pathetic thing, entirely cut off from its own folk wisdom and earnestly learning the trite moralisms of a society in which he was, as a child and would be as an adult, denied any legitimate place. (P. 319)

Besides McKay's views on education, numerous passages scattered throughout the book warn of the dangers posed by "the poisonous orchids of civilization" to the instinctive life that derives from "contact with African racial roots" (p. 56). He makes these dangers look real by attacking the lifeless "gray respectability" that rules the lives of Afro-Americans, a group of blacks "enfeebled by self-effacement before condescending patronage, social negativism and miscegenation" (p. 320). However, more than once in *Banjo*, McKay undercuts his notion of a racial mystique by showing blacks from different parts of the world communicating not on the strength of a shared "soul," but by means of food, wine, and sex. Toward the end, Ray joins Banjo in a vagabond life because he persuades himself that he was very close to the beachboys in "spirit" and "they represented more than *he or the cultured minority* the irrepressible exuberance and legendary vitality of the black race" (p. 324; emphasis mine). Ray's taking off with Banjo might be compared to Huck Finn's flight from civilization, but Ray, whose character is formed by a tentative and unconvincing synthesis, does not fit in Banjo's world. The *New York Times* reviewer (12 May 1929), who gave *Banjo* one of its most sympathetic early reviews, perhaps tried to articulate the same dissatisfaction when he said: "We should like to see a novel devoted to Ray in which he would be forced to think and feel his way out of some real problem."

Critics are in general agreement that in *Banana Bottom*, the third and last of his published novels, "McKay achieves an aesthetic structure which permits the formulation of a viable resolution to the predicament of the educated black man."[15] McKay returns to the setting of his native Jamaica in *Banana Bottom*, in which, as both Robert Bone and Michael Stoff have shown, "McKay expands and sustains the tension of contrary value systems"[16] in the characters and events of his simple, quiet tale. "On one side is the Christ God, the Calvinist austerity, and the naive ethnocentrism of the Mission. On the other is the Obeah God, the primitive sexuality and the simple values of the folk culture."[17]

Bita Plant, raped at the age of twelve by Crazy Bow and adopted by the Craigs as the subject of an experiment, in one sense tests the artificial synthesis McKay imposed on the character of Ray at the end of *Banjo*. Educated in an English missionary school, she returns to Jubilee, Jamaica, and is expected to marry Herald Newton Day, a divinity student at Kingston, to help the Craigs fulfill their plans of having a cultured native couple succeed them at the Mission. Bita realizes that she could not love the fawning and pompous Herald Newton Day, but decides to go along with the Craigs' plans for her, partly out of gratitude and partly because, as a dark brown girl, she could not expect to marry "better than a parson."

At this point, McKay keeps the plot from getting out of hand, as far as his search for a resolution between the two cultures is concerned. Found copulating with a goat, Herald Newton Day leaves suddenly for Mexico. Also, McKay has already introduced Squire Gensir,[18] an Englishman of means who has deliberately chosen to live a simple life in the Jamaica countryside. He is an agnostic who has internalized the values of peasant life. At first the Squire is prejudiced against Bita's education, but soon finds she is different from the generally priggish and genteel educated blacks of Jamaica. In time, Bita and Gensir become close friends, but McKay prevents another derailing of his plot by making Gensir "a thin, middle-built" man of sixty, with a reputation for a sexual aloofness that is as formidable as his intellectual prowess. In the conflict that naturally develops between Bita and the Craigs, Gensir's friendship and influence serve as a catalyst in Bita's choice of a life-style. Bita feels that Gensir's enjoyment of the native "tea-parties," customs, and traditions must be "merely cerebral"; however, she herself has "a surging big feeling" for the simple life of her childhood days.

Early in the story, Bita is attracted to Hopping Dick, known in the area as "a grogshop customer, a horse-gambler and a notorious feminine heart-breaker." Bita spends long hours with Hopping Dick and this leads to a confrontation with Mrs. Craig and a return to Banana Bottom to live there with her parents. With some help from Jubban, her father's dragman, she successfully resists the advances of Marse Arthur, the mulatto son of a powerful British landlord in the area. She also rejects proposals from the light-skinned educated blacks whom she finds uninteresting. Later, she decides to marry the honest but uncouth Jubban, who is proud, sensitive to nature, respectful of Bita's artistic and intellectual interests, and who grows in time into a dynamic farmer.

Bita thus represents McKay's successful synthesis of "instinct" and "intellect," which is achieved by making a new and important distinction: "For the first time, McKay distinguishes between education, or the cultivation of the intellect, and the necessary acceptance of the value system implied by that education."[19] However, McKay's resolution in *Banana Bottom* is achieved at a great loss of complexity; by choosing a rural Jamaican setting for his novel, McKay bypasses many urban and international issues raised in *Home to Harlem* and *Banjo*.

According to Nathan Huggins, Jake (or Banjo) is not in the "noble savage" tradition in American literature. "Most notably, he is completely and enthusiastically urban; there is not the slightest whimsy about his living by rural or country values."[20] And if Harold Cruse is correct in saying that the crucial problems of Afro-American existence are likely to be resolved in Northern cities rather than on Southern plantations,[21] it is unfortunate that McKay did not concern himself more with the issues raised in *Home to Harlem* and *Banjo*. The apparent aesthetic gain of *Banana Bottom* is our cultural loss, because issues such as the self-hatred of the oppressed or the possible cultural and political uses of the shared history of oppression of nonwhite nations continue to demand our serious attention.

McKay avoids these issues by preventing tedious discussion from obstructing the narrative and by making his protagonist in *Banana Bottom* a woman whose major conflicts are sexual.[22]

Placed in the midst of real situations in a rural world, Bita resolves the conflict between her "racial roots" and her white education without the agonizing uncertainties of Ray's thinking. She asserts her confidence in herself in perhaps the clearest and strongest statement on the subject in McKay's writings: "I thank God that although I was brought up and educated among white people, I have never wanted to be anything but myself. . . . I can't imagine anything more tragic than people torturing themselves to be different from their natural unchangeable selves" (p. 169).

The literary ancestors of *Banana Bottom* are not McKay's two earlier novels, nor the works by his Afro-American contemporaries or predecessors. As a carefully drawn idyllic picture of rural Jamaica, *Banana Bottom* compares with Thomas Hardy's novels of local color. Jubban and his "folksy" wedding to Bita are too reminiscent of Gabriel Oak and the parallel scenes in *Far From the Madding Crowd* to preclude influence. The use of the hurricane, the flood, and other natural elements is similar to that of the Brontë sisters and the early George Eliot. *Banana Bottom* has a Victorian simplicity and is characterized by nostalgic and panegyrical evocations of mango trees of Martha's Basin in the middle of the forest, of town markets and tea parties, and of the "unconscious freedom" in the unrepressed, instinctive life of the natives.

Discussing the Harlem Renaissance writer's use of primitivism in defining black identity, Nathan Huggins observes that "it is especially a male fantasy. It is easier to imagine men as roustabouts, vagabonds, bums and heroes, harder to draw sympathetic females whose whole existence is their bodies and instinct. . . . Without women, and without children, there can be no race or race consciousness."[23] One must admit that both in the world of Little Augie (the protagonist in Bontemps' *God Sends Sunday*) and that of McKay's Jake Brown, women appear almost always as sex objects—pretty, painted, and dressed-up. Nearly all of them are prostitutes or semi-prostitutes, who sell their bodies for cash or acquire "sweet men," or pimps, in exchange for sexual favors. Of course, since they live in a world where "miserable cockfights, beastly, tigerish, bloody" settle matters of sexual possession, often with the help of knives and guns, they cannot afford to be soft and delicate. They imbibe the ways of the male world around them, drive hard bargains with men, fight brutal "hen fights" that may permanently disfigure one or both of the antagonists, derive sadistic pleasure from watching brutal beatings of their former lovers by their present lovers, and show themselves capable of despica-

ble coarseness and depravity once "they set their hearts on con-
quering someone sexually." They are seen by Jake as down-to-
earth "realistic and straight-going . . . . the real controlling forces
of life" (*Home to Harlem*, p. 69). Woman here is seen as an ines-
capable part of the man's world, a necessary evil: "Ain't no place
on earth with the womens and there ain't no life anywhere without them," says Zeddy in *Home to Harlem* (p. 34).

But nowhere do we get a glimpse of the inner lives of these
women except as they express the sexual or sex-related gratification they receive from male partners—as in the case of Felice, the
little brown beauty of *Home to Harlem*, who returns fifty dollars to
Jake to express her satisfaction; or of Rose, who loses herself in an
ecstasy of desire and gratitude after she provokes Jake into hitting
her; or of Della Green in *God Sends Sunday*, who is pleased when
Little Augie performs the ultimate in giving the "lumps" by hurl-
ing the lamp at her. In the world of the roustabout, beating is generally seen as "an act of singular intimacy between a girl and her
man" (*God Sends Sunday*, p. 94). Augie's code tells him that
"giving a woman her knocks" is a manly man's privilege and anyone interfering with it is assaulting his "manliness." When the Big
Biglow gives Della a beating, Little Augie loses his mind; if Biglow "had been intimate with her in some other way, it would not
have been so bad." But his beating Della "invaded the one prov-
ince that Augie believed to be his own" (p. 85).

God Sends Sunday, which came under heavy attack from genteel black critics who had earlier panned McKay's *Home to Harlem* and *Banjo*, reads like a period piece. Bontemps shows little
interest in using primitivism to define ethnic identity. Recently, in
his "The Awakening: A Memoir,"[24] Bontemps explained how *God
Sends Sunday* evolved out of "a first novel with autobiographical
overtones about a sensitive black boy in a nostalgic setting"—
something that did not interest the publishers in the year of the
stock market crash. At least three editors turned it down, suggesting that they would like to have a novel about one of the minor
characters in the original story. And thus Bontemps wrote the story
of Little Augie and fed the market successfully tapped three years
earlier by *Home to Harlem*. The story is structured simply in two
parts; part one depicts Lil Augie riding the wave as the most famous jockey of his time, and part two cuts him down to his real size.
Both parts are dominated by the vagabond-picaroon motif, and the
protagonist spends his later years trying to bask in the glory of his
youth. But Lil Augie refuses to accept himself or others for what
they really are; he insists on measuring Della Green in terms of
Florence Dessau, the yellow girl whom he desires intensely, but

who prefers to remain the mistress of Augie's white boss, Mr. Woody. Augie's manliness comes to the fore only when he is threatened by giant-sized men like Biglow and Lissus, and the result in both cases satisfies his ego, but is fatal to the other men.

Bontemps' simple identification with black folk contrasts to McKay's interest in primitiveness—as a search for positive meanings of blackness—and in his more progressive views of women. In *Home to Harlem*, Jake Brown quits Rose as soon as he discovers her pleasure in being beaten—Jake's mother had taught him never to hit a woman. He also refuses to be any woman's "sweet man," though he would not pass harsh judgments on anybody else who chooses to be one. Ray's educated girlfriend, Agatha, inspires respect and admiration in Jake. And Ray's story of Jerco's suicide introduces a norm of higher love even in the world of prostitutes and pimps. Still, McKay fails to create a full-fledged woman character.

But in commenting on the exclusion of women and children from the world of the roustabout, Huggins is guilty of oversights. Latnah, the Arab woman in *Banjo*, is a female roustabout, and, within her Oriental aloofness, she is as much a beach bum as any of the male characters. She is as free with men as they are with women, and she uses her tiny argent-headed dagger effectively for self-defense. In a passage that parallels the opening paragraph of Joyce's *Portrait of the Artist As a Young Man* and Benjy's monologue in Faulkner's *The Sound and the Fury*, McKay provides a glimpse of her racial consciousness in a moment of aroused sexual jealousy over Banjo's renewed friendship with Chère Blanche, the white prostitute:

> So, thought Latnah, he no like my kind. He no man. He no good. He no got no pride of race. Me give him sleep. Me give him eat. Me give him love. Me give him money for go buy that thing. Even my money he took. . . . For the benefit of their two-legged white rats. Banjo an ofay lover. (P. 169)

As if to make up for a major omission of family life, Jake is introduced in *Banjo* as happily married to Felice with a son named after Ray. Although Jake's vagabond spirit lures him from the household hearth from time to time, he does not "feel like running away from Felice no moh" (p. 293). Ray finds warm group life impossible without colored women. And when McKay wrote *Banana Bottom*, with Bita as his heroine, he had realized that woman is central to his racial vision and therefore is the means to resolve the conflicts between folk and educated black cultures.

When a student from the Ivory Coast insinuatingly remarks on the number of mulattoes in the United States, Ray explains that "the colored women like it as much as the white men."

> I know that the American Negro press says that the American colored women have no protection from the lust and passion of white men. . . . But the world today is too enlightened about sex to be fooled by white or black propaganda. . . . Woman is woman all over the world, no matter what her color is. She is cast in a passive role and she worships the active success of man and rewards it with her body. . . . If she [the black woman] is not inhibited by race feeling, she'll give herself to the white man because he stands for power and property. Property controls sex. (P. 206)

This basic definition of interracial sex fits many sexual relationships in Harlem Renaissance novels. The "yaller" Florence, in *God Sends Sunday*, lives openly and proudly as the mistress of the white and powerful Mr. Woody. Angela in Jessie Fauset's *Plum Bun*, Mimi in Walter White's *Flight*, and Clare in Nella Larsen's *Passing* all "pass" into the white world, and become concubines or wives of white men in order to have greater economic and professional opportunities. Unconsciously, however, the near-white heroines of the "passing" novels suffer from "yellow fever"—a color-conscious distaste for Negroes of darker skins. We see other examples of this psychology in the characters of Gin-Head Susy in *Home to Harlem*, Olivia in *Comedy: American Style*, and Emma Lou Morgan in *The Blacker the Berry*.

Neither in the case of Gin-Head Susy nor anywhere else in his work does McKay elaborate on "yellow fever"; but scattered throughout his novels are comments that reveal the range of white and black attitudes toward interracial sex. In *Home to Harlem*, Jake leaves London in the wake of East End race riots. Black and white men fight like fools while cheap women egg them on. Lost before in the swirl of "monster" dances with his white woman, Jake suddenly feels homesick for the all-black Harlem. At Madame Suarez's buffet-flat, the "downtown" white's curious interest in the primitive black is only complemented by this black version of the white women: "Sometimes there were two or three white women, who attracted attention because they were white . . . but they appeared like faded carnations among those burning orchids of a tropical race" (p. 106). A judge expresses society's official view of miscegenation by his approval of whipping white women who associated with black men. Some black women cannot love white men; Madame Laura, in *Home to Harlem*, claims she has "got no loving inclination for any skin but chocolate," and Latnah, the Arab woman in *Banjo*, sums up her attitude quite simply: "I go with white man, but only for money. White race no love my race. My race no love white" (p. 169). Carrying McKay's thesis of black primitiveness to its logical conclusion, Ray, in *Banjo*, sees "a war joined between civilization and sex" that supports a parallel war between black and white: "It was as if the white man considered sex a nasty, irritating thing, while a Negro accepted it with primitive joy. And maybe that vastly big difference of attitude was a fundamental, unconscious cause of the antagonism between white and black brought together by civilization" (p. 253).

Chef "Rhinoceros" in *Home to Harlem* accentuates the strange contradictions that color creates in the lives of most Americans. Dark-skinned and gross in size and manner, he is "a great black bundle of consciously suppressed desires" (p. 160). The Chef lets everybody know that he is "no regular darky" and shows a violent distaste for all the stock things the whites associate with the blacks: "He would not eat watermelon, because white people called it 'the nigger's ice-cream.' Pork chops he fancied not. Nor corn pone. And the idea of eating chicken gave him a spasm" (pp. 161-62). The Chef's "color complex" runs deep and determines his preferences among women too. He "hated yellow men with 'cracker' hatred, but he loved yellow women with 'cracker' love" (p. 180). The mere sight of a yellow girl transforms his face "into a foolish broad-smiling thing" and is enough to distract him from his habitual efficiency, giving the pantryman his long-awaited chance to get even with him.

In contrast to McKay's use of sexuality to sketch the contours of the black experience, some Renaissance writers asserted the American-ness of the Afro-American by depicting or satirizing the irrationality of America's color complexes. Jessie Fauset, like Walter White, depicted the limitations and humiliations suffered by educated, middle-class blacks in Northern cities and suburbs in order to arouse the American conscience; and George S. Schuyler's *Black No More* took white and black Americans to task for their deep-seated color hang-ups.

As the blurb of the recent reprint of Schuyler's book reads, "*Black No More* is coruscating satire with a Voltairean touch—and the kind of double-edged irony from which no one emerges unscathed."[25] Schuyler, unlike McKay, had no romantic notion of black "primitive joy," nor had he any use for talk about African roots. "The Aframerican is merely a lampblacked Anglo-Saxon . . . it is sheer non-sense to talk about 'racial differences' . . . between the American black man and the American white man. . . . In the homes of the same cultural and economic level, one finds similar furniture, literature and conversation."26 It is from such a vantage point that Schuyler seems to have satirized in *Black No More* the beliefs and activities of major black cultural and political figures: Dr. Shakespeare Agamemnon Beard (W.E.B. DuBois); the National Social Equality League (NAACP); *The Dilemma* (*The Crisis*, NAACP's journal); Santop Licorice and the Back-to-Africa Society (Marcus Garvey and the Universal Negro Improvement Association); and many others.

Schuyler makes America's constant reiteration of white suprem-acy look ludicrous. The plot of *Black No More* centers around the discovery by the brilliant Negro doctor, Junius Crookman, of a process to turn dark skins white. Max Disher, the coffee-brown pro-tagonist, undergoes Dr. Crookman's treatment, because he is tired of stuck-up "yellah" women and frustrated in his ambition to "feel like an American citizen." With his newfound Caucasian freedom, Max heads toward Atlanta in search of a Southern white girl he had once seen in a Harlem cabaret and had fallen in love with. At first, Max—now Matthew Fisher—did not find his new life as a Cauca-sian "the rosy existence he had anticipated":

> As a boy he had been taught to look up to white folks as just a little less than gods; now he found them little different from the Negroes, except that they were uniformly less courteous and less interesting. . . . The unreasoning and illogical color prej-udice of most of the people with whom he was forced to as-sociate infuriated him. He often laughed cynically when some coarse, ignorant white man voiced his opinion concerning the inferior mentality and morality of the Negroes. (P. 57)

Meanwhile, Dr. Crookman and his partner, Hank Johnson, open their centers all over the country and manage to turn all Negroes white-skinned. Since their process does not guarantee the change for the next generation, they have to open more hospitals to ac-commodate white women who continue to embarrass themselves and their families by bearing Negroid babies. In a matter of ten years, however, the pigmented skin disappears from America. Then, to help fulfill the American urge to find an underdog, Dr. Junius Crookman, by now the Surgeon-General of the United States, declares that as a result of his treatment, the new Caucasians in practically every instance are two or three shades lighter than the old Caucasians. Schuyler measures the effect on the American public of Dr. Crookman's announcement in the last few pages of his book:

> What was the world coming to, if the blacks were whiter than the whites? Many people in the upper class began to look askance at their very pale complexions. . . . The new Caucasians began to grow self-conscious and resent the curious gazes bestowed upon their lily-white countenances in all public places. They wrote indignant letters to the newspapers about the insults and discriminations to which they were increasingly becoming subjected. . . . Those of the upper class began to look around for ways to get darker. . . . Beauty shops began to sell face powders named *Poudre Nègre, Poudre le Egyptienne* and *L'Afrique*. (Pp. 245-48)

The only salvation for America and even the world, in Schuyler's view, was to become "mulatto-minded."[27] No one among Schuyler's Harlem Renaissance contemporaries would have agreed more with the views he expressed in his *Nation* article and in *Black No More* than Jessie Redmon Fauset. Fauset, for years the literary editor of *The Crisis* and the most prolific of the Renaissance novelists, developed and dramatized the thesis of the black's shared Americanness in her four novels: *There is Confusion* (1924), *Plum Bun* (1928), *The Chinaberry Tree* (1931), and *Comedy: American Style* (1933). Fauset denied that she propagandized, but her fiction easily fits the norm set by the DuBois-Brawley school of black critics during the twenties. (She showed wider sympathies as a critic and editor by defending and encouraging writers with many different styles and interests.) As the vehement attacks of DuBois and Brawley on *Nigger Heaven*, *Home to Harlem*, and *The Blacker the Berry* indicate, these critics saw the need for new literature that would help weed out the widespread American stereotypes of the black as coon, pimp, lecher, primitive, minstrel, or roustabout. And Fauset, more than any other Renaissance novelist "so thoroughly offsets the artificial glamor associated with the Negro."[28] Fauset wrote about, to use her phrase, "the better class of colored people." Set in the colored communities of Philadelphia and New Jersey, her novels concern the petty excitements and disappointments of mulatto heroines in their search for happiness in love and marriage. *Plum Bun* and *Comedy: American Style* explore secondary interests that make them the most readable of her four books; *Plum Bun*, a novel of "passing," uncovers the many layers of irony in America's color complex, while *Comedy: American Style* embodies a not so distinguished treatment of Olivia's "color me white" psychology. The black drama critic Theophilus Lewis (*Amsterdam News*, 5 May 1934) sums up the world in Jessie Fauset's novels:

> It is a planet where all the women are lovely and the men handsome enough to illustrate collar ads. The highest virtue in that halcyon world is respectability. The most precious possession is an old Philadelphia ancestry, or next to that, an old Red Brook background. A comfortable income, derived from pill mongering, embalming cadavers, the catering business or some other traffic, is taken for granted. A finishing school o.k. is desired but not required of young ladies. Young men must present a college degree and no back talk. With those preliminary qualifications clutched tightly in their fists, the boys and girls are ready for action in a realm where love is the sweetest thing—and the greatest thing. They are, in short, ready to live, move and have their being in a world God would take pleasure in having created if God were a top-crust colored woman—which perhaps He is.

Fauset's third novel, *The Chinaberry Tree*, developed from her story "Double Trouble" (published in *The Crisis*, August 1923), exemplifies this pattern in its stark simplicity. Zona Gale had to come to Fauset's rescue with a preface, because the book was accepted reluctantly by the white publishers. ("White readers just don't expect the Negroes to be like this," they said.)[29] In *The Chinaberry Tree*, Fauset's intention was to depict "something of the home life of the colored American who is not being pressed too hard by the Forces of Prejudice, Ignorance and Economic Injustice. And behold he is not vastly different from any other American, just distinctive."[30] The story presents two illegitimate girls, Laurentine Strange and her cousin, Melissa Paul, and their efforts to break through the Puritanical barriers of the colored community of Red Brook, New Jersey, in order to win happiness in love and marriage. Laurentine, born of the scandalous affair between the mulatto Sal Strange and the rich-and-white Frank Halloway, trains herself as a seamstress with generous help from her white half-sisters. At sixteen, Melissa comes to live with Sal and Laurentine because her mother, Judy Strange, decides to leave for Chicago with her latest lover. Seventeen years earlier, Judy Strange had lived with her sister, Sal, and Melissa was born as a result of Judy's affair with Sylvester Forten, the Red Brook caterer, who dies soon after Melissa is born. But Melissa knows nothing about it and derives great satisfaction in thinking that she, unlike Laurentine, was born in wedlock. Laurentine, aloof and rejected by the community, is crossed in love with Phil Hackett, but soon catches the eye of Dr. Danleigh, a widower who shows great understanding of Laurentine's situation, partly because of his own unhappy first marriage. Melissa is drawn into a love affair with Malory Forten, neither of them being aware of their sibling relationship. Finally, after a few foreseeable obstacles, Laurentine is united with Dr. Danleigh and Asshur Lane is shown rushing to the scene to offer love and security to his old flame, Melissa.

The Chinaberry Tree was hailed by many reviewers, including Rudolph Fisher, as a well-written story about a neglected but important section of American life. Jessie Fauset's emphasis on the desirability of respectability was condoned and praised. Reviewing the book in *Opportunity* (March 1932), Edwin Berry Burgum defended the ideal of respectability, because "for any race that suffers consciously from surrounding prejudice, the attainment of respectability is the one sort of imitation that can eradicate it." It warmed the New England Puritan heart of W.E.B. DuBois to see a book that did not confine black sex experience to "frank prostitution or careless promiscuity." Reviewing the book in *The Crisis* (April 1932), DuBois wrote: "It is, therefore, not at all according to Hoyle that an interracial sexual lapse should fasten itself upon a little colored community like a pall and be worked out only in generations. Or that sexual looseness within the race should literally blast a household."

But other voices found the portrayal of the black community's Puritan ethos overdone. Shaemas O'Sheel, the *New York Times* reviewer, had this to say: "Social life among the intelligent, cultivated Negroes of Philadelphia and New York is a thing of dignity and beauty, but to present it as a thing so primly Victorian, with never a hint of another side, is a dubious service" (*New York Times*, 7 April 1929). Even Edward Berry Burgum, quoted above, thought that Fauset's "characters [had] acquired a veneration for chastity which was certainly not caught from white Montclair but from Queen Victoria." No wonder, then, that Fauset's race pride does not carry her far on the road to ethnic definition. Her uncritical attitude toward the complexities of intraracial class problems and her repeated attempts to recreate a brown-skinned replica of the white American world seem, in retrospect, to limit her work's aesthetic and cultural value. "Her characters are so commonplace as to seem actual transcriptions from unimaginative life, and her novels often bear a striking resemblance to the duller novels of white middle-class society."[31]

Between Claude McKay on one hand, and Jessie Fauset and George Schuyler on the other, and yet also outside the matrix defined by them, stands Jean Toomer. *Cane* was published in 1923 and is generally recognized as the highest literary achievement of the Harlem Renaissance, but it baffled the reviewers in the twenties and continues to puzzle Toomer's critics to this day. "A critical analysis of *Cane* is a frustrating task, for Toomer's art, in which outlines are reduced to essences, is largely destroyed in the process of restoration. No paraphrase can properly convey the aesthetic pleasure derived from a sensitive reading of *Cane*."[32] It is difficult to see *Cane* as a novel after reading the facts marshaled by Darwin T. Turner in his excellent biocritical essay on Toomer.[33] But the unity of mood and the distilled social consciousness of Toomer's book justify treating *Cane* in a study of Harlem Renaissance novels. "At first glance it [*Cane*] appears to consist of assorted sketches, stories and a novelette, all interspersed with poems. Some of the prose is poetic, and often Toomer slips from one form into the other almost imperceptibly. The novelette is constructed like a play."[34]

Cane is divided into three parts. The first contains sketches of five black women and one white woman of rural Georgia, as well as nine poems, some of which reinforce the motifs expressed in the prose pieces. The second part consists of six stories set in black Washington, D.C., and one in Chicago, as well as five poems. The third part is "Kabnis," a dramatic narrative that returns to Georgia. The book abounds in Blakeian "contraries," and Toomer shows himself a master of the paradox. In *Earth Being*, an autobiography written in the early 1930s, Jean Toomer said he saw life "as comic and tragic, as chemical and sacred, as natural and divine."[35] In *Cane*, Toomer works, by his own definition, as "an essentialist" rather than as a classicist or a realist. What gives *Cane* its unity is the mystical sensibility that flows through the poet-novelist's keen observation of people, places, and events. In his fascinating career, and in *Cane*, Toomer was led almost entirely by his interest in discovering roots, distilling essences, and achieving a wholeness through them.

Toomer is the only Harlem Renaissance writer whose experiments in form and style had a direct connection with the white literary scene of the twenties. Toomer had read both Sherwood Anderson's *Winesburg, Ohio* and Waldo Frank's *Holiday* before he wrote *Cane* and was deeply affected by the self-conscious art of the Imagists. Notwithstanding the hostility of the early Fugitives to blacks and black writing, Toomer's *Cane* parallels the works of John Crowe Ransom and Allen Tate.[36] Toomer's vision is also rooted in a Southern agrarian culture, and, like early Ransom, Toomer appreciates the mysteries and beauties of nature. In the uncensoring attitude Toomer displays toward his characters and their responses to the elemental forces that surround them, Toomer shares the Fugitives' rejection of the New England puritanism that pervades American literature from the North. The lyrical intensity that so completely absorbs any undercurrent of protest in *Cane* parallels the emphasis on form in the creative and critical output of the Fugitives. At the same time, Toomer's interest in Robert Frost's poetry is evidence of his sympathy with Locke's efforts to develop a "local color" school of black American literature.[37]

Toomer's world view, as dramatized in *Cane*, reveals his mystical wonder in the objects, people, and events around him. Symbols of the dusk, the moon, and the soil run through the book and color the actions and meanings of different stories. The human actors and the landscape are mutually indispensable. Events are characterized by an inevitable round of joy and pain, of agony and relief. That goes for plants and animals and for cane and cotton as much as for men and women. Fear, hate, love, and superstition stalk the actors wherever they go, whatever they do; the mood is often resigned, but sometimes it is existential, that is, the characters are sometimes completely and unselfreflectingly involved in their experiences.

But to stop with Toomer's mystical lens would be to miss the deeper meaning of *Cane*. Toomer's search for a satisfying answer to the problems of black existence on the American continent seems to have been as intense as Claude McKay's. Unlike McKay, however, Toomer had no use for a vague and romantic identification with the African motherland. The tenor and quality, if not the breadth, of Toomer's vision in *Cane* is Whitmanesque. He saw himself, like Whitman before him, as part of an exciting democratic experiment, as someone who is "naturally and inevitably an American."

Thus in *Cane*, Toomer, the poet of the "Song of the Son," returns to the "mystical" Georgia soil of his father and grandfather in search of his cultural roots. Toomer confronted and accepted the checkered history of blacks in the United States with all its beauties and brutalities, its shames and prides. The South was inevitably the black's homeland—with its blues and spirituals, its miscegenation and lynchings. Toomer used the black American as Tolstoy or Turgenev had used the Russian peasant.[38] The intimate

link between Toomer's literary exploration of Afro-American identity and his personal search for consciousness is revealed in the
biographical note he wrote for *The Liberator* in 1922:

> My family is from the South. . . . Racially, I seem to have (who
> knows for sure) seven blood mixtures: French, Dutch, Welsh,
> Negro, German, Jewish, and Indian. Because of these, my
> position in America has been a curious one. I have lived
> equally amid the two race groups. Now white, now colored.
> From my own point of view I am naturally and inevitably an
> American. . . . Within the last two or three years, however, my
> growing need for artistic expression has pulled me deeper and
> deeper into the Negro group. And as my powers of receptivity
> increased, I found myself loving it in a way that I could never
> love the other. It has stimulated and fertilized whatever cre-
> ative talent I may contain within me. A visit to Georgia last
> fall was the starting point of almost everything of worth that I
> have done. I heard folk-songs come from the lips of Negro
> peasants. I saw the rich dusk beauty that I had heard many
> false accents about, and of which till then, I was somewhat
> skeptical. And a deep part of my nature, a part that I had re-
> pressed, sprang suddenly to life and responded to them. Now, I
> cannot conceive of myself as aloof and separated. My point of
> view has not changed; it has deepened, it has widened.[39]

Toomer also differed from McKay in his artistic and spiritual
impulses, which inclined him more toward a Hegelian synthesis
than toward the Manichean opposition that marks McKay's novels.
Cane, as well as an earlier unpublished play, "Natalie Mann"
(1922),[40] contain the dialectical elements of a Hegelian construct
despite the strong mystical overlay. The evocation of Georgia's
red, fertile land and the six women who display their unappreci-
ated elemental strengths in defiance of traditional morality contrasts with the life of black Americans in Washington, D.C., that is,
under increasing pressure from white middle-class values in an
urban and industrial environment. The highly symbolic structure
of the third part, "Kabnis," brings to full circle the artist's quest for
a cultural and spiritual synthesis which will embrace all the dis-
cordant elements of his Afro-American existence. But it is a measure of Toomer's artistic integrity that this search ends in confusion and self-doubt. Ralph Kabnis and Lewis are dramatic pro-
jections of the Afro-American's double-consciousness.[41] Lewis fails
to realize his mission as a Christ figure, and Kabnis is incapable of
embracing the harshness of his Southern roots. Toomer's vague

hope lies in the potential of Carrie Kate, who, through her ties with Father John, might achieve the wholeness that Kabnis and Lewis individually lack.[42]

Toomer achieves his lyrical rendition of the powerful drama in the lives of his characters from rural Georgia and urban Washington, D.C., through his intricately woven, elusive style. Intensity is created with images and similes consonant with the mood and motif in each section. Karintha is "as innocently lovely as a November cotton flower." The air is "sweet like clover," when the narrator in "Avey" gets close to Avey for the first time on an excursion down to Riverview. This rush of images is supported throughout by numerous uncanny and evocative descriptions such as, "Her soul is like a little thrust-tailed dog that follows her, whimpering," or "The Dixie Pike has grown from a goat path in Africa," or "Her mind is a pink mesh-bag filled with baby toes." These descriptions, which make no sense at the realistic level and for which analysis does not yield precise definitions, give *Cane* a unique status in American literature.

Even more powerful than imagery is the remarkable empathy with which Toomer portrays each main character. This quality is nowhere more evident than in the well-rounded portraits of women characters who give their bodies freely to men who have no inkling of their souls. Karintha, a growing thing ripened too soon, "carries beauty perfect as dusk when the sun goes down." Young men bring her love and money, but they have no notion of the "smoke" that curls up about her soul, of the guilt she carries in her breast for the death of her child. Becky, the white woman with two Negro sons, who would not reveal the identity of her lover, dies a lonely death as an outcast, and her sons "beat and cut a man who meant nothing at all in mentioning that they lived along the road." Carma, full of life and "strong as a man," drives her husband to murder and into the chain gang. The near-white Esther, forced for long years to live with her father's crass materialism, centers all her sexual and religious fantasies on the muscular black preacher, King Barlo, till she discovers his "hideous" self among the town prostitutes, and then "there is no air, no street, and the town has completely disappeared" (p. 48).

Toomer deftly manipulates the form of the dramatic narrative in "Blood-Burning Moon," which is the best realized unit of the book both in form and theme. Toomer draws the characters with swift strokes, evoking the whole gamut of feelings that emerge in a Southern interracial sex triangle. It is the story of Louisa, whose "skin was the color of oak leaves on young trees in Fall. Her breasts, firm and up-pointed like ripe acorns. And her singing had the low murmur of winds in fig trees." Louisa is loved by both the black Tom Burwell and the white Bob Stone. Her ambivalence toward her two lovers is artfully fused into the mood of the story:

> A strange stir was in her. Indolently, she tried to fix upon Bob or Tom as the cause of it. . . . Separately there was no unusual significance to either one. But for some reason, they jumbled when her eyes gazed vacantly at the rising moon. And from the jumble came the stir that was strangely within her. Her lips trembled. (Pp. 52-53)

In his analysis of the story, the black novelist Waters E. Turpin[43] points to a similar ambivalence in Bob Stone and praises Toomer's ability to capture "the flavor, the essence, the epitome of a Southern factory town."

> Up from the deep dusk of a cleared spot on the edge of the forest a mellow glow arose and spread fan-wise into the low-hanging heavens. And all around, the air was heavy with the scent of boiling cane. . . . The scent of cane came from the copper pan and drenched the forest and the hill that sloped to factory town, beneath its fragrance. . . . And from factory town one could see the soft haze thrown by the glowing stove upon the low-hanging heavens. (Pp. 53-54)

Later, when the lynch mob chases Tom Burwell, Toomer increases the tempo of the action with short, staccato sentences:

> The mob pushed in. Its pressure, its momentum was too great. Drag him to the factory. Wood and stakes already there. Tom moved in the direction indicated. But they had to drag him. They reached the great door. Too many to get in there. . . . Taut humming. No words. A stake was sunk into the ground. . . . Tom bound to the stake. His breast was bare. . . . The mob was silent. . . . Only his head, lean, like a blackened stone. Stench of burning flesh soaked the air . . . Tom's eyes popped. His head settled downward. The mob yelled. (Pp. 66-67)

In "Blood-Burning-Moon" "Toomer achieves both form and perspective. He is not primarily concerned with anti-lynching propaganda, but in capturing a certain artistic quality in Southern life which defies the restraints of civilized life."[44]

Toomer, like McKay, opposed the values of black folk to the increasing standardization of urban and industrial life. In his concern for the issues of color and class as they affect the Afro-American's self-image, Toomer displays an empathy similar to that found in the works of Langston Hughes and Rudolph Fisher. The "dicty," materialistic Rhobert "wears a house, like a monstrous diver's helmet, on his head" (p. 73). John, the theater-manager's brother in "Theater," desires Dorris but is too class-conscious to love her. The middle-class narrator in "Avey" can respond either to the girl's soul or her body, never meeting the challenge that the fullness of her womanhood demands. Direct and oblique references to class abound in the prose sketches of *Cane*.

The Harlem Renaissance novelists—with the partial exception of Claude McKay—overwhelmingly confirm that the black American's cultural roots lie within his American experience. *Cane*, as the most profound and provocative effort of the Harlem Renaissance writers to define Afro-American identity,[45] also contains a mature and humanistic view of race and sex. In contrast to McKay's unpersuasive emphasis on the black's African primitiveness, Toomer searches for positive black images strictly in the American context. As an artist he unhesitatingly and completely accepts the Afro-American's cultural and historical past. In doing so, he implicitly rejects Fauset's approach to improving the black's status by asserting that middle-class black Americans were as good, as colorless, as narrow-minded and caste-ridden, and perhaps more puritanical than the white Americans of the same class. Toomer sums up his outlook—entrenched deeply as it is in the poetry and mysticism of *Cane*—in two aphorisms:

> We should have feeling. We should have taste, and the ability to discriminate. We should have intelligence.

> We should have a standard of excellence, values and a real purpose.[46]

THE DICTIEƒ AND THE ƒHINEƒ

CLAƒƒ IN BLACK AMERICA

Those of us who have forged forward are not able as yet to go our separate ways from the unwashed, untutored herd. We must still look back and render service to our less fortunate, weaker brethren. And the first step toward making this a workable attitude is the acquisition not so much of a racial love as a racial pride.

Jessie R. Fauset, Plum Bun

The majority of black Americans during the twenties were working-class or common folk,[1] but a distinct black middle class already existed—insofar as the middle class is "that highly elastic American social category which starts as the first economic level above that of want."[2] There was also a minute black upper class, whose status, unlike its white counterpart's, depended more on education and achievement in the white world than on wealth. Domestic servants, waiters, bellhops, barbers, and chauffeurs made up the black middle class; college teachers, lawyers, businessmen, and doctors formed the upper classes. The black middle and upper classes could not be rigidly defined; in fact, in view of their small number in contrast to the black masses, the two classes could be seen as one continuous middle-income group with middle-class or aristocratic values. These social classes enjoyed some petty monopolies in service occupations and small-scale businesses in addition to supplying most of the black leadership during the Renaissance period. Small middle-class black communities existed all over the country and, to some extent, thrived in urban centers such as Baltimore, Philadelphia, Washington, D.C., Atlanta, and Durham, North Carolina. There was—as there is today—hostility between the black upper classes ("dicties") and the black folk ("shines"). This hostility stemmed from social distance, skin color, racial pride, and the closeness of the black bourgeoisie to "white" values.

All the novelists of the Harlem Renaissance came from middle-class backgrounds, and most of them received college and graduate school education at prominent universities around the country.[3] Therefore, it should not come as a surprise that the majority of Renaissance novels by black writers concern middle-class characters, mostly light-skinned mulattoes.

The Harlem Renaissance novelist most dedicated to the depiction of the black middle class is Jessie Redmon Fauset. In her first three novels, Fauset pictures middle-class black Americans—their values, manners, emotions, activities, dilemmas—with conscious emphasis on similarities to their white counterparts, and on the absurdities of the color line that thwart the progress of her protagonists toward happiness, a goal they invariably attain. In *Comedy: American Style*, her fourth and last published novel, she goes a step further to expose the sickness and tragedy caused by America's convoluted color complex. The novels of Nella Larsen and Walter White also deal with the black bourgeoisie, but their critical perspective is quite different from Fauset's. The early pages of Larsen's *Quicksand*, for example, offer a sharp critique of Southern black schools and educationists, and White's *Flight* underscores the intolerance and provincialism of the black community in Atlanta. DuBois' *Dark Princess* contains both a well-intentioned but ludicrous attempt by a middle-class hero to become proletarian by working on the railroad tracks and a detailed picture of the corruption and opportunism of the middle-class black leadership entrenched in the Chicago machine. Wallace Thurman also explores intraracial color caste; in *The Blacker the Berry* he describes the discriminations suffered by a dark-skinned girl of middle-class background among black Americans.

The world of middle-class black American life in Renaissance novels is like that painted by E. Franklin Frazier in his classic study, *Black Bourgeoisie* (1957).[4] The black bourgeoisie—unable to identify itself with the Negro masses on the one hand and suffering the contempt of the white world on the other—has developed a deep-seated inferiority complex. Middle-class blacks created a make-believe world in seeking compensation for their feeling of inferiority. Among the compensations Frazier lists are the false importance assigned to "Negro business"; the emphasis placed in the black press (the most successful black business) on "society" and achievement among black bourgeoisie; the privileged position of the black bourgeoisie at the top of the social pyramid behind the walls of segregation; their pride in white heritage; their righteous conformity to the values, morals, manners, and canons of respectability of the white middle class; their desire to gain education and display academic degrees, especially from white schools. According to Frazier, middle-class black Americans exhibit considerable confusion and conflict in their personalities because of their constant striving for status within the Negro world, as well as in the estimation of the whites. Their ambivalence toward the black masses stems largely from the fact that while the black folk are more exposed to white violence, they, the bourgeoisie, are more exposed in a spiritual sense. Although they cannot bring themselves to identify with the black masses, their rejection by the white world makes them extremely sensitive to the slights and discriminations which all blacks suffer. Many novels discussed in this chapter convey this general impression, but it will suffice to briefly consider two novels by Jessie R. Fauset.

Fauset was acclaimed by W.E.B. DuBois, Aubrey Bowser, W.S. Braithwaite, Alain Locke, and many others, for her sympathetic understanding of educated, middle-class blacks. The portrayal of decent, respectable black Americans satisfied a deeply felt need of the black bourgeoisie; it affirmed their values, and compensated for their stunted status in American society. Perhaps for that reason alone, Fauset's literary shortcomings were overlooked by early middle-class black critics. However, some white reviewers, especially Edwin Berry Burgum[5] and Gerald Sykes,[6] did point to Fauset's near-Victorian preoccupation with respectability and elegance. Her style and diction merely reflect her thematic interests and this, coupled with her "inability to structure a plot effectively,"[7] almost assure unexciting reading. Robert Bone, however, does Fauset less than justice by sarcastically and uncritically dismissing her four novels in one sentence each.[8] Fauset is of more than historical significance, her subject alternates between the safe formulas of a genteel fictionist and the exploration of challenging themes such as incest and self-hatred. Moreover, Fauset's second novel, *Plum Bun*, stands solidly among the "passing" novels in Afro-American literature. Olivia in *Comedy: American Style* parallels Thurman's Emma Lou in *The Blacker the Berry*; these two novels anticipate more recent Afro-American novels such as Chester

Himes' *The Third Generation* (1954). The primary value of her novels is, however, sociological. Intentionally or otherwise, she sheds light on the conflicting impulses that middle-class blacks exhibited in adjusting to the American color caste.

There is Confusion (1924), Fauset's first novel, demonstrates both her strengths and weaknesses as a novelist. It is an ambitious book in which she attempts to explore many themes that appear in her later short stories and novels. "The consequences of illicit relationships between master and slave are illustrated in the chronicle of white and black Byes. Legal injustice, peonage, and lynching are not overlooked. The operation of prejudice is revealed in schools, colleges, graduate and professional institutions, stores, restaurants, hospitals, theaters and even in the world of art."[9] Through the characterization of Maggie Ellersley as a poor black girl with social-climbing ambitions, Fauset also deals with class conflict within the black group—a subject she unfortunately ignores almost completely in her later work. She shows how, in the caste-ridden world of colored Philadelphia, this conflict hinges on the need and desire to acquire lineage and respectability. Unfortunately, there is too much for Fauset to cope with in one novel and the result is a chaotic plot.

The story concerns Joanna Marshall, the daughter of a successful New York businessman, who hopes to achieve greatness as a singer and dancer. At school, Joanna attracts Peter Bye, whose bitterness about his family's history of exploitation always threatens to overwhelm his life and career. However, inspired by Joanna's own sense of direction and sustained by his dream of happiness with her, he goes to medical school in Philadelphia, where he faces severe financial and racial difficulties. A determined careerist, Joanna fails to sympathize with Peter's frustrations as a black male trying to succeed in a hostile environment, leading to an estrangement between the two. Because of her class snobbery, Joanna writes a nasty letter to Maggie Ellersley, who is in love with Joanna's idealistic brother, Philip, and causes much suffering in the lives of both. Unable as a black artist to receive the attention she deserves, she finally begins to see Peter Bye's problems in a new light. Meanwhile, Peter Bye enlists in the army during World War I and meets Meriweather Bye, "a fatalistic white relative whose liberal racial views lessen Peter's bitterness and give him hope."[10] He returns to Joanna as a fully qualified medical doctor and she renounces her dreams for a stage career to live happily ever after with Peter and their children.

There is Confusion might have made a better narrative if Joanna's determination had proceeded to its logical, tragic, end—and Joanna had not sacrificed her genuine ambition for a career to the happiness of spouse and children. Instead, Fauset draws a close connection between the success and happiness of her heroes and heroines, and the harsh realities of the American color caste. "Being black is something like being poor or having some slight deformity."[11] In *The Chinaberry Tree*, Melissa, conversing with Malory about Aunt Sal's notorious affair with Colonel Halloway, suddenly realizes how purely artificial, how man-made "the American color barrier is and that life must continue in spite of it."[12] Anna, the heroine in the story "There was One Time" (*Crisis*, April-May 1917), contends that "life was the main thing—teaching school, being colored, even being poor, were only aspects." In *Plum Bun*, Mattie Murray wants her daughters, Angela and Virginia, to remember that "being colored or not is just one thing more or less you have to contend with" in life. The thrust of Fauset's work is toward an adjustment to the American caste system. She seems to be telling her black readers not to be so obsessed with problems of discrimination as to forget that there are many interesting things in life—even for colored Americans—and that the American color complex cannot last forever.

Although the apparent sanity of such an approach cannot be denied easily, an incident in *The Chinaberry Tree* illustrates the "make-believe" nature of such sentiments. In *The Chinaberry Tree*, Fauset has, to use her own words, "depicted something of the homelife of the colored American who is not being pressed too hard by the Furies of Prejudice, Ignorance and Economic Injustice."[13] But the quiet and peaceful homelife of black Americans in Red Brook, New Jersey, seems unreal, almost farcical, under the powerful shadow of the only incident of discrimination treated in the book—when Laurentine and Dr. Danleigh are refused by a white waiter in a New York restaurant. Rudolph Fisher understated the disastrous effect of including this incident in the novel when he described it as "so much more dramatic than other episodes" in the story.[14]

In *Comedy: American Style*, Fauset depicts the sad career of a woman who wants to escape the consequences of being black in America. The title is obviously ironic, since the story is really an Afro-American tragedy. Having failed to marry a white man herself, Olivia, a near-white mulatto, tries to realize her dream through her children. Her only brown-skinned son, Oliver, is driven to suicide because he feels unwanted by Olivia. She stalls her daughter's plans to marry a black graduate of M.I.T., takes her for a trip to Europe, and forces her to settle down with a provincial, miserly Frenchman. She leads her husband, a black physician, to bankruptcy by indulging in what Frazier describes as the black bourgeoisie's "delusion of wealth."[15] She is always buying things and entertaining white women at social gatherings where she presents her son, Oliver, as a hired butler in order to hide her racial identity. Surprisingly, no one in Olivia's family, including her husband, rebels against her "psychopathic Aryanism."[16] The only partial exception is her elder son, Cary, who achieves a degree of happiness in his marriage with the near-white Phebe Grant. At the end of the novel, Olivia, rejected by her French son-in-law and promised a paltry monthly allowance by her husband, is shown miserable and alone in Paris.

The conscious intent of *Comedy: American Style* is clear: it is best for blacks, however light-skinned, to seek happiness within their own group, instead of warping and wasting their lives trying to become white. This thesis is akin to the accommodation with American color caste idea that runs through all of Fauset's fiction. However, she lacked the distance necessary to provide a fictional critique of black bourgeoisie that would parallel Frazier's sociological study. Fauset does mildly criticize the unholy stress on lineage, respectability, and class snobbery among black middle classes, but her conscious purpose seems belied by her unconscious identification with the values she condemns. According to Blyden Jackson, "for all the nobility of her intentions, because she is herself so naively philistine, so breathless with adoration for good-looking people Nordic style (even when they are tinted with the tar brush), good-looking clothes, good-looking homes and country-club ideas of *summa bona,* Jessie Fauset's defenses of the Negro middle-class backfire into an indictment of her horrid copycatting of the wrong values."[17] A harsh but essentially sound judgment.

Some Renaissance novelists grappled with the problem of developing life-styles based on Afro-American values rather than succumbing completely in their artistic vision to the middle-class mores of the dominant society. In some novels, the lower-class black's "cake-eater," jazzy style or his apparent shiftlessness become symptoms of an inability to accept the values and manners dictated by the white society. In no position to live in open hostility to the white society and unable to submit to the servility and complacency of most Negroes, these free spirits were forced to seek comfort and freedom in actions and modes of behavior that, to this day, remain more of a folkway than a socially accepted life-style. These "social misfits" include the leading characters in McKay's *Home to Harlem* and *Banjo*, Jimboy and Harriet in Hughes' *Not Without Laughter*, and, to a lesser degree, Sam Lucas in *One Way to Heaven*, Shine in *The Walls of Jericho*, and Hopping Dick in *Banana Bottom*. It is no coincidence that these characters (with the exception of Ray in McKay's novels) are drawn from the lower strata of society and that they are looked upon as irresponsible by other characters in the books in which they appear and by middle-class American readers.

But this is not the only fashion in which lower-class characters appear in Harlem Renaissance novels. Some novels dealing with the lower-class Negroes have what Alain Locke called the "saving grace of realism." McKay's *Banana Bottom*, Hughes' *Not Without Laughter*, and Countee Cullen's *One Way to Heaven* contain persuasive descriptions of lower-class life. McKay and Hughes also project visions of a black style fusing the values represented by the two major strata of Negro society. Bita successfully combines the folk values with her Western training and education; her attraction to Hopping Dick and the tea parties and her aversion to the stiffness of middle-class Negroes indicate a successful fusion of upward mobility and the capacity to share the simple joys of rural folk. Sandy, the sensitive young hero of Hughes' novel, never unlearns to admire Jimboy or Harriet, yet is determined to pursue the dreams for education and accomplishment which Aunt Hager has instilled in him. Also, Rudolph Fisher's *The Walls of Jericho*, the only Harlem Renaissance novel written in a predominantly comic mode, projects Fisher's vision of cooperation between the classes in the equal partnership between the "dicty" Fred Merrit and the working-class Shine.

Hughes' *Not Without Laughter* comes closest among the Harlem Renaissance novels to giving a realistic, if not naturalistic, portrayal of black folk. Alain Locke's review acclaims *Not Without Laughter* as "one of the highwater marks of the Negro's self-depiction in prose," despite its immaturity of narrative technique. "Indeed it [*Not Without Laughter*] was born in Mr. Hughes' poetry, which aims to evoke the folk temperament truly and reverently; and in its best chapters, *Storm*, *Guitar*, and *Dance*, its style palpitates with the real spiritual essence of Negro life."[18] As James O. Young points out, "*Not Without Laughter* was an important novel because it was one of the first by a black writer in which the life of the common folk was examined on its own terms, not for its humor or propaganda value."[19]

At the center of Hughes' novel is Sandy, an imaginative young boy growing up in a poor black home in Stanton, Kansas. More than anything else, *Not Without Laughter* is an episodic, at times lyrical, narrative of Sandy's growth from childhood to early youth. Besides the slights and insults by whites in and out of school, Sandy's education includes an active participation in his grandmother's Protestant work ethic, listening at night to sounds of his parents' lovemaking and to conversations of poverty and politics among adults, his first job at the barber shop where he learns "the protective art of turning back a joke," and his disillusionment in love when he discovers his idol, Pansetta, to be a common hussy. As time passes, Sandy is hardened by the harsh realities of his existence and is inspired by his grandmother's tough fiber to cope with them. He comes to learn that "no matter how hard life must be, it was not without laughter."

However, the two influences out of many that seem to stay with Sandy as he is poised at the beginning of a new hope at the end of the book are his grandmother and his aunt, Harriet. Working as an elevator boy in a Chicago hotel, he recalls his grandmother's ambitions for him and determines to get his education despite his mother's opposition. He is inspired by the examples of Booker T. Washington and Frederick Douglass, who pursued their education against the odds of extreme poverty and slavery. Sandy admires Aunt Harriet for her impatience with white patronage, her ambition and initiative that lift her from carnival dancing and streetwalking to her fame as "the Princess of the Blues." It is no mere coincidence that Harriet promises to see Sandy through his struggle to realize Aunt Hager's dreams for his education.

Sandy is thus a good example of "a middle-class Negro developing from the Negro masses, as these masses themselves become increasingly middle-class."[20] But with a difference. After his grandmother dies, Sandy has to live with his aunt and uncle, Tempy and Arkins Siles, who have acquired a few material advantages and socialize only with "high toned colored folks." Late in the book, Sandy thinks to himself, "I want a house to live in, too ... like Tempy's and Mr. Siles's.... But I wouldn't want to be like Tempy's friends—or her husband, dull and colorless ... ashamed of colored people."[21] Bone finds Hughes' characterization of Sandy "an untenable half-way house, which Claude McKay and Jessie Fauset would equally scorn to occupy,"[22] but it is not clear what is so untenable in Sandy's imbibing Harriet's self-respect and sprightliness, while he seeks the material advantages possessed by his "dicty" aunt.[23] Bone also fails to observe that the "cultural dualism" of Bita Plant in *Banana Bottom* parallels Sandy's "half-way house" and hinges on a similar conscious choice on the part of the heroine. Bita enjoys the intellectual advantages of a

Western education without adopting the values behind it.

Hughes creates a double sense of time in *Not Without Laughter*.[24] An obsessive concern with the flow of time from day to day and year to year in everyday life contains as well the weight of the whole Afro-American experience. To invoke the past in epic style, old Aunt Hager and Uncle Dan Givens talk about slavery; and Sister Johnson tells how all the Negroes of Vicksburg, Mississippi, were run out of town by the whites. Hughes also evokes the ideologies that have always had relevance to black life in America. In "Nothing but Love," for example, Aunt Hager expounds the philosophy of love, consideration, and forgiveness that she lives by. In literature, this philosophy has been dramatized in countless characters, from Uncle Tom in Stowe's *Uncle Tom's Cabin* (1852) to Vyry in Margaret Walker's *Jubilee* (1966). Hughes' use of the blues and the spirituals is even more effective. Aunt Hager counters Sandy's rising resentment against the whites for denying him entrance to the amusement park by singing

> From this world o' trouble, free,
> Stars beyond!
> Stars beyond!

As the tempo of Hager's song rises, Sandy hears in it "a great chorus out of the black past—singing generations of toil-worn Negroes, echoing Hager's voice" (p. 214). When Harriet dances to the tunes Jimboy plays on his guitar, Sandy sits and listens, the songs having set him to dreaming. At the end of the book, when Sandy and his mother return late to their one-room Chicago flat after spending the evening with Harriet, the young man's hope for the future is well-crystallized in the sound of spirituals being sung in a little Southern church on the block, "An' we'll understand it better by an' by!" (p. 304).

However, Hughes the poet is at his best in the ironic humor that characterizes his treatment of middle-class black Americans. Tempy becomes the main vehicle of Hughes' satire on the manners and values of black bourgeoisie. She is given a house by Mrs. Barr-Grant, a rich white woman she had served conscientiously as a maid for many years. This enables her to marry Mr. Siles, a mail clerk, and the two of them settle snobbishly into the upper strata of the Stanton black society. The upgraded Tempy is ashamed of her family connections and compensates in every possible way. She acts stiff and high-toned with poor people and shows contempt for anything "niggerish." She leaves the spiritual-singing Baptists and joins the Episcopal Church where the best people go.

She buys at stores where whites buy and reads journals they read. Harriet, a perfect foil to Tempy, finds her so "stuck-up and dicty" that one cannot "touch her with a ten-foot pole" (p. 45). At Christmas, Tempy visits her poor relatives to fulfill the obligation of giving them gifts. "When she had gone, everybody felt relieved—as though a white person had left the house" (p. 165). She and her husband are so busy proving themselves in the eyes of the whites, they have no time to act natural or show human consideration for others. At Aunt Hager's funeral, Tempy dismisses Harriet coldly and takes over the property in a businesslike manner. She also decides to bring Sandy up as "a perfect colored boy." "Such a boy," she believes, "certainly wouldn't be a user of slang, a lover of pool and non-Episcopalian ways" (p. 297).

Like Langston Hughes, Countee Cullen—another poet turned novelist—tried to portray the black folk as well as the black middle class in a single novel, *One Way to Heaven*. The main plot is the love story of Sam Lucas, a one-armed handsome dark man from Texas, who lives by his wits, and Mattie Johnson, a pretty and dark brown working-class girl of Harlem. Sam is always on the move and makes his living by gambling and by shamming a dramatic conversion to religion at least once in every town he visits. He arrives in Harlem on New Year's Eve and walks into a big revival meeting at the Mount Hebron Episcopal Church. Deeply moved by the feigned conversion of Sam, Mattie gives up her stubborn resistance to conversion and decides to become a church-going Christian. Simultaneously with her conversion, she falls in love with Sam and they get married.

The emphasis in Cullen's story, unlike Hughes', is not on the economic hassles of the working-class life, but on the ups and downs of Mattie's love for Sam. Thus, except for the fact that Cullen's main characters come from the lower strata of black life, the thrust of Cullen's tale is not very different from that of Fauset's novels. True to character, Sam never converts seriously to religion and finds an outlet for his roving impulses in the arms of Emma May, the only usher at the theater where he works as a doorkeeper. Mattie continues to show the new convert's fervor, while Sam moves farther away from her with each passing day. Pregnant with Sam's baby, Mattie despairs at the prospect of losing Sam completely, and, when her baby dies within hours of its birth, Sam goes to live with Emma May. The last act of this love drama is the con man Sam's final performance. Suddenly taken ill with pneumonia and brought home by Mattie to lie on his deathbed, Sam overhears a conversation between Mattie and Aunt Mandy that expresses the former's concern about his lack of grace. As a recompense for all his neglect of Mattie, Sam obliges her by feigning visions of light and sounds of celestial music all around him as he dies.

Although Cullen does not dwell on the indignities perpetrated by the American color line or on the miseries of poor blacks, he deals at greater length with religion and the black church. Hughes mentions the rivalry between the revival and the carnival, but describes only the latter; Cullen, the adopted son of an Episcopalian minister in Harlem, gives the church a sympathetic, though not uncritical, treatment.[25] Cullen observes that middle-class blacks politely neglect the church, but the poor blacks at the church are "like chronic bargainers . . . . they continue to buy, hoping to find a real bargain in the end" (p. 25). The watch-night services at the Harlem church where Mattie first meets Sam are described elaborately. Cullen effectively uses the irony that marks his treatment of middle-class blacks in the subplot of the novel. He describes the newly converted Mattie trying to persuade Sam to get some religion:

> She eyed him sorrowfully, as if she had grown wise between the intaking and releasing of a breath, and she cautioned him firmly in words she had heard at many a meeting with Aunt Mandy, and which she had unwittingly buried deep in herself for this moment's harvesting:
> "You must lean hard on the Lord." And she felt as if she had uttered some pearl of wisdom which she alone had discovered and released to a weary, despondent world. (Pp. 45-46)

Cullen's treatment of religion extends to some minor characters. The Rev. Clarence Johnson of Texas recognizes Sam Lucas as the man who had feigned a similar conversion at Memphis, Tennessee, and tells Sam: "I am not sure that you are not the most despicable man I've ever come across—or an unwitting instrument in the hands of Heaven" (pp. 30-31). The aloof Rev. Drummond assumes the contours of a kindly but shrewd man of the world when, arriving at Mattie's flat for dinner, he finds Sam in a nasty mood over Mattie's refusal to wear a kimono that Sam has brought from the theater. However, among the minor characters in the religious sections of the book, Aunt Mandy stands out with her curious mixture of Christian belief and paganism. Aunt Mandy is practical and sympathetic; she understands Sam's indifference to the church and more than implies that her niece is to blame for their family problems.

The story of Sam and Mattie is only tenuously and unconvincingly linked to the elaborate social gatherings at the house of Mattie's mistress, Constancia Brandon. Constancia, the beautiful wife of Dr. George Brandon, a black physician who is also an oil magnate from Oklahoma, is "the mirror in which most of the Social Harlem delighted to gaze and see itself" (p. 90). Her money gives her the freedom to be "willful, capricious and rude whenever she desired to deviate from her suave kindness" (p. 90). She enjoys bringing together people of disparate temperaments and interests and forcing them to make embarrassed conversations. Gifted with wit and intelligence, she does not suffer from any complexes because of her race. She is light enough to "pass" but "enjoys life too much and enjoyment isn't across the line—they don't know what it is" (p. 187). Cullen's gentle and delightful satire is directed more at Constancia's friends than at her. In describing Constancia's relationships with each of them, Cullen treats all her friends with an ironic but not bitter humor. Cullen demonstrates his ability to handle six or eight people by "rapidly moving from character to character, interjecting slices of repartee among the asides that he, as narrator, makes about his characters."[26]

It is not important today to try to match Cullen's satirical portraits with their real life models. That he did have real people in mind is clear from his peculiar prefatory note: "Some of the characters in this book are fictitious." The guests at Constancia's soirées include Mrs. Vanderbilt-Jones who moves to Sugar Hill from Brooklyn to avoid New York's expensive cabs; Donald Hewitt, an Englishman who says he has been writing a book for years and now plans one on Negroes; Walter Derwent, a white writer interested in black life and culture; Mrs. DePeyster Johnson, a New York public school teacher who feels responsible for the birth and protection of the New Negro; Samuel Weinstein, a Columbia graduate student who embarrasses Negroes by taking black literature far more seriously than they do; the Duchess of Uganda, née Mary Johnson, a "Back to Africa" zealot; her friend, Lady Hyacinth Brown, velvet-skinned and seductive, an excellent foil to the soot-black face and huge shapeless body of the Duchess; Lawrence Harper and Lottie Smith, black artists who give only their own works as gifts; Miss McCoffin, the Irish-American missionary who tries to teach spirituals to her African charges. Cullen's satire reaches its climactic point when Constancia prankishly invites the white Southern professor who has gained fame for his tract, *The Menace of the Negro to Our American Civilization*. Constancia not only manages to cajole and orders others to sit through the professor's talk but also insists on applause from everyone else at its end.

Cullen's book highlights, unintentionally perhaps, the contrast between the classes but fails to weave the two strands of the narrative into a cohesive picture of Harlem life. At one point, a sensitive and suggestive evocation of spring in Harlem reinforces the distance that separates the fashionable Harlem from the life that Sam and Mattie live:

> In Constancia's neighborhood one does not change one's winter clothes precipitately for the habiliments of Spring, but one goes through all the nuances of diminishing warmth. One's skin is tender, one's lungs are delicate; April is treacherous, and one safeguards one's health. . . . Where Sam and Mattie live one cannot take time to mince words. . . . Spring is in the air. Your windows go up with a bang that is everything but studied and proper. (Pp. 213-14)

When Constancia patronizingly insists on having Sam and Mattie's wedding at her place, she prepares also to measure her success by the attention she would get in the society columns of the local newspapers the next morning. In return for an occasional favor from Constancia—such as her help in getting Sam a job—Mattie has to put up with the dubious reputation among her equals of working for "uppity" colored people.

Since the publication of *One Way to Heaven* in 1932, reviewers and critics have pointed out Cullen's failure to weld "a high life and high society theme into the same story."[27] Critics have wondered why Cullen did not write two books. "One feels that a superb short novel has been sacrificed to convention or that Mr. Cullen has been unwilling to regard Sam and Mattie as important enough to justify devoting all his novel to them."[28] Rudolph Fisher, who had successfully won a wager by writing a cohesive story of low and high life in Harlem years earlier in *The Walls of Jericho*, compared the juxtaposition in *One Way to Heaven* of "two so different subjects so differently handled" to "exhibiting a lovely pastel and a cartoon in the same frame."[29]

Fisher's own novel, however, differed from *One Way to Heaven*. *The Walls of Jericho* stands alone among Harlem Renaissance novels as a high comedy that intersperses hilarious social satire with brilliant passages of personified description. Cullen's Miss McCoffin, delightful enough in herself, seems pale beside Fisher's bold and devastating portrait of Miss Agatha Cramp, the

white philanthropist. Also, Fisher's novel envisions an alliance between the poor and the well-to-do blacks that goes much beyond
the condescending and distorted relationships pictured by Hughes
and Cullen.

The thin plot of *The Walls of Jericho* mainly follows the love
story of a piano mover, Joshua Jones, nicknamed Shine, and Linda
Young, a housemaid who works for Miss Cramp. Woven into their
story are the inconstant fortunes of Fred Merrit, an extremely
race-conscious Negro lawyer, who is otherwise light enough to
pass as white. Rudolph Fisher, a brilliant physician who established his practice in Jamaica, New York, outreaches his middle-
class background in effectively delineating lower-class characters
in *The Walls of Jericho* and many short stories. Fisher shows little
of Hughes' interest in black folklore, but he dramatizes the lives of
common people with a rich use of dialect. Pearl Fisher, his sister,
has rightly claimed for him "a peculiar superiority of orientation
and awareness usually totally lacking in the writings of minority
group members who write about their own people."[30] In *The
Walls of Jericho*, this superiority shows through in the fine class
consciousness of the "rats" or "shines" in contrast to the "dicties,"
their mutual distrust and the exploitation of that distrust by a variety of people, including bootleggers and racketeers.[31]

But nowhere does Fisher's superiority over other Renaissance
novelists show more than in his humor and satire. Walter White
hailed *The Walls of Jericho* as "the first light novel of Negro
life."[32] Jinx Jenkins and Bubber Brown—characters Fisher would
use again in his mystery novel, *The Conjure Man Dies* (1932)—
provide many examples of the Negro's characteristic irony that
disavow fact and repudiate reality, "a markedly racial tendency to
make light of what actually was grave" (p. 29). They joke constantly at each other's cost and their "kidding" threatens to erupt
into violence any moment. Described by Fisher as the Damon and
Pythias of Harlem, they reminded early reviewers more of Miller
and Lyles, or the vaudeville team of Glenn and Jenkins. They
fight over everything—siding with "dicties" against whites, the
chances of Shine getting "soft" over Linda, the past participle
form of "smite," or even whether they feel hot or cold. It is interesting to record in passing that although most early readers delighted in the keen repartee of Jinx and Bubber, DuBois found
them "only moderately funny, a little smutty and certainly not
humanly convincing."[33]

Fisher excels even more in the section entitled "Uplift," a
Chaucerian gallery of portraits that forms part of the background
for the Annual Costume Ball of the General Improvement Associa-

tion at Manhattan Casino. The Ball is attended by "the rattiest rat to the dictiest dicty" and attracts many black and white luminaries. There is J. Pennington Porter, "proud, loud and pompous," who argues quite logically that "only admixture produced harmony between races." Porter's wife is "round, brown and expansile . . . always . . . bursting with something to say, but had never been known to say it; a woman so inflated with her husband's bombast that one felt she'd collapse at a single thrust" (p. 98). Honorable Buckram Byle, an ex-alderman, is seen standing "motionless, silent, scowling," while his wife Nora eagerly obliges every Nordic's request for a dance. Among the white guests is Noel Dunn, "the Nordic editor of an anti-Nordic journal, who missed no item of scene or conversation that he thought he could use for copy" (p. 99). He and his wife find the Pennington Potters ("Popeyed Potters" as Cornelia Bond, a rich black beauty, calls them) "convenient wedges in effecting several profitable entrances" into Harlem life. Cornelia Bond's invitees include Conrad White, the white writer who claims he is only passing downtown, and Betty Brown, his fiancée who complains that all Harlem girls have beautiful hands.

The star presence at the ball is, of course, Miss Agatha Cramp, the white do-gooder who is overwhelmed by her first experience of seeing "so many Negroes in one place at one time." She is also outraged by the large number of fair-skinned people—she does not suspect that some of them are blacks—who move among the crowd on the floor, apparently enjoying themselves without guilt or inhibition. Fisher introduces Miss Cramp in an earlier chapter with a terse irony that is reminiscent of Jane Austen. Miss Agatha Cramp, we are told, had "a sufficiently large store of wealth and a sufficiently small store of imagination to want to devote her entire life to service" (p. 59). For the last fifteen years, she has devoted her time and money to different ethnic groups, to which her successive maids have belonged, but "now, with a colored maid on hand, she had no outlet for her urge" (p. 59). Suddenly one morning she notices how amazingly pretty Linda is, triggering in her mind the startling possibility that "Negroes might be mankind, too." At the ball, she is introduced to Fred Merrit, who unmercifully vents his bitter hatred on whites on Miss Cramp's ignorance of his racial identity. Inwardly chuckling with glee at Miss Cramp's awkward enthusiasm for the black's uplift, Fred Merrit finally extracts an invitation from Miss Cramp to call on her. A bit later, Miss Cramp, not knowing how to cope with Nora Byle's inadvertent revelation of Fred Merrit's identity, sits in her box with uncomprehending eyes, "eddies and currents of heads swirling about in a stream below her" (p. 139).

Although there is no lack of variety in Fisher's humor or satire, his book is enriched by a masterly use of personification. "A piano," he tells us "is a malicious thing; it loves to slip out of your grip and snap at your toes, with an evil chuckle inside. Push up its lip and see it sneer; touch it and hear it rumble or whine" (p. 23). Fisher also employs this figure of speech in describing Manhattan streets: "Court Avenue is a straight, thin spinster of a street which even in July is cold. . . . Twice a day, when sunlight touches the windows . . . Court Avenue smiles a chilly, crystalline smile. . . . In short, Court Avenue is a snob of a street" (p. 44). Fisher describes the horror and blankness that Fifth Avenue expresses in Negro Harlem; he imagines Broadway trying without success to escape Fifth Avenue's lot: "Broadway, seeing its fellow's fate, veers off to the west as it travels north, avoiding the dark kingdom from afar. A futile dodge, since the continued westward spread of the kingdom threatens to force its side-stepping Broadway any moment into the Hudson" (p. 189). The skillful humanization of inanimate objects permits elements of the backdrop to become actors in the racial and human drama. But Fisher is just as skillful in his use of the opposite approach; he describes the dancing couples at the Manhattan Casino Ball as "the leaves and petals of flowers strewn thick on a stream; describing little individual figures and turns, circling capriciously in groups here and there, but all borne steadily onward in one common undertrend" (p. 102).

The central metaphor, which provides the book's title and resolves its major conflicts, is provided by Reverend Tod Bruce in his sermon at St. Augustine's Episcopalian Church. As Aubrey Bowser puts it, "The brilliant preacher manhandles a Bible story into proving what he wants it to."[34] To Bruce, the story of Joshua has meaning for every individual's life; the walls of Jericho represent "the self-illusion which circumstance has thrown around a man's own self." And Bruce adds:

> A man may think he is black when he is white; boast that he is evil and merciless and hard when all this is but a crust, shielding and hiding a spirit that is kindly, compassionate and gentle. . . . No man knows himself till he comes to an impasse . . . to some disrupting impact that shatters the wall of self-illusion. This, I believe, is the greatest spiritual battle of a man's life, the battle with his own idea of himself. (Pp. 185-86)

The metaphor has obvious relevance to the situation of Shine and

Linda, both of whom as lovers vie with each other to act cool and indifferent, till the walls come "tumblin' down" and they realize how deeply they care for each other.

For Shine, however, it has further meaning; accustomed to acting hard and rough in the world of men, and unable to forgive himself before for not avenging Merrit's alleged assault on Linda, he recognizes his essentially humane nature and tells himself: "The guy that's really hard is the guy that's hard enough to be soft" (p. 264). Later, discovering that Patmore, the poolroom man, not Merrit, was the real villain, he suspends his general distrust of middle-class blacks to enter a business partnership on an equal basis with Fred Merrit, an uncommon "dicty." Merrit offers the partnership as a "race proposition" by which the walls between the classes can be scaled down. "That's what we Negroes need, a business class, an economic backbone. What kind of a social structure can anybody have with nothing but the extremes—bootblacks on one end and doctors on the other. Nothing in between. No substance" (pp. 282-83).

There is, however, something between the extremes of the bootblack and the doctor in Harlem society. And Fisher carefully exposes that part of the black social structure in order to insure against being misunderstood. Between the two worlds of the "rats" and the "dicties" is "the glittering, big time sphere of Mr. Patmore with its aristocracy of numbers bankers, cabaret owners and poolroom Kings."[35] Henry Patmore is "a perfect ladies' man . . . with a constant large supply of bank notes on his person . . . and an excellent taste in dress. Further, there was about him the reassuring deliberateness of complete self-confidence. . . . Never did Patmore's manner suggest his motive" (pp. 76-77). We never know whether it is mere chance or his Jake-like (*Home to Harlem*) instinct that makes Shine turn down the offer of partnership in bootlegging. The danger that lurks behind Mr. Patmore's power and intelligence is evidenced in the manner he settles an old grouse with Fred Merrit by burning Merrit's new house on Court Avenue under the mask of hostility from white neighbors. In Fisher's vision of peace between the classes, there is no room for Patmores, but certainly for honest and industrious working-class people, such as Shine and Linda (with Huggins, one might call them the "field hand" and "house servant," respectively),[36] as they rise to fill the gap between the extremes of affluence and poverty.

Considering the confusion and division that other Renaissance novelists reflect in their thinking about the issues relating to class among blacks, the firmness and clarity of the alliance Fisher envisions is remarkable. In reviewing *One Way to Heaven*, Fisher had complained that in satirizing his upper-class characters, Cullen had become "a caricaturist, suppressing all his sympathies, sketching with a sharp and ingracious pen."[37] In Fred Merrit, Fisher created a middle-class black character—who with the partial exception of Joel Marshall in Fauset's *There is Confusion*—stands alone among the literary characters of the Harlem Renaissance in viewing the problems of poor blacks with sympathy but without condescension. *The Walls of Jericho* abounds with caricatures of black bourgeoisie, but Fisher also portrays a few sympathetic characters of middle-class background—something almost completely absent in Hughes and Cullen. His work also does not suffer from the twisted perspective that mars Fauset's treatment of the black middle class. There is a serious voice behind the visible sprightliness of Fisher's book, "a voice that says neither Yea nor Nay, but merely suggests that all this is worthy of thought."[38]

Frazier discusses the Negro Renaissance in *Black Bourgeoisie* and credits much of the fiction from the period with "not only an objective attitude toward the past but a sympathetic understanding of the lives of the Negro masses."[39] It is, of course, beyond the scope of Frazier's book to substantiate his statement with illustrations from the works written during the Harlem Renaissance. However, as my analysis suggests, Frazier overstated his case. After weighing all the evidence, it is not easy to disagree with Faith Berry, who has charged that most of the Renaissance writers did not deal with the issues and dilemmas that confronted the black population at that time.[40] Only Rudolph Fisher described in some of his short stories the impact of the black urban migration. But the class consciousness reflected in the work of Langston Hughes and Rudolph Fisher is a positive heritage in times when class conflict continues to dominate the Afro-American scene.

"FOOLING OUR WHITE FOLKS"

COLOR CASTE IN AMERICAN LIFE

I submit that here is the gift par excellence of the Negro to America. To spur ten times our number on to great heights of achievement; to spare the nation the enervating presence of a destructive social caste system, such as exists elsewhere, by substituting a color caste system that roused the hope and pride of teeming millions of ofays—this indeed is a gift of which we can well be proud.

George S. Schuyler

In America a fairly rigid caste system defines the status of blacks. "Being colored is like being born in the basement of life, with the door locked and barred—and the white people live upstairs."[1] Using a caste framework to explain black status in America originated with W. Lloyd Warner and his associates in the thirties and forties, and, when applied to Americans of African origin, is a useful conceptual tool. Middle-class blacks might have life-styles and values parallel to their white counterparts, but they nonetheless share with the lower-class blacks certain limitations on their "life-chances."[2] Despite increasing desegregation and the new opportunities for middle-class blacks during the last two decades, the color caste persists.

Although biological theories are used to justify the artificial division into black and white, Afro-American writers have always exposed the dilemmas arising from the classification of individuals according to caste. In this tradition the Harlem Renaissance writers insist that caste is a matter of social designation; it is not based on scientific evidence. As early as 1853, William Wells Brown's *Clotel, or The President's Daughter: A Narrative of Slave Life in the United States*, the first published novel by an Afro-American, tried to arouse white sympathy for the abolitionist cause by portraying the fluctuating fortunes of Currer, a mulatto woman whom the author introduces as President Jefferson's discarded concubine, and her two near-white daughters, Clotel and Althesa. Brown's main characters reveal the injustices and humiliations suffered by black slaves and confirm the truism that white people treat light-skinned Negroes better than their dark-skinned counterparts. But in *Clotel* and in other works by Brown's black contemporaries, the authors try to arouse sympathy for their mulatto characters "less because they are colored than because they are nearly white."[3]

During the post-Reconstruction period, the half-century following the first publication of Brown's *Clotel*, an elaborate caste system replaced slavery. By the turn of the century, the related themes of the mixed-blood and "passing" attracted black and white writers of disparate background. The white writers were interested primarily in the social effects of miscegenation or in the melodramatic possibilities of the theme. Numerous sensational works appeared; Thomas Nelson Page's *Red Rock* (1898) and Thomas Dixon's *The Leopard's Spots* (1902) and *The Clansman* (1905) stand out for their portrayal of the mixed-blood "as the embodiment of the worst qualities of both races and hence as a menace to the dominant group."[4] On the other side, George Washington Cable's *Old Creole Days* (1879) and *The Grandissimes* (1880) sympathetically treated the Louisiana mulatto's social and psychological problems. In his *An Imperative Duty* (1892), William Dean Howells uses the theme of miscegenation to attack the morbid devotion to duty that Puritanism bequeathed to Americans. Albion Tourgée, in his reformist novels, *A Royal Gentleman* (1881) and *Pactolus Prime* (1890), does not censure mulattoes who choose to cross the color line. Mark Twain's *The Tragedy of Pudd'nhead Wilson* (1894) traces the layers of irony embedded in the American color caste through his antebellum story of a near-white slave, Roxana, who exchanges her own infant son with the master's, the two being nearly identical. Twain's concern is then the effects of environment in determining an individual's personality.

But it is Charles W. Chesnutt's *The House Behind the Cedars* (1900) and James Weldon Johnson's *The Autobiography of an Ex-Colored Man* (1912) that develop the passing theme. After writing a collection of stories concerned with the life of an American mulatto, entitled *The Wife of His Youth and Other Stories of the Color Line* (1899), Chesnutt wrote *The House Behind the Cedars,* about the attitudes toward passing of a brother and sister, John and Rena Walden. John has no qualms about having crossed the color barrier, once he is convinced he has rights he must enjoy. But when Rena decides to pass, she cannot take lightly the consequences of the deception involved. Chesnutt treats interracial love with the respect and seriousness that marked his statements on the subject elsewhere. Like George Schuyler during the twenties, Chesnutt saw miscegenation as the ultimate solution to America's racial problem: "The races will be quite as effectively amalgamated by lightening the Negroes as they would be by darkening the whites."[5]

Johnson's use of the passing theme in *The Autobiography of an Ex-Colored Man* gave him the freedom to deal with American life on either side of the color line, and to reflect "his sharp insights, his definitive understanding of the 'problem,' and his broad human sympathy."[6] The nameless narrator in the *Autobiography,* who presents his story as a "human document," goes through a most commanding range of experience in American and European life. Leaving the North for Atlanta University, he moves on to Jacksonville, where he works in a cigar factory. He returns to the North to become part of Harlem's cabaret society as a gambler and ragtime pianist, until a murder compels him to leave for Europe as a traveling companion to a millionaire. Having tired of Europe and his employer, he returns to the American South with the long-term objective of transforming black folk music into classical jazz. Disgusted by a Georgia lynching, he returns to the North where he passes, marries a white woman and lives a comfortable life. His regret at the end of his career is that he chose money, which he saw as the primary measure of a white man's success, over "making history" as a black musician. As Hugh Gloster points out, in his unbiased interpretation of men and conditions as he knew them, Johnson became an important precursor of the Harlem Renaissance.[7]

Passing as a theme in literature or as a happening in real life could not have taken the twenties by surprise. But disappearing into the white world is more than an Afro-American phenomenon;[8] immigrants of different backgrounds have accelerated their social mobility through assimilation. For a black, the risks in passing have always been higher, but the possibilities that lie beyond have been more tempting. For obvious reasons, individuals from white ethnic groups find it easier to assimilate, but even in cases where it proves difficult, they have advantages over their black counterparts. For one thing, they were not humiliated by a legally and socially sanctioned system that segregated them on the basis of their ethnicity. Moreover, even when the hyphenated Americans were discriminated against, they always had the dubious freedom of feeling superior to American Negroes.[9]

But blacks did not have such options. They either grudgingly accepted their subservient status, or tried to maneuver themselves onto the other side of the fence. In his now famous article, "Why I Remain a Negro," Walter White commented on the extent of the passing phenomenon:

> Every year approximately 12,000 white-skinned Negroes disappear—people whose absence cannot be explained by death or emigration. Nearly every one of the 14 million discernible Negroes in the United States knows at least one member of his race who is "passing"—the magic word which means that some Negroes can get by as whites, men and women who have decided that they will be happier and more successful if they flee from the proscription and humiliation which the American color line imposes on them.[10]

White wrote this article in 1947, and without going into statistics, we can surmise that at least as many Negroes were passing into the white world in the 1920s. In addition, light-skinned Negroes, living with their families in black neighborhoods, occasionally passed in order to enjoy a downtown meal or the theater.

Langston Hughes, in "Fooling Our White Folks,"[11] tells how most Negroes enjoy seeing black people call white America's bluff by passing as white, whether temporarily or permanently. However, since the first literary treatment of passing in William Wells Brown's *Clotel*, its humorous side has scarcely surfaced in Afro-American novels. It is the serious side of the theme which has received attention from a number of Renaissance novelists. Ephraim A. Berry wrote in 1929 that passing is "a jazz theme, suitable for the swift staccato of the evening tabloid, the roar and flash of the gas buggy or the clash and clang of 'black and tans.' "[12] The Renaissance novels of passing match Berry's description in their variety of style and effect even if they lack the breadth of Johnson's framework in the *Autobiography*.

The first novel on the theme of passing published during the Harlem Renaissance years was Walter White's *Flight* (1926). Then within a year of one another, Jessie Fauset's *Plum Bun* (1928) and Nella Larsen's two novels, *Quicksand* (1928) and *Passing* (1929), were published. Coming from black families with middle-class predilections, these novelists emphasized, for example, the desire of their protagonists to explore avenues, economic or otherwise, that would have been open to them in American life but for their racial identity. Their treatment of the theme also confirms McKay's contention in *Banjo* that passing was relatively a nonissue among lower-class blacks. In the world of Jake and Banjo, there is little talk of "passing white and the specter of the Future that were the common topics of colored intelligentsia."[13]

In his excellent introduction to the 1971 reprint of *Passing*, Hoyt Fuller points out that passing is no longer among the interests of the black community and that not "many Black people were worked up over passing even in the twenties."[14] Evidently, there are fewer reasons today for blacks to pass. But the appearance of so many passing novels during the twenties is evidence of its predominantly middle-class orientation. The novelists who dealt with the theme were at ease with it, considering their potential closeness to the phenomenon in real life. But the more important reason for the preponderance of the theme among Harlem Renaissance novelists has to be their feeling that its treatment would give them the leverage to say things that, to them, seemed important to say at that particular juncture in the history of American race relations. The passing novel might also represent a conscious effort to inculcate black pride, or as Bone puts it, to make "a symbolic rejection of the writer's unconscious desire to be white."[15]

The three major Renaissance novels of passing—*Flight*, *Plum Bun*, and *Passing*—all reflect the same pattern in their octoroon heroine's life—yielding to the temptation of passing as white, living as mistress or wife to a bigoted white man, and finally returning to the fold of black life when she begins missing the warmth, the color, the vivacity of black life. The three books are set in different cities for the early portions of their heroines' careers, but in each case the lure of Harlem plays a part in the heroine's decision to return to black life. Like other novels dealing with the lives of middle-class black Americans, the novels of passing "portrayed people, who, while black by the definitions imposed in America, looked and behaved very much like whites."[16] Thus, at one level there is an attempt to delineate a dimension of culture and values which the middle-class blacks shared with white Americans. At the same time, these novels inform white readers that middle-class blacks have no intention or desire to relinquish the joy and abandon of black life for the dullness of the white bourgeoisie. The fleeting but exaggerated pictures of the lower-class black, who enjoys himself in spite of his problems, indicate the magnetic pull that brings the heroines back to black life.

The heroine in *Flight* is a girl of Creole background who does not even consider herself seriously as a Negro until she is forced to watch the killing of innocent, unknown blacks in downtown Atlanta during the race riots in 1906. The Atlanta riots are the last step in the conversion of Mimi Daquin into a full-fledged, race-conscious Negro—a conversion that starts with her moving from an ethnically mixed and easygoing New Orleans to a segregated and caste-ridden Atlanta. Mimi had regarded race as an insignificant factor in her life as an individual; now, she thinks of everything in terms of race or color. Soon, she grows away from the gentle and broad-based philosophy of her father, Jean, and also fails to sympathize with Jean's painful surrender to his ambitious second wife's "sordid" values. Mimi finds a young friend in Hilda Adams, who is madly in love with Carl Hunter, a sharp but weak-willed youth who does not care much for Hilda.

Carl, however, becomes an instrument for the next major move in Mimi's life. He is attracted to Mimi and, together, they enjoy common cultural and intellectual interests. After dallying with her sense of loyalty to Hilda, Mimi realizes she is in love with Carl and gives herself to him in an impulsive moment. Soon after, Jean Daquin, still full of nostalgia for his calm and beautiful days in New Orleans, suddenly dies of a heart attack. The sudden death of her father and Carl's timid reaction to her pregnancy force Mimi to think and act independently; she decides to keep "her own soul free" rather than marry a "worthless scamp." Against the entreaties of Carl and his parents and "the Niagara of words" from her stepmother, Mimi leaves Atlanta for Philadelphia. There, she gives birth to a male child and supports him and herself by working at odd sewing jobs. Finally, stuck with a huge bill for an intestinal operation on her child, she requests and receives help from her aunt, Mrs. Rogers, who, in turn, invites her to come and live with her in New York. Enrolling her son in a white Catholic orphanage, she moves to New York. There she enjoys her newfound-land of Harlem social life, till gossip catches up with her in the form of Mrs. Plummer from Atlanta, forcing her to pass and later marry James Forrester, a Wall Street broker.

The heroine of *Flight* is portrayed as a beautiful, intelligent, and sensitive girl, who reminded Carl Van Vechten of the self-reliant heroines of Ellen Glasgow.[17] White also manages to place the stereotype of the unwed black mother in a new perspective—Mimi would not compromise in her "soul" even if it meant loss of comfort and social reputation. Yet White is too concerned with the demands of his thesis to allow Mimi's career to develop freely.

Mimi is one of the most manipulated heroines in literature. Just as Mrs. Rogers and Mrs. Crosby abruptly enter to serve as links in the chain of the plot, Mimi unconvincingly makes decisions quite incompatible with her character. Reviewing the book in *The Crisis* (July 1926), Nora E. Waring wrote that "Mimi seems deprived of her individuality and becomes a mechanical accomplice to the plot rather than an intelligent woman striving to break through the whims of fate to a spiritual freedom." The motivation that supports Mimi's decision to pass, considering her great love for her race, is weak, and the exploration of her feelings toward her son, Jean, Jr., in the final section of the narrative, is unsatisfactory. The highly coincidental plot is further undermined by the author's poor anticipation of questions that Mimi's actions raise in the reader's mind. For example, why does Mimi suffer several years of deprivation in Philadelphia before making her plea to Mrs. Rogers? White glosses over Mimi's failure to carry out her intention of telling James Forrester about Jean, Jr., and her own racial identity before marrying him. Further, although Mimi's spiritual alienation from her husband and his beliefs is understandable, her expectation to find peace in the gossip-ridden and narrow-minded world, which she had fled unhesitatingly eight years earlier, is not entirely plausible. And, finally, the social and psychological possibilities of the passing theme tend to become submerged as White generalizes about the rising trend of machine and money, East versus West, and the hypocrisy of Christian institutions. Perhaps Blyden Jackson justly singled out *Flight* as a conspicuous attempt by a black novelist to execute a conception beyond his capacity.[18]

But reviewers recognized that *Flight* was a better novel than White's earlier *Fire in the Flint*, a hastily written narrative about the savage lynchings in Central City, Georgia, of Bob and his elder brother, Dr. Kenneth Harper. The most significant thing about *Fire in the Flint*, according to DuBois, was that "a book like this can at last be printed."[19] *Fire in the Flint* does not need the helping hand of either art or propaganda and lives and breathes by "the terrible truth and reality of its substance."[20] But *Flight* is an attempt to carefully construct a detailed narrative of a young girl who goes from New Orleans to New York through Atlanta and Philadelphia in search of her spiritual salvation. Some of the better writing depicts black life in Atlanta and Harlem. In his review of *Flight*, Carl Van Vechten praised White's calm detachment, of which the earlier novel contained no hint.[21]

Jessie Fauset also emphasizes the social and economic aspects of the passing theme in *Plum Bun*. Fauset's approach to passing is well expressed in the nursery rhyme epigraph that supplies the titles of her novel's five sections:

> To Market, to market
> To buy a Plum Bun
> Home again, Home again
> Market is done.

The heroine, Angela Murray, passes as white to seek greater opportunities for herself as a young girl and artist. Although the unfolding of Fauset's thesis in *Plum Bun* runs parallel to White's in *Flight*, Fauset shows a finer craftsmanship in anticipating the turns and twists of her plot and manages to write a story whose exploitation of the black-white ironies in American life parallels that of Mark Twain's in *Pudd'nhead Wilson*. A successful device is the presence from the beginning to the end of Virginia Murray, Angela's brown sister, a perfect foil to the heroine. Fauset also avoids the cluttered multiplicity of interests that had plagued *There is Confusion* and tries to concentrate on related aspects of one significant theme; *Plum Bun* is easily her most successful novel.

Angela and Jinny grow up in a small house on Opal Street in Philadelphia where their honest and hardworking parents shower warmth and affection on both. Yet the two sisters are as different as can be. Jinny has a simple ambition in life—to be able to keep house like Mattie, her mother, for a man like Junius, her father. Angela, restless and ambitious, feels cramped in the drab little house. With her mother, she passes for fun in downtown restaurants and theaters. But although her mother never gives thought to serious passing, Angela is fascinated with the idea of taking a short cut to "the paths which lead to broad thoroughfares, large bright houses, delicate niceties of existence."[22] When Junius and Mattie both die within days of each other (Fauset is good at getting rid of people who have served their purpose for the plot—sometimes two or three characters die on a single page), Angela decides to take her share of the estate and disappears into the white world as Angèle Mory.

Arriving in New York, Angela admits that she is breaking with her family and race to seek greater opportunities less as an artist and more as a young white girl. Her artistic "gift was not for her the end of her existence; rather it was an adjunct to a life that was to know light, pleasure, gaiety and freedom" (p. 116). Failing to invite serious matrimonial interest from the rich and suave Roger

Fielding, she overcomes her "fastidiousness" to become his mistress. Even though she does not love Roger, she develops in time "a beautiful feeling" for him. For a while, she even forgets her intention of marrying in order to secure her future. She and Roger both know that "her surrender was made out of the lavish fullness and generosity of her heart" (pp. 203-4). Yet Roger deserts her abruptly and she turns in her loneliness to Anthony Cross, her classmate from an art class at Cooper Union, whose earlier attentions she had politely ignored. In a curious turn of events, Anthony reveals that he is part Negro and that he is already engaged to Jinny, even though still in love with Angela.

Meanwhile, Angela analyzes her career to date and comes to accept what her mother and sister have always understood—that "when one is taken up with the problem of living, with just life itself . . . being colored or not is just one thing more or less you have to contend with" (pp. 251-52). She realizes that she has been selfish in her pursuit of happiness and learns to appreciate close family connections and the warmth of black life. She fights her new malaise with inspiration from the values of black life in America, particularly the endurance blacks have long shown in the face of heavy odds. Now she begins to see blacks "as a people powerfully, overwhelmingly endowed with the essence of life. They had to persist, had to survive because they did not know how to die" (p. 309).

In handling Angela's return to black life, Fauset skillfully avoids both the sharp reversal in the finale of *Flight* and the melodramatic ending of *Passing*. Some early reviewers justifiably denounced the excessive use of coincidence in the book—especially in the hackneyed device by which Anthony Cross and Angela Murray are both shown to be of the "same race"—they also gave the author due credit for her remarkable restraint in the treatment of a potentially sensational subject. Her interest is primarily sociological rather than psychological, in situation rather than character, and she uses it in *Plum Bun* to her maximum advantage. She does not allow genealogy, glimpsed briefly in the case of Anthony Cross, to overwhelm *Plum Bun* as it had *There is Confusion*. She draws both her black and white characters clearly enough as individuals to meet the demands of her theme and weaves their reactions to passing into the general pattern of the narrative.

Fauset introduces protest without resorting to pages of introspection or self-pity. Angela's black friend, Rachel Powell, along with Angela, is granted a fellowship to study at the Fountainebleu School of Fine Arts near Paris in an open competition; but the award to Rachel is withdrawn when the Selection Committee learns of her racial identity. A committee of concerned citizens meets at the house of Martha Burden, Angela's white liberal friend, to fight on behalf of Rachel, who refuses to take part in any such effort. Anthony Cross dramatically announces his racial identity and justifies Rachel's attitude by emphasizing that blacks sometimes "have to stop their fight for the trimmings of life in order to hang on to the essentials which they've got to have and for which they must contend too every day just as hard as they had the first day" (p. 338). Anthony's revelation of his racial background causes confusion among his white listeners, many of whom are shown to harbor deep prejudices behind their liberal postures. However, it is Angela who must rescue the beleaguered Rachel from a horde of journalists eager to exploit her story for sensation. Pestered by questions from newsmen and frustrated in her attempt "to explain to these smug, complacent people Rachel's ambition . . . her only too obvious endeavour to share their training and not their friendship," Angela announces that she is turning down the American Committee Fund grant for the same reason (p. 345). In absorbing the reactions of her white friends to her avowal of black ancestry, Angela discovers how Rachel Salting, the Jewish girl of high ideals, hurt deeply over anti-Jewish prejudice, is herself full of antiblack sentiment; how the rich and lonely Mrs. Denver finds the courage to continue her friendship with Angela, and how Elizabeth and Walter Sandburg, the young white couple, pass the test as genuine friends of the Negro.

Nella Larsen is clearly Fauset's superior in craft and language; Larsen has greater success in infusing her material with dramatic form[23] and she writes effectively and economically, maintaining artistic unity and the proper point of view.[24] In addition to its neat execution, *Passing* reflects a psychological interest in passing that is missing in both Walter White and Jessie Fauset. Aubrey Bowser, in his 5 June 1929 review in the New York *Amsterdam News*, described *Passing* as "a story for the sake of the story and not for the sake of the race problem." Larsen's tone and diction are reminiscent of "society novels." For Hoyt Fuller, Larsen's approach "falls somewhere between the easy worldliness of Katherine Mansfield and the deliberate scene-setting of a mediocre home magazine story teller."[25]

The plot of *Passing* involves two near-white women, Clare Kendry and Irene Redfield. Clare, passing as white, is married to John Bellow, a white man who hates "niggers" and is unaware of Clare's black ancestry. Irene Redfield has married a black physician and seems to relish the security of her marriage and social life. Nella Larsen chooses to tell the story from Irene's point of view so that the main interest of the book is not the psychology of the woman who is passing but the complex and ambivalent responses of the woman who could have passed. Irene and Clare, childhood friends, have not seen each other for twelve years when they accidentally run into each other on the roof of the Drayton Hotel in Chicago. Clare, almost too beautiful to be true, is married to a rich banking agent with whom she spends a good part of her time in Europe. Clare uses her chance encounter with Irene to inquire about her old Chicago friends; she is curious about what they have thought of her and her disappearance all these years. Clare also expects to satisfy her longing to associate more with blacks through Irene. On the other hand, Irene instinctively senses danger in renewing her friendship with Clare even though Clare evokes in her a strange and compelling fascination for having done "this rather dangerous and . . . abhorrent thing successfully" (p. 44). Clare, who has a very nonchalant attitude to passing, wonders why Irene never passed. She tells Irene, "It is such a frightfully easy thing to do. If one's the type, all that's needed is a little nerve" (p. 37). Irene, at best a casual passer, is what she is partly because she considers serious passing a "hazardous business." Yet she wants to know how someone like Clare adjusted to a strange and unfriendly environment.

Unfortunately, Irene's fascination and curiosity about Clare's life on the other side of the fence lack substance enough for Nella Larsen to sustain her plot. Irene sums up the attitude of most middle-class blacks toward passing: "It is funny about 'passing.' We disapprove of it and at the same time condone it. It excites our contempt and yet we rather admire it. We shy away from it with an odd kind of revulsion, but we protect it." Failing to fully exploit the germ of drama in the above view, Larsen lets her story decline into a treatment of sexual jealousy between her two women characters over Brian, Irene's husband, with Irene strangely torn between self-interest and racial loyalty. However, the Jamesian quality of the scenes relating to this triangle saves the book from becoming a sentimental melodrama. Notwithstanding Nella Larsen's skills as a writer, the reader fails to understand the curious logic by which Irene's racial loyalty becomes identified with Clare, who poses a serious threat to Irene's security, the most desired thing in the world for her. Nella Larsen tries unsuccessfully to gloss over Irene's pseudoconflict:

The instinctive loyalty to a race. Why couldn't she get free of it? Why should it include Clare? Clare, who'd shown little enough consideration for her, and hers. What she felt was not so much resentment as a dull despair because she *could not change herself in this respect, could not separate individuals, herself from Clare Kendry.* (P. 184; my emphasis)

In addition to this unreasonable demand on the reader's credulity are the numerous allusions to Irene's perception of Clare's "cat-like" temperament, and to Clare's self-proclaimed ability to "get the things [she wants] badly enough" even if she has to hurt her friends in the process. Why Irene would not do anything sooner or less drastic than push (did she really push?) Clare out of a high-rise window at the end of the book is not at all clear. A more serious flaw is the failure to give any inkling of Clare's motives, feelings, or thinking except from the outside; she is not even given the benefit of a confidante in a drama that owes most of its action to her character.[26] It is unfortunate that Larsen—who exhibits the sensitivity and literary skill to match the challenge of her theme—does not choose to deal with passing from Clare's point of view, exposing the many subtle shades of feeling in the life of a woman who chooses to cross the color line. But, then, that would have been a very different book.

Larsen's first novel, *Quicksand* (1928), the tragic story of a mulatto, was acclaimed by critics and awarded the Harmon Foundation annual prize for "distinguished achievement among Negroes," E. Merrill Root, in *The Christian Century* (18 October 1928), gave the book an eloquent review, describing it as "a significant document of the contemporary human tragedy." Among the more recent critics, Robert Bone considers *Quicksand* the best novel of the period with the exception of Jean Toomer's *Cane*.[26]

Told from the point of view of its heroine, Helga Crane, *Quicksand* is the study of a woman who is bright, inhibited, and neurotic—"a pretty, solitary girl with no family connections" (p. 34). She is "a race-divided soul, [who] does not know what she wants—but she knows that she wants it."[28] Helga's neurosis may be defined as her failure to identify her emotional and sexual needs and find appropriate channels for them. As the novel opens, Helga gives up her teaching career at Naxos, a black school in the South, because she is fed up with its servility and snobbishness, hypocrisy and self-satisfaction. She arrives in Chicago only to be turned away from her white uncle's door by his new wife, and to suffer indignities at the hands of white employment agencies. She travels to New York as personal assistant to the autocratic and self-sufficient Mrs. Hayes-Rore, who, as the widow of a black Chicago politician, receives invitations from all over the country to lecture on race. Mrs. Hayes-Rore introduces Helga to her niece, Anne Grey, a young widow, who welcomes Helga's company as a roommate. Soon Helga finds herself absorbed in the social life of the upper crust in Harlem; "their sophisticated cynical talk, their elaborate parties, the unobtrusive correctness of their clothes and homes, all appealed to her craving for smartness, for enjoyment" (p. 95). Here she meets again Dr. Anderson, the former president of Naxos College, a man she would have always loved, had she let herself.

With signs of spring in Harlem, Helga's restlessness returns. She is tired of race talk by Anne Grey, who constantly apes the white woman's clothes, manners, and ways of living. Driven by "some imp of contumacy" from the man she loves, and released— like Henry James' Isabel Archer—by an unexpected gift of $5,000 from her Chicago uncle, Helga decides to leave for Europe to live with her Danish mother's sister, Katrina, and her husband, Poul Dahl, in Copenhagen. In Denmark, Helga is a great success as an exotic presence at social affairs, exhibited proudly like a strange species of pet dog. The Dahls, warm and affectionate, see Helga as an instrument in their own plans for social climbing and she disappoints them greatly by refusing the proposal of Axel Olsen, an aristocrat turned artist. She begins to develop a growing sense of "incompleteness" about her life in Denmark and feels "homesick, not for America, but for Negroes" (p. 207).

Not until she meets Dr. Anderson again does Helga realize the sexual nature of her vague yearnings. In an effective and significant dramatization, Dr. Anderson, now married to Anne Grey, stops in the hall and passionately kisses Helga. She resists strongly till "all power seemed to ebb away, and a long hidden, half-understood desire welled up in her with the suddenness of a dream. Helga Crane's own arms went up about the man's neck" (p. 233). When Anderson soberly ignores her invitation for an affair, she walks the Harlem streets on a rainy night, finding release for her libidinal reticence not in a bar but in a storefront church.

Nella Larsen introduces this unexpected atavistic turn quite effectively. Helga watches the performance at the church with shock and fascination until there creeps upon her "an indistinct horror of an unknown world." Before she can get away from it, she is overwhelmed by "the same madness." As churchwomen surround her in a "thunderclap of joy," she experiences a miraculous calm. As a premonition of the simple life she is about to choose, Helga feels "a happiness unburdened by the complexities of the lives" she has known. The Rev. Pleasant Green, a fattish yellow man who sat beside her at the church, escorts her with fatherly protection to her apartment. In a surprising move, she marries him and they move to Alabama where she bears a child every year and lives among a set of Fundamentalist sharecroppers. Her mindless routine during the day is made bearable for her by the challenge and anticipation signified by the approaching night: "all that was living in her sprang like rank weeds at the tingling thought of night, with a vitality so strong that it devoured all shoots of reason" (p. 273).

Helga's neurosis is convincingly explained by the emotional deprivation of her childhood. She grew up without the benefit of love from either her Danish mother or her black father; and she is extremely self-conscious about her illegitimate birth. Her internal conflict over the two races is created by the absence in her early life of the family and community acculturation through which a child discovers a group identity. In her unquestioning acceptance of white America's contemporary assumptions about miscegenated children (including their potential reversal to hereditary primitivism), Helga never achieves more than a tentative identification with either blacks or whites.

The narrative structure of the novel derives from the central, unifying metaphor contained in its title. If Helga could have seen herself as an individual rather than a human organism dominated alternately by black or white blood, she might have been reasonably happy with Axel Olsen or even happier with Robert Anderson. Driven instead by a short-sighted view of her mixed parentage, Helga Crane finds herself unable to accept her blackness and incapable of adapting to whiteness. Helga's quest for happiness leads her floundering "through a succession of minor bogs, until she is finally engulfed by a quagmire of her own making."[29] Her insistence on seeing her deeply personal and sexual longings in racial terms is closely linked to the repetitive design of her life, a "manic depressive" pattern evoked by recurrent images of appalling confusion, insistent desire, suffocation, chronic vaccilation, and intense hatred for males she attracts or is attracted to. Yet Helga's tragedy cannot be explained away in purely psychological terms; she is as much a victim of a self-image based on the prejudices of the people around her as a case of asphyxiation.

Roark Bradford grasped the mixed nature of Helga's dilemma when he reviewed *Quicksand* for *Herald Tribune Books* (13 May 1928). "But always it is there—a wistful note of longing, of anxiety, of futile searching, of an unconscious desire to balance black and white blood into something that is more tangible than a thing that merely is neither black nor white, of a nervous, fretful search for that will o' the wisp called happiness." *Quicksand* thus is not, as Robert Hemenway describes it, a study of "the human effects of miscegenation,"[30] but instead a study of the impact on a black individual's—especially a black woman's—character and behavior of her acute consciousness and helpless acceptance of white myths and shibboleths about her miscegenation.[31] Helga insists on viewing her deeply personal and emotional problems in terms of race. Nella Larsen extends Helga's predicament to all black Americans and relates it to the general theme of an existence determined largely by images and definitions supplied by others. This is especially true of the passages in the tightly written novel concerned with middle-class blacks and their values ("their constant slavish imitation of traits not their own"), or about the black as a mere beggar for security and happiness, or about the pathetic patriotism of black Americans.

By exploring Helga Crane's neurosis, Larsen effectively uses the stereotype of the tragic mulatto to provide a moving commentary on the repercussions of American color caste at a personal level. The tragic mulatto stereotype predicates the mixed-blood as a victim of divided inheritance; "from his white blood come his intellectual strivings, his unwillingness to be a slave; from his Negro blood come his baser emotional urges, his indolence, his savagery."[32] Helga Crane would most likely measure herself in terms of the above stereotype. The distinction of Larsen's novel, as of Langston Hughes' play *Mulatto* (1935), lies in attributing the mulatto's tragic sense of nonbelonging to individual and family problems rather than to the biological fact of miscegenation. *Quicksand*'s focus makes it complementary to Zora Neale Hurston's detailed study of a different kind of black woman in *Their Eyes Were Watching God* (1937) and anticipates by many decades the intensity and emotional tenor of works such as Sylvia Plath's *The Bell Jar* (1963).

The Harlem Renaissance writers concerned with the lives of near-white Afro-Americans bring out the black American's lukewarm acceptance of the American caste line at the same time that they stress the need for a new racial solidarity to cope with the unwholesome effects of racial segregation. If they do not recommend violent revolt or argue for the establishment of a black nation in Africa or the United States in the Afro-American's search for equality and human dignity, they also do not favor pious,

Christian patience. In line with the contemporary sociocultural thinking of Alain Locke, Charles S. Johnson, E. Franklin Frazier, and the leadership of the NAACP and the Urban League, they expected to break down the caste barrier by developing increasing contacts between black and white Americans, by asserting new images of black life through art and literature, and by contributing to the growing reservoir of scientific information regarding the Negro's past.

The near disappearance of the passing novel during the last three decades is partly a measure of the inadequate objectives that the earlier black novelists wanted to convey through their near-white protagonists and partly a reflection of the changes in America during the same period. Contending that mulattoes have never really been representative of black people, Blyden Jackson argues that since the forties, the black novelist has come to find the tragic mulatto protagonist "inadequate for his larger hopes."[33] Some Renaissance novelists, especially Jessie Fauset and Walter White, did use their mulatto heroines to bear the weight of racial protest. White and Fauset moved away from the earlier novelists' misdirected sympathies in dealing with the tragic mulatto as someone isolated from both races and provided a nonbiological motivation for their main characters; they followed the lead of James Weldon Johnson's *The Autobiography of an Ex-Colored Man* and foreshadowed later sociocultural and literary Afro-American developments. A significant contribution in this context is Nella Larsen's miscegenated heroine in *Quicksand*. But the issue of color engaged some other Renaissance novelists in a different and broader context than the one defined by novels whose near-white heroines debated whether to pass or not to pass.

THE BURDEN OF BLACKNESS

COLOR IN AFRO-AMERICA AND BEYOND

The problem of the twentieth century is the problem of the color line.

W.E.B. DuBois, Souls of Black Folk

How is it better to be enslaved by the Spaniards than by the Bubis?

Zo in Schuyler's Slaves Today

The predominantly light-skinned Negro "middle-class" precariously maintained its position in American life as an intermediate color caste between the white power structure and the black masses. But the color issue runs deeper than class or caste in Afro-America: Wallace Thurman looks closely at color in *The Blacker the Berry*; George Schuyler internationalizes color in *Slaves Today* by depicting the exploitation of the Liberian native; and DuBois, in *Dark Princess*, raises the same question in an even wider context—that of what is today known as the "third world." These works provide a meaningful and interrelated commentary on color in the modern world.

For a treatment of the discrimination suffered by dark-skinned blacks at the hands of their light-skinned counterparts, Wallace Thurman differentiated the more frequently noticed color caste in American life from the deeper obsession among blacks with the shade of skin regardless of class. His young protagonist is Emma Lou Morgan, a jet black girl born in an otherwise "blue vein" family of Boise, Idaho, whose motto was "whiter and whiter every generation," until their descendants might assimilate easily into the white race "so that problems of race would plague them no more."[1] The exhaustive series of situations in black life which Emma Lou encounters show how her rejection by her group and her consequent self-rejection become hopelessly complete. Thurman exposed a rarely admitted and, for most blacks, an embarrassing aspect of life, and gave it its first fictional treatment.[2] *The Blacker the Berry*, among the better achievements of the Harlem Renaissance, has merit both for what it achieves and for what it does not. It is a testimony to the high standards of art and craft by which Thurman attempted to judge himself and other black novelists.[3]

The assumption behind the extended treatment of "blackness" in *The Blacker the Berry* is starkly simple—a dark skin is as human and as beautiful as any of the myriad shades that are found within the black community and generally in life. That such a commonsense notion needed an extended literary demonstration then, and does even today, is an ironic commentary on American life, black and white. Early in the novel Thurman relates this intraracial color prejudice to the profound color complex that exists in American life:

> Emma Lou had been born in a semi-white world, totally surrounded by an all-white one, and those few dark elements that had forced their way in had either been shooed away or else greeted with derisive laughter. It was the custom always of those with whom she came into most frequent contact to ridicule or revile any black person or object. A black cat was a harbinger of bad luck, black crepe was the insignia of mourning, and black people were either evil niggers with poisonous blue gums or else typical vaudeville darkies. It seemed as if the people in her world never went half-way in their recognition or reception of things black, for these things seemed always to call forth only the most extreme emotional reactions. They never provoked mere smiles or mere melancholy, rather they were the signal either for boisterous guffaws or pain-induced and tear-attended grief. (P. 13)

Notwithstanding Melville's "whiteness of the whale" symbolism in *Moby Dick*, black is so firmly established as a portent of evil or bad luck in the West,[4] that a character as dark as Emma Lou cannot escape the prejudice engendered by the rigid color line that divides black from white in American life. In Boise, Idaho, white and black wives gossip over back fences and lend one another needed household commodities, but there is little social intercourse between their husbands. "And it was not a matter of the difference in their respective husbands' businesses," adds the narrator. "It was purely a matter of color" (p. 17). Emma Lou is all the more embarrassed by her friendship with the vibrantly human but uncouth Hazel Mason, because she parades "her darky-like clownishness" in front of white people in an integrated institution. Later in the book, when Emma Lou's employer, the white actress Arline, is away in Chicago, her response to being asked to work as a maid for a black actress is: "Imagine her being maid for a Negro woman! It was unthinkable" (p. 138). Emma Lou wants to associate with black people "who [are] different from whites only in so far as the skin color was concerned" (p. 46). She would have fully agreed with William M. Ferris, the author of a two-volume study called *The African Abroad*, who in 1913 exhorted the Negro to become a Negrosaxon: "He cannot bleach out his complexion or straighten his hair, or sharpen his nose, or thin his lips. But in mind and character and disposition he must become a black white man. After the Negrosaxon has been made over into the likeness of the white man, he can hope to be made over into the image of God."[5]

Truman Walter, a likely spokesman for Wallace Thurman— whom Emma Lou meets through her Filipino-mulatto lover, Alva, at a house-rent party of Harlem[6] writers and intellectuals—states the issue in more sophisticated terms:

> We are living in a totally white world, where all standards are the standards of the white man. . . . It merely explains, not justifies the evil—or rather, the fact of intraracial segregation. Mulattoes have always been accorded more consideration by white people than their darker brethren. They were made to feel superior even during slave days. (P. 166)

Truman Walter's analysis gives the question an interesting psychological turn. Thurman frequently attacks the white stereotyping of blacks by accentuating the reactions of the light-skinned Negro toward the darker Negro. According to Truman Walter:

> People have to feel superior to something, and there is scant satisfaction in feeling superior to domestic animals or steel machines that one can train or utilize. It is much more pleasing to pick out some individual or some group of individuals

on the same plane to feel superior to. This is almost necessary when one is a member of a supposedly despised, mistreated minority group. . . . Negroes are, after all, human beings, and they are subject to be influenced and controlled by the same forces and factors that influence and control other human beings. . . . It is no wonder that even the blackest individual will seek out some one more black than himself to laugh at. (P. 167)

But while Truman Walter (a slender dark youth who—like Thurman himself—is from Salt Lake City and has gone to school in Southern California) can sit back and rationalize about the intraracial color prejudice in intellectual terms, Emma Lou must face it as a real thing in a real world. Her family—with the partial exception of her Uncle Joe—rejects her from the day of her birth:

Emma Lou had always been the alien member of the family and of the family's social circle. Her grandmother, now a widow, made her feel it. Her mother made her feel it. . . . to say nothing of the way she was regarded by outsiders. As early as she could remember, people had been saying to her mother, "What an extraordinarily black child! Where did you adopt it?" . . . "Try some lye, Jane, it may eat it out. She can't look any worse."[7] (Pp. 22-23)

For four years she is the only black pupil in an all-white high school. At the University of Southern California, she is spurned by a color-conscious group of black students. It would have been easier for Emma Lou to find acceptance within her family and among black people had she been a boy. A dark-skinned man could perhaps work his way up to a decent economic level; but even such a man would seldom marry a dark-skinned woman. Emma Lou is frequently insulted with labels such as "hottentot," "inkspitter," "dark meat," "crow-like." A coffee-colored fat man walking down Seventh Avenue in Harlem shouts within her hearing: "Man, you know I don't haul no coal" (p. 108). She is turned down for a secretarial position with Angus and Brown, a successful Negro real estate firm in Harlem. A West Indian landlady shuts the door in her face because "Persons of color didn't associate with blacks in the Caribbean Island she had come from" (p. 137). Frustrated in her unequal competition with the light-skinned female, Emma Lou wishes time and again "to effect a change of sex or at least a change of complexion" (p. 26). Snubbed constantly by both employers and males because of her dark skin, she tries all kinds of creams, skin preparations, bleaching aids. She even eats arsenic wafers, which serve only "to give her pains in the pit of her stomach." Perhaps she would have found happiness in the world of George Schuyler's *Black No More* where Dr. Junius Crookman discovers a process to turn black skin white forever.

Thurman, himself a highly self-conscious, dark-skinned person, delineates the predicament of Emma Lou Morgan with skill and understanding in a terse prose style. He portrays with sympathy the drive of his heroine to grab at any chance of securing happiness. Trapped in the Negro world that allows her little love and even less hope, she is in for a career of sexual and economic exploitation by one male after another. The first of these is Weldon Taylor, whom she meets upon her return home from her freshman year in California, at the Sunday School Union picnic— the one annual gathering of the black community where color and class differences are temporarily forgotten. Soon Emma Lou finds "an incomparably satisfying paradise" of physical pleasure in Weldon's arms, and starts dreaming about the time when she would marry him, "keep a home for him and spur him on" in his medical career. Even though she is not entirely happy with Weldon's dark brown skin, she soon finds herself, as others in her family find her also, a changed creature, "a vibrant, joyful being."

Emma Lou's psychological and emotional drives result from her having "lived to herself for so long . . . shut out from the stream of things in which she was interested for such a long period during the formative years of her life, that she considered her own imaginative powers omniscient. Thus she constructed a future world of love on one isolated experience, never thinking for the moment that the other party concerned might not be of the same mind" (pp. 64-65). When she discovers that after all Weldon "did not feel toward her as she did towards him," she interprets the situation the way she has been taught: "Hadn't she been told that they would use her for their sexual convenience? . . . She was a black girl and no professional man could afford to present such a wife in the best society" (p. 69). Her life repeats this pattern of hopeful expectation and painful withdrawal. Later, during her lonesome days in Harlem when her eyes are vainly searching for the warm and pleasing color of Alva, Jasper Crane meets her in a movie theater and cozens money out of her by promising to see her the next day and then never showing up.

But there is another and perhaps more engrossing side to Emma

Lou's rejection and exploitation by the black society. That is her own paradoxical rejection of herself. Her early conditioning in her "blue-vein" family makes her a snob. "She had absorbed this trait from the very people who had sought to exclude her from their presence" (pp. 45-46). She cannot warm up to many people, male or female, who offer her their company or friendship. At college, Emma Lou recognizes Hazel Mason's infectious good nature, yet she cannot accept her Southern accent and manners. Grace Giles, a music student at the University of Southern California, befriends Emma Lou and introduces her to many people, mostly from Grace's home state of Georgia. Emma Lou finds them all "dull" and "commonplace," and labels them "fuddlers" because she finds their clothes and their attempts at politeness too clumsy for her taste. Emma Lou is determined not to go out of her class, determined either to associate with the "right sort of people" or else to keep to herself. Of course, she really does not know what she means by the "right sort of people." "She had a vague idea," Thurman comments, "that those people on the campus who practically ignored her were the only people with whom she should associate." Her almost neurotic obsession with the "right sort of people" sends Emma Lou on an odyssey—comparable in many ways with Helga Crane's flight from her intensely personal desires in *Quicksand*—that ends in her Pyrrhic victory. She realizes that although she has never been more than "a commercial proposition" to Alva, she had exercised "the same discrimination against her men and the people she wished for friends that they had exercised against her—and with less reason" (p. 259). This is well illustrated in her attitude toward John, the first man she meets in Harlem, and in her treatment of Benson Brown, and of the Columbia law student she meets at the Casino.

Emma Lou's intense, excruciating experience with Alva encompasses both the social and the personal dimensions of her situation. She meets Alva first at Small's Paradise, where she has gone with Arline and Arline's white-liberal brother from Chicago. Alva, sitting at the next table with two male friends, casually asks her for a dance, mutters a polite "thank you" at the end and turns away. Later, Emma Lou sees him at the Renaissance Casino and boldly expresses her desire to see him again. Braxton, Alva's parasite friend, teases him: "The only thing a black woman is good for is to make money for a brown-skin papa" (p. 153). Having this in mind himself, Alva starts seeing Emma. Alva blames her for being "a trifle too color conscious" when she reacts touchily to a show at the Lafayette which ends with a little black girl riding a mule and singing mournfully:

> A yellow gal rides in a limousine,
> A brown-skin rides a Ford,
> A black gal rides an old jackass
> But she gets there, yes my Lord. (P. 204)

Later, discovering Alva helplessly sick, and stuck with the care of his and Geraldine's idiot child, Emma Lou sacrifices her more recently acquired YWCA friends and ignores the respectability that her new job as a public school teacher demands by moving in with Alva—only to be treated by him as "Alva Junior's mammy" as soon as Alva recovers.

Thurman ends *The Blacker the Berry* on a hopeful note. Emma Lou rejects the possibility of going home because "that would mean beginning her life all over again." Like Lord Jim in Conrad's novel, she realizes that her attempts to escape herself by flights—from Idaho to California to Harlem—have not helped. She finds comfort in the philosophy of Campbell Kitchen (possibly Thurman's version of Carl Van Vechten), who said that "everyone must find salvation within one's self, that no one in life need be a total misfit, and that there was some niche for every peg, whether that peg be round or square" (p. 256). She blames mainly herself for her problems and intends "to balance things. Life after all was a give and take affair. Why should she give important things and receive nothing in return?" (p. 260). She determines to accept her black skin as "real and unchangeable" and to begin life anew "not so much for acceptance by other people, but for acceptance of herself and by herself" (p. 257). She plans from now on to "find—not seek," and contends that "life was most kind to those who were judicious in their selections" (p. 258). But in spite of Emma Lou's new self-awareness, the reader is not entirely convinced that her future will be happier or less painful.

George S. Schuyler, seven years Thurman's senior, was the younger writer's predecessor in the offices of *The Messenger*, the Negro magazine published by political radicals A. Philip Randolph and Chandler Owen. Schuyler was acutely aware of Thurman's theme in *The Blacker the Berry* and took America, both white and black, to task on the question of color in his delightful and scathing piece of satire, *Black No More*. But while readers were still absorbing the shock of his *Black No More*, Schuyler was already on his way to Liberia to write another book at the request of publisher George Palmer Putnam. Schuyler left the United States for Liberia on 24 January 1931, and spent three months observing and recording conditions there. The result was *Slaves Today*, in which Schuyler focused on Africa without yielding to the temptation of romanticizing it—a tendency of some Renaissance artists and poets. Liberia had remained an area of special interest for American Negroes since 1847, when it was established as a black Republic by freedmen from the United States sent there through the efforts of the American Colonization Society. A contemporary cause for commotion in Afro-America over Liberia was the report from a League of Nations Commission which found that most Liberian government officials were reaping huge profits from a flourishing system of "pawning" and forced labor. The thinly veiled fictional treatment of Liberian conditions in *Slaves Today* was Schuyler's significant contribution to the controversy that raged then in prominent Afro-American newspapers and journals.[8]

Before Schuyler left the United States, he met with Bishop Davis, who had just returned as U.S. Minister from Liberia. Davis conveyed to Schuyler his personal impressions about the corrupt politicians who ran the government in Liberia. On arrival in Monrovia, Schuyler was unimpressed with its "unpaved, rock-covered streets," the weeds, the odors, and the mosquitoes. "Compared to it, such all-Negro American towns as Boley, Oklahoma, and Mound Mayou, Mississippi, were palatial," he tells us in his autobiography, *Black and Conservative* (1966).[9] After getting through the formalities in Monrovia, Schuyler trekked 600 miles through the hinterland with the U.S. Vice-Consul William George and a crew of native "boys." Schuyler found the hinterland trip exhausting, but educational:

> Villages ranging from fifty to five hundred huts were from fifteen to twenty miles apart. The chiefs were hospitable and always provided a neat guest house for us and "dashed" [furnished] George and me whatever food, rice, palm oil, and palm wine we needed. We paid for what was supplied to the carriers, but they ate separately according to tribe and did not look upon each other as brothers. They also slept separately with their respective tribesmen. They were all black but there any similarity ended. They spoke only rudimentary English and when I had to address them it was through Blackie. Talk about uniting the black brothers was grimly laughable.
>
> At each town I interviewed the chief, "dashed" him salt, tobacco, safety razor and blades, mirrors and a bottle of gin,

and pumped him for information relative to the recently
"suppressed" slave trade. I got a lot of information, too, some
of it accompanied by tears, as they related how they had been
treated for failing to "recruit" enough of their young men for
Fernando Po. A typical punishment was to spread-eagle the
chief on the ground with wrists and ankles tied down, and
then have one of the soldiers vigorously flog him as his people
were forced to look on. Some towns had been visited by tax
gatherers as often as four times a year. In one town the people
grew so tired of these visitors that they just abandoned their
home and went far into the bush where they erected a new
town. I was taken there by a circuitous route along an almost
indistinguishable trail.[10]

It was to arouse the attention of the American public to these
grievous conditions that Schuyler wrote *Slaves Today*, as well as
numerous pieces in the journals and newspapers in 1931. *Slaves
Today*, as an attempt to crusade against a social evil, is a direct
literary descendant of Harriet Beecher Stowe's *Uncle Tom's Cabin*
(1852). Also, in successfully weaving the narrative interest into the
documentary fabric, Schuyler anticipates Steinbeck's method in
Grapes of Wrath (1939). Zo and Pameta, especially Zo, are just
"real" and complex enough to enlist our sympathy, and it is this
thread of separated lovers in the plot that keeps one reading,
whereas a pure exposé of Liberian corruption would have been
much less compelling.

In the foreword, Schuyler clarifies the propagandistic and documentary intent of his book. All the characters, natives as well as
Americo-Liberians, are taken from real life. The exposé of Liberian conditions is to be seen against the global backdrop of forced
labor that prevails "under various euphemisms today." His un-
stated contention is that political corruption and tyranny are
neither a national monopoly nor a racial heritage, and that the
helpless black masses of Liberia were no better off under their
aggressive and self-seeking Americo-Liberian rulers than they
would have been under their white counterparts.

Schuyler's picture of the deplorable Liberian conditions is unre-
lenting. The native is helplessly trapped in the Liberian aristo-
crat's yoke, with no escape either in town or in the hinterland. He
is "pawned" for cheap labor in Spanish colonies and forced to
work on the road; at the same time, he faces the most cruel consequences if his monthly levy of palm oil and rice is deficient or
delayed because of manpower shortage on the farms. In Boloba,
Zo observes that natives were freely going in and out of the dis-

trict commissioner's bungalow. "The reason seemed to be," adds the author mischievously, "that those going in were carrying something while those leaving were empty-handed" (pp. 87-88). In many aristocratic homes, the Americo-Liberian's other crimes are being compounded by the unforgiveable one of child abuse. David Jackson gets young boys to work as house servants by making their parents the never-kept promise of educating them. "Other Liberian families sent their pawns to school but usually to carry the books of their pampered children" (p. 232). With very few exceptions, every Americo-Liberian shares responsibility for this heartless oppression, either through silence or active participation. The Right Reverend Henry Biggs, the Bishop of Liberia, indulges in sophistry to rationalize his apathy to the native's lot. We also get a glimpse of "justice or its Liberian equivalent"—a brief Kafkaesque drama in which natives, just returned from their two-year labor in Fernando Po, are stripped systematically of the wages given by the Spanish consul in Monrovia.

The central metaphor in *Slaves Today* is that of an ancient and peaceful African community, living in harmony with nature, being assaulted by a stealthy leopard that emerges from the blackness of the surrounding jungle. The peace of the African community— guided by the father figure of a chief and protected from evil by the mysterious powers of a witch doctor (counterparts of the ruling and priestly classes respectively)—is disturbed by David Jackson and other Americo-Liberian aristocrats for the sole purpose of exploitation. The virtual slavery of the Liberian native is not redeemed in any way by the fact that his oppressor has the same skin color as he does. Schuyler tells us, "It was no more difficult for them [the Liberian aristocrats] to oppress and exploit fellow black men than it usually is for powerful whites to do the same thing to fellow white men. Color did not enter here—it was class that counted" (p. 100). But the fact that the forefathers of the current Liberian leadership had come from the United States filled with "Christian ideals" and "the true spirit of pioneers" does sharpen "the living irony that is Liberia." In his foreword, Schuyler states that the Liberian Republic was founded by the American freed slaves "as a haven for all oppressed people. Its proud motto reads, 'The Love of Liberty Brought Us Here,' but the aborigines find little liberty under their Negro masters" (p. 5). Thus, while Schuyler tries not to lose sight of the international dimensions of human exploitation through forced labor and slavery, he attempts also to bare the intricate ironies of a class line which separated the Liberio-Americans (Afro-Americans) from the native Liberians (Africans) within the Negro world.

Schuyler's writing in *Slaves Today* varies both in style and quality. Some variety seems intentional, introduced deliberately to arouse the civilized world's conscience to the atrocities committed against the native population of Liberia by a group of Americo-Liberians, who see natives as nothing more than "the rungs on the ladder to riches and power." One device Schuyler uses successfully to achieve his end is to picture the native African and his surrounding landscape as living in perfect harmony with each other—except when government representatives from Monrovia intrude.

> The jungle is a great green prison, impregnable by virtue of the amazing network and screen of vines and creepers that bind tree to tree. . . . The trail is the only visible evidence of humanity in the jungle. . . . It is the corridor that connects one center of life with another; the artery of communication between town and town. One holds to it as a child to its mother, following it religiously, faithfully. It means life to the inexperienced; the jungle spells death. This waving, pulsating mass of green on either side of the pedestrian, touching him at times, is almost bursting with life, breeds life in amazing, bewildering quantities and varieties, but it is, in the main, life inimical to man. . . . It is not so much the larger animals he has to fear, but the small ones, and the insects—rodents, gnats, beetles, ants and an infinite, uncountable variety of others. These dispute possession of the earth with man and he has yet to prove himself the victor. (Pp. 86-87)

The passages which describe the community life, the customs and traditions, and the rites and festivals of the Africans win the reader's sympathy for the native, and, by implication, indicate the seriousness of the Americo-Liberian's crimes against man and nature. Schuyler's writing about Africa and Africans in 1931 is sometimes moving:

> Africa loves to dance. Almost every night when the tropical moon illumines village streets as if they were lighted by arc lights, the variously pitched drums tap out their intricate rhythm and the close-packed crowd shuffles, leaps and hops to exhaustion. Few forms of entertainment prove superior to the African dance in all of its variations. The roll-tap-and-boom of the drums sends peculiar tingles over the body. The inhibitions of industrial society drop gradually from even the most civilized person until he also wants to join the gyrating,

stamping black folk. The dance, the drums, the horns—these musical instruments are ages old. They have come down from the dawn of humanity. They are a part of our heritage. No wonder all humans are drawn to them. (Pp. 32-33)

But describing the daily life of Liberians, who are controlled by Americo-Liberian rulers, necessitates a different style and technique. Without lapsing into sentimentality, Schuyler frequently uses the devices generally associated with the reform school of naturalistic fiction. The plot, for example, hinges upon an incident at Takama, a day after the marriage of Zo, the protagonist, and Pameta, the beautiful daughter of Chief Bongomo. David Jackson, the Commissioner of the First District, visits the village on short notice. Angered by the inadequate preparations of the villagers to receive his entourage, he decides to punish Chief Bongomo for delay in delivering his monthly requisition of rice and palm oil. When Bongomo yanks his sword from its scabbard to get revenge for being whipped in front of his people, Jackson's sergeant shoots him to death. Then, in a volley of random shots, many other natives are killed or wounded. Before Jackson leaves, he multiplies his excesses by fining the village twenty-five pounds, and by abducting Pameta, the young bride of Zo. This pattern of arbitrary rule, sadistic cruelty, and inhuman killings by Americo-Liberians is repeated throughout the book.

The only things the Americo-Liberian cares for are living well and accumulating money, and he pursues these ideals without restraint or scruples. David Jackson has excellent meals and plenty of scotch and wine to drink, even when he is in the hinterland. Two or three native women travel with him as part of his harem. "Why rule half a million natives unless you were to live well?" (p. 52). He has a free hand from Monrovia to use the natives in any way he deems fit and he always does so without compunction. He "pawns" the natives for cheap labor in the disease-infested plantations of Fernando Po, forces them to work on building the roads, and kills them when they hesitate or refuse to do his bidding. When his soldiers prod native women working on the road from behind with rifles or small branches, Jackson enjoys it immensely in his "boys will be boys" attitude. Jackson somehow remains immune to the effects of venereal disease, but he infects many of his concubines, including his favorites Gonda and Pameta, and then discards them like worn-out clothes instead of providing medical treatment. Mrs. Jackson, a graduate of an American Negro college and an incurable romanticist, takes out the bitterness of her unhappy marriage on her maids and servants. She relieves her tensions and soothes her nerves by relentlessly whipping a young boy.

To such vivid descriptions of the ruling class' cruelty and intransigence, Schuyler adds detailed pictures of the disease and deprivation that the African native suffers in his virtual slavery to the Americo-Liberian elite. Schuyler powerfully describes the case of forty men who are taken to Monrovia to be drafted into forced labor. Here are "forty men with very few exceptions who knew not where they were going. . . . Forty men who did not expect any pay for their labor and were not going to get any" (p. 124). Each of them is made to carry a weight of sixty pounds to Monrovia by an arduous jungle route encumbered with roots, rocks, and driver ants. Then, all of these forty men—through the courtesy of John Collins, the Spanish consul, and despite the warning of Tom Saunders, the liberal party boss—are loaded as "human cargo" into the bottoms of three big boats, under the seats of the oarsmen. When the men feel plagued by both suffocation and seasickness, their attempt to get fresh air is countered by the bite of the Spanish sailor's whip. In Fernando Po, the plantations swarm with mosquitoes and tse-tse flies. Men sleep in a long, low warehouse on narrow beds constructed of cocoa staves and banana leaves. They are fed poorly and paid a meager six pesos for thirty days of twelve-hour-a-day toil. The planters furnish "all facilities to regain the men's money" by permitting a swarm of peddlers and prostitutes to sell their wares at exorbitant prices on their payday. "Only occasional trips to the hospital broke the monotonous routine of labor" (p. 170). Schuyler describes the patients and their diseases at length in his campaign to arouse the reader's disgust at the system that causes all the human misery reigning in the hospital. Yellow fever, elephantiasis, and frambesia (yaws) contend for supremacy, rivaled by venereal diseases.

Schuyler's characters in *Slaves Today*, unlike those in his *Black No More*, are carefully portrayed, and it is in his characterization that he most effectively employs the satiric skills that made his jouranlistic columns (such as "Shafts and Darts" in *The Messenger*) so famous and widely read in the 1920s. He gives a finishing touch to his portrait of Liberia's President Sidney Cooper Johnson by pointing out that as Secretary of State, he had won

> international fame for saying nothing adroitly. The long, involved sentences which characterized his diplomatic notes had caused the foreign ministers of great powers to scratch their heads in puzzlement and admiration. His state papers were always masterpieces because they could be interpreted

in many ways, but they seldom contained anything definite. (Pp. 11-12)

David Jackson's personal attendant, Joe, traveled across the hinterland with a woman explorer "managing not to steal enough to arouse her suspicions. Joe had soon learned that a perpetually smiling countenance, speedy service and unfailing courtesy very effectively cover a multitude of sins" (p. 61). In the last chapter—which is comparable in its effect to the last scene in George Orwell's *Animal Farm* (1945)—the President gloats over his party's victory in the elections and appoints Captain Burns to take the place of the late David Jackson because Burns "understands the natives so well" and "isn't burdened with scruples."

Schuyler deserves credit for not romanticizing the native. In fact, the early reviewers praised Schuyler for not falling into the pitfalls of "sentimentality and high-flown descriptive writing"[11] that were inherent in his assignment. Schuyler never fails to emphasize the shared humanity of his native characters. Tolo, the Takama witch doctor, is a self-conscious skeptic, who "like those of his craft the world over" finds it prudent to surround his findings with an aura of mystery and uncertainty. The Africans in the novel, like most people elsewhere, blame their tragedy on a scapegoat and would have nothing to do with Zo once he has been chosen as scapegoat by "the ordeal of the whip." Perhaps Schuyler's three-month exposure to Liberian natives was not enough for him to completely avoid the hazards of stereotyping. Some natives show little ingenuity or resourcefulness in avenging their insults or accomplishing their objectives. For example, the reader is likely to be puzzled by what Zo does in order to recover Pameta from Jackson's clutches. Schuyler credits Zo with "a level head, common sense and a supreme confidence in his ability" (p. 118). Like an individualistic Westerner, Zo hesitates to reveal his plans for recovering Pameta to his Boloba compatriots. All the same, why he does not think of entering the commissioner's house as a newly hired servant or does not wait for a better chance to achieve his objective is difficult to explain. Again, Schuyler makes no attempt to penetrate the psychology of Soki, who endures his ill-treatment by the overseers in Fernando Po for two years only to turn his bared teeth and raised fists upon Big Carlos on the last day, with foreseeable consequences.

In *Slaves Today*, Schuyler does not hold America directly responsible for the practices that thrive in Liberia, but he more than implies that the United States could intervene if it were sufficiently concerned, and he does reveal many small but significant connections between Liberia and America. He sees the Liberian political structure as modeled on pre-Civil War America. Also, most Liberian aristocrats have had their academic or political education in the United States and apply their American training stringently to the situation at home. Having been incarcerated in the States for forging a check, Sammy Williams, the Vice-President of the Republic, spent a jail term at Sing Sing, "where he learnt much from his associates that was useful when he entered Liberian politics later on" (p. 137). Schuyler, in fact, suggests that the Americo-Liberians were using the same tactics to maintain the status quo in Liberia that the Southern whites employed in the United States to keep their Afro-American ancestors from a full participation in the political process:

> According to Liberian law, only owners of property can vote. To assure the Conservative Party of continuance in power, each President signed thousands of blank deeds, which were distributed throughout the civilized section of the republic to those who could be depended upon to vote Conservative. Of course, all deeds presented for registration by members of the Liberal Party were carefully scrutinized for the slightest error. (P. 283)

The party leaders "had not studied American political practices in vain." Considering Schuyler's allusions to America, it appears that, in 1931, he intended his *Slaves Today* not only as a strong argument for American intervention in Liberia to avert further deterioration of conditions there, but also as a reminder to white European colonists to give better treatment to the colored masses in their Asian and African colonies. "If this novel can help arouse enlightened world opinion against this brutalizing of the native population in a Negro republic, perhaps the conscience of civilized people will stop similar atrocities in native lands ruled by proud white nations that boast of their superior culture" (p. 6).

After looking back at the history of colonialism in Asia and Africa for the twenty years following the publication of Schuyler's book, it seems that *Slaves Today* had little, if any, success in arousing the "conscience of civilized people." But it did add fuel to the already burning controversy over Liberia in the black American press. Among those who did not see eye to eye with George Schuyler was W.E.B. DuBois. This was, of course, not the first time the two of them had disagreed, nor would it be the last. Schuyler had attacked DuBois for asking blacks to support Woodrow Wilson in 1912—an error of judgment which DuBois regretted later. Again, in 1934, when DuBois recommended voluntary separation of blacks from whites in a succession of editorials in *The Crisis*, Schuyler attacked his position as "a complete surrender to segregation and therefore acceptable to every klansman, Fascist and Nazi."[12] In 1931, however, DuBois had praised Schuyler's *Black No More* as a piece of frank, courageous, and all-embracing satire on America's race problem, and he had taken good-naturedly his own caricature as Dr. Agamemnon Shakespeare Beard that the book contained. But in reviewing *Slaves Today* in the February 1932 issue of *The Crisis*, DuBois charged that Schuyler "did not realize the history of Liberia," did not know enough about its present conditions, and had played into the hands of white imperialists by writing *Slaves Today*. Responding in the March issue, Schuyler accused DuBois of permitting "belligerent and commendable Negrophilism to warp [his] vision in the case of the Liberian racketeers." He had also begged the question that lay at the heart of *Slaves Today*: "are we not to expect that Negro colonists who are so excessively religious . . . will be more humane to their black native wards than would white colonists? Especially so when these black rulers boast of their race patriotism?"[13]

Slaves Today answers this question negatively by tracing the tragic careers of Zo and Pameta through pain and suffering to their unnecessary and untimely deaths. In fact, DuBois himself shows in his second novel, *Dark Princess*, the inadvisability of such expectations from individual or group behavior in a world of unpredictable human responses. In *Dark Princess*, he shows his Afro-American protagonist not as an aggressor but as a victim—not only of the white American society, but also of a group of Asian aristocrats who profess to be working for the emancipation of the world's darker nations from Western imperialism, but who themselves exude the miasma of their prejudice against the Negro, African or American. Being a dreamer and idealist, however, DuBois expresses his hopes and fantasies in *Dark Princess* by depicting the triumph of his hero and his heroine, an Indian princess, over this form of prejudice within prejudice. In contrast, Schuyler's hardcore realism does not allow him to endorse any illusory or self-deceptive notion that would credit the Afro-American with an extra dimension of humanity based on his own heritage of exploitation. Schuyler might agree with Truman Walter in *The Blacker the Berry*—and with the more recent findings of some psychologists[14]—that the members of "a despised, mistreated minority-group" often suffer a great urge to treat other individuals or groups the way they have been treated by their oppressors.

DuBois' *Dark Princess*, like Schuyler's *Slaves Today*, was admittedly propagandistic. But the direction and substance of their books presage their later careers, besides indicating the wide gulf that always separated them as persons. Schuyler's self-portrait in his autobiography is that of a "man continually walking further apart from the beliefs of his fellow black Americans, ridiculing both their failures and their successes."[15] The classic testimony to Schuyler's alienation is the final chapter of *Black and Conservative*, wherein he condemns any kind of civil rights protest, including the March on Washington, "as part of the Red techniques of agitation, infiltration and subversion," defends the use of force by police and praises them for their restraint, and pronounces Martin Luther King "quite undeserving of any prize as an apostle of peace . . . his entire activity [being] to the contrary."[16] Schuyler makes these statements solemnly—without any of the Mencken humor that marked his earlier writings. DuBois, on the other hand, remained alert and sensitive to his times to the very end of his long career; he crusaded all over the globe on behalf of Afro-Americans and Africans, even through the bitter final years of his life, greatly misunderstood by most Americans and strangely cold-shouldered by black leaders, many of whom were his old friends and colleagues. Schuyler's book dealt with one concrete situation that invited the attention of the Afro-American in a style that matched the documentary nature of his assessment; DuBois' *Dark Princess*, of a piece with many of his later works such as *Color and Democracy* (1945) and *The World and Africa* (1947), raised many issues of a more basic and philosophical nature, in a style best described as prophetic.

At the turn of the century, DuBois had declared, "The problem of the twentieth century is the problem of the color line—the relation of the darker to lighter races of men in Asia and Africa, in America and the islands of the sea."[17] As if to dramatize the implications of this, he wrote *Dark Princess*;[18] here the color line involves the most important nations of the civilized world. A Committee of Darker Nations working for independence from Western colonial powers occupies a central place, and DuBois anticipated by several decades the present-day talk of "third world" solidarity. But the prognostic vision implies more than that. Ironically, the book also highlights the need for the darker nations (as well as individuals and groups) to cope with international prejudice, a form of cancer that continues to eat into the growth of any sense of unity—African, Afro-American, or "third-world." In showing that this global internal prejudice—like its counterpart in the Afro-American world of *The Blacker the Berry*—has its roots in color and a caste system based on color, *Dark Princess* bears testimony to the long-term aberrations—emotional, psychological, and sociological—that are sometimes attributed to the unnatural and oligarchical dominance of the globe by the white race. As in the world of the Afro-American, so in the colonies of Asia and Africa, the colonial powers have needed to develop a class of people—sometimes described as bourgeois—which, while keeping the natives in their place, thrives on the petty favors of the ruling class. This middle class, varying in its size and power in different colonies, used many rationalizations—of which color was an important one—to justify its hostility toward the lower classes and to exercise its control over them. *Dark Princess* was decidedly ahead of its time in exposing the prejudice that cut across cultural and national barriers.

Dark Princess, a ponderous novel of over three hundred pages, traces the career of Matthew Towns, who flees from his frustrations as a medical student in a racist society only to experience the prejudices of an Asian aristocracy. Returning to the United States, he is drawn into the banal practices of a city machine before he is spiritually rejuvenated through Kautilya, a bright and elegant Princess from India. The climactic points in the plot, which also converge with the major turns in Towns' career, are a series of accidental meetings between Matthew and Princess Kautilya. Having been rebuffed in his effort as a medical student to register in an obstetrics course at the University of Manhattan, Matthew leaves for Europe by the first ship available. Sitting in the Viktoria Cafe in Berlin, he dramatically rescues a colored girl from a white American assailant. The imperious and elegant brown beauty he rescues turns out to be "H.R.H. the Princess Kautilya of Bwodpur, India," who is working with a revolutionary committee of aristocrats drawn from India, Japan, China, and Egypt. Matthew meets with this committee but is discouraged by the shadow in the air "of a color line within color line, a prejudice within prejudice." The Princess herself, however, inspires his love and admiration, and he goes home to dedicate his career to transforming the living conditions of lower-class Negroes. In order to sensitize himself to the needs and feelings of common people, he leads a rough life as a Pullman porter, sharing the hassles and humiliations of the job. It is as a Pullman porter that he encounters the Princess again—this time on a Southbound train, the destruction of which he has conspired to achieve earlier with Perigua, a West Indian revolutionary. At this point, he takes the next important step of his life and decides against violence as a solution to the American racial problem. Without compromising the confidence that Perigua has placed in him (Perigua dies because the bomb explodes early), Matthew takes the blame on himself and is sentenced to ten years of hard labor. Sara Andrews—secretary to Sammy Scott, the political boss of black Chicago, and a shrewd climber—learns of Towns' case, manages to get him released and decides to put him to political use first for her boss and later for herself. She gets Towns elected to State Legislature, marries him, and maneuvers to get him the Republican nomination for Congress. It remains for Kautilya again, by now turned into a working-class woman, to emerge mysteriously with Matthew from his library and to rescue him from a corrupt and stultifying career that lies before him as a candidate for Congress.

Dark Princess is undoubtedly more important as a social or political document than as literature. It is more a fantasy than a realistic novel; its characters, except for Sara Andrews, are wooden and lack motivation; the dialogue is artificial, bordering sometimes on the ludicrous; the diction is often archaic or flamboyant or both. As one early reviewer pointed out:

> It [*Dark Princess*] is by no means a dull novel, for the author's passion alone is enough to give it vigor and interest. Beyond that it is hard to go. The melodramatic plot, with its bewildering complications, its incredible coincidences, its overemphatic climaxes; the grand style, lapsing into poetry with or without justification; the one-dimensional characters, existing not for their own sakes but for the author's special purpose— these are the paraphernalia of a second-rate novelist of the nineties. The truth is, of course, that DuBois is not a novelist at all, and that the book judged as a novel has only the slightest merit.[19]

The nonliterary uses of *Dark Princess*, however, are manifold. As Harold R. Isaacs points out, DuBois poured into *Dark Princess* his "racial fantasies, his view of the world, his obsession with color, his public judgments and his secret hopes and some of his innocent dreams."[20] The psychologist might find *Dark Princess* a valuable tool for explaining the enigmatic personality of one of the central figures of this century. Isaacs himself suggests that DuBois' life story, both in its public and private dimensions, offers most of the standard materials for a psychoanalytical study like Erik Erikson's *Young Man Luther* (or Erikson's more recent *Gandhi's Truth*). By DuBois' own admission and by the consensus of people who worked with him at different times, DuBois was not an easy man to know. He was often thought to be "too cold, too aloof, not human enough with ordinary people."[21] It is helpful to remember that DuBois' inherited New England puritanism was compounded in his case by "the veil of color." He responded to his first discovery of himself, as a black man in a hostile white society, by withdrawing into himself and by identifying with the whole mass of nonwhite humanity in the world—the twin tendencies that would seem to characterize also the career of Matthew Towns in *Dark Princess*.

DuBois saw art, particularly black art, solely as a means to improve or enhance life; he criticized those artists—for example, Carl Van Vechten and Claude McKay—who concerned themselves only with the lurid or flamboyant aspects of Harlem life and neglected to depict the ordinary models of honesty, hard work, and decency that were as much a part of black America. "All art is propaganda and ever must be, despite the wailing of the purists . . . whatever art I have for writing has been used always for propaganda for gaining the right of black folk to love and enjoy. I do not care a damn for any art that is not used for propaganda. But I do care when propaganda is confined to one side while the other is stripped and silent."[22] Thus, *Dark Princess* is what would today be called a "consciousness-raising" book, and, together with Thurman's *The Blacker the Berry*, and Claude McKay's *Banjo*, it is a literary counterpart to Garvey's "Back to Africa" idea. DuBois intended to extend his readers' horizons beyond the harsh realities of the American scene—to enlighten the black American about the global dimensions of his struggle for dignity and equal rights, and to indicate to the white American the importance and urgency of realizing the democratic experiment America represents.

Dark Princess belongs to the primary strand of Afro-American thought which attempts to define the complexities and ironies of the Negro's peculiar situation in the West without distorting or simplifying facts. DuBois was responsible for a memorable and seminal statement on the American Negro's double sense of himself:

> The Negro is a sort of seventh son born with a veil, and gifted with second sight in this American world . . . one ever feels his two-ness—an American, a Negro; two souls, two thoughts, two unreconciled strivings; two warring ideals in one dark body, whose dogged strength alone keeps it from being torn asunder.[23]

Dark Princess underscores the paradoxical existence of the black American in the West when Matthew Towns reacts to the Asian aristocrats' prejudice against the black, not by listing (as he is at first tempted to do) the achievements of the black to date, but by asserting his faith in the uniqueness of the American democratic experiment: "America is teaching the world one thing and only one thing of real value, and that is, that ability and capacity for culture is not the hereditary monopoly of a few, but the widespread possibility for the majority of mankind if they only have a decent chance in life" (p. 20).

Unlike some nineteenth-century radical black nationalists such as John Bruce and Bishop Henry M. Turner, DuBois did not reject the West.[24] As *Dark Princess* indicates, by 1928 DuBois had traveled far from the theory of the talented tenth" he had propounded in *Souls in Black Folk* (1903); his protagonist, Matthew Towns, suddenly (and unconvincingly in terms of the narrative) learns the importance of the masses, when faced with the prejudice of a highly Europeanized Asian aristocracy. After explaining to the Asian revolutionaries the relative insignificance of his light skin ("Black blood with us in America is a matter of spirit and not simply of flesh"), he moves on to identify himself completely with "the great sodden masses of all men and even in Black Africa" (p. 25). DuBois had visited Russia in 1926 and was impressed with the accomplishments of the Revolution, but he remained unconvinced of its relevance to America. *Dark Princess* evidences DuBois' persistent faith, despite his increasingly Marxist orientation, in the potential superiority of a broad-based democracy.[25] Matthew Towns tells the Revolutionary Committee of Darker Peoples: "We come out of the depths—the blood and mud of battle. And from just such depths, I take it, come most of the worthwhile things in this old world" (p. 23). On the other hand, his campaign to unite the darker nations of the world against their white imperialist adversaries has obvious connections with the need he expressed in 1934 for Afro-Americans to voluntarily segregate themselves in order to develop their own social institutions and become a force for positive change in the United States and the rest of the world.

The most readable passages in *Dark Princess* develop DuBois' political insights—about the nationhood of black America and its inevitable link with Afro-Asian colonies, the crucial role of the common man in the future, the need to redistribute power and wealth to benefit all nations, and the possibility of eliminating hate, poverty, disease, and war from the realm of human life. DuBois demonstrates his close kinship with the romantic idealism and unflinching optimism of his New England predecessors, such as Emerson, Thoreau, Whittier, and Higginson, who fought the proslavery forces of their times with real if varying degrees of commitment.[26] Unfortunately, DuBois did not have the opportunity to develop fully the myriad possibilities of his humanitarian approach as a man of letters in the crucial area of race relations in the modern world and was forced time and again in his long and checkered career to settle for halfway houses.

The theme of internal prejudice, traced by Thurman in *The Blacker the Berry*, comes full circle in *Dark Princess*. The progress is from an internal enigma of black America in *The Blacker the Berry* through a sociopolitical disorder of American-Liberian proportions in *Slaves Today* to the deep-seated color complex that cripples any movement toward Afro-Asian solidarity in *Dark Princess*. *Slaves Today*, whose naturalistic plot and ending demanded that the civilized world immediately solve a concrete problem, ends most unhappily. The other two books are clearly hopeful in their drive to instill an awareness of two deep-rooted and interrelated strains in Afro-American and Asian life. However, although Emma Lou's self-realization has some psychological validity at the level of characterization, the effectiveness and success of Kautilya in DuBois' novel belong only to the world of fantasy. The Indian Princess, possessed at a young age with extraordinary moral strength, political maturity, and worldly experience, moves at a jet-age speed all over the globe, managing always, like a Greek goddess, to be by Matthew's side during his critical moments. She also unconvincingly seems to have convinced other members of her Revolutionary Committee, including its Japanese chairman, of the Negro's great potential for participating in and leading the nonwhite's international struggle for liberation and power. As if all this were not enough, she also successfully establishes a black republic in Virginia, with Towns attending the coronation of their out-of-wedlock son, Madhu Chandragupta Singh, as the "Maharajah of Bwodpur and Maharajah-dhirajah of Sindrabad."

These three books are the high achievement of the Harlem Renaissance in progress in ideas, even though they fail to achieve their full literary potentials. They raise and attempt to answer thorny questions surrounding color that have more recently engaged figures of such diverse backgrounds as Frantz Fanon and Malcolm X. Thurman made a singular contribution by providing the first treatment in fiction of self-hatred, a challenging and elusive theme. *Slaves Today* is both narratively and historically interesting, despite its lack of originality in conception and execution; it strips naked the illusion that a dark skin somehow makes a human being invulnerable to the corruption and intransigence of power. *Dark Princess*, although a poor novel, is socially, psychologically, and politically significant. In fact, with the exception of *Banjo, Dark Princess* is the only novel from the Harlem Renaissance that exhibits a full awareness of the African and Asian nonwhite masses, who, along with the Afro-Americans, form a colored majority in the world. *Dark Princess* dramatizes DuBois' belief that the rise of the black masses in America is inseparable from and mutually dependent upon the rise of the nonwhite nations throughout the world. As Harold R. Isaacs puts it, "Written in 1928, his prophecy that the 'Dark World' would go free by 1952 was not bad, not bad at all."[27]

Black literary expression of the American twenties was marked both by variety and vitality. Black journals such as *The Crisis*, *Opportunity*, and *The Messenger*, besides many short-lived "little" magazines all over the country, encouraged and published black poets, short story writers, novelists, playwrights, essayists, reviewers, critics, and journalists in a vigorous display of intellectual and creative activity. Other journals also encouraged black writers, and major publishers opened their doors to black poets and novelists for the first time. The Harlem Renaissance is an important phase of black American self-expression for this reason alone, if for nothing else. Some of the ideas that have come to public attention only in the 1960s can be traced back to the earliest expressions of Afro-American thinking, and the twenties provide a reservoir of the black feelings and attitudes familiar today.

The novels of the Renaissance reflect an extraordinary range of thinking on the basic issues of black American existence. On one hand, novels by writers such as Jessie Fauset, Nella Larsen, and Walter White deal primarily with the values and lives of the black middle class. These novelists also explore the American color caste, especially the dilemmas faced by characters light enough to "pass" as white. At the other extreme Jean Toomer's *Cane* and Langston Hughes' *Not Without Laughter* achieve fascinating blends of lyricism and naturalism. Closely related to the work of Toomer and Hughes are the novels of Claude McKay, who searches for new and positive life-styles through his shrewd inversion of familiar black stereotypes. In *One Way to Heaven*, Countee Cullen pictures the masses of ordinary, churchgoing men and women that peopled black communities, while Rudolph Fisher's *The Walls of Jericho* projects a new vision of alliance between the two discrete classes of Afro-American life. McKay's *Banjo* and DuBois' *Dark Princess* reflect a high degree of consciousness of the emotional and political connections that exist between Afro-Americans and colonial peoples elsewhere in the world. Thus, from the intraracial issue of prejudice against the dark-skinned

Emma Lou in Thurman's *The Blacker the Berry* to the international implications of color in Schuyler's *Slaves Today* and DuBois' *Dark Princess*, the novelists of the Harlem Renaissance traverse a long road in terms of color, caste, and class.

The styles and techniques of Renaissance novelists establish them firmly in the European-American literary tradition. Many show literary affinities with their white American contemporaries. Jessie Fauset and Walter White occasionally overcome the limits of their essentially genteel tradition in sharp pictures of black middle-class life. Nella Larsen's rendering of subtle shades of feeling and her handling of scenes indicate her closeness to the tradition of Henry James and Edith Wharton. Jean Toomer's *Cane*, parallel in structure with Sherwood Anderson's *Winesburg, Ohio* and Waldo Frank's *Holiday*, achieves a lyrical intensity uniquely its own. In *The Blacker the Berry*, Wallace Thurman deals with his heroine's bittersweet delusions over color in a tight, ironic prose style. Claude McKay experimented with the plotless novel in *Home to Harlem* and *Banjo* before attempting a "local color" story of his native Jamaica in *Banana Bottom*. His male protagonists, like the hero in Hemingway, have simplicity, toughness, and a private code. Arna Bontemps develops a style appropriate to the decadence and nostalgia that surround his subject in *God Sends Sunday*. Rudolph Fisher, who makes a masterly use of O. Henry's "sting in the tail" device in many short stories about black migrants from the South, has written a high comedy in *The Walls of Jericho*, which is a remarkable satirical portrait. George Schuyler takes both black and white Americans to task for their confusions over color and race in his Menckenian satire, *Black No More*. In *Slaves Today*, he combines the narrative and documentary interests of a tale, anticipating Steinbeck's method in *The Grapes of Wrath*. Countee Cullen's hilarious satire on upper-class blacks in *One Way to Heaven* and Langston Hughes' ironic portrayal of black bourgeoisie in *Not Without Laughter* are complemented by Thurman's bitter satire on the writers of the Harlem Renaissance in *Infants of the Spring*.

This creativity does not necessarily clear the movement of charges of political naiveté, of believing that black cultural and literary contributions increase the prospects for political equality in the United States. White patronage made the Harlem Renaissance "a misnomer, a fad ... an emasculated movement."[1] The Renaissance, it is charged, had a bourgeois orientation and failed to grasp and mirror the lives of black masses in its output.[2] At the same time, many critics think that the New Negro movement failed because the black middle class did not support it morally, aesthetically, or financially.[3]

These harsh charges, made from the vantage point of the sixties and the seventies, are only partially valid or apply only to particular writers or works. It is difficult to make generalized criticisms which apply to the short-lived, multifaceted movement as a whole. For example, what is the precise effect of white patronage or the degree of dependence on white models? It is only fair to judge the movement by its high points, and the works of many Renaissance writers, such as Langston Hughes, Rudolph Fisher, and Jean Toomer, demonstrate artistic independence of white or black patronage.

There is no doubt that Alain Locke and Charles S. Johnson failed to grapple fully with the economic and political implications of their philosophy of cultural pluralism. In terms of art alone, however, their call for a return to black folklore and a stress on uninhibited racial expression were significant, and the best writing of the Harlem Renaissance came from writers who, independently or under the influence of Locke and Johnson, chose to write within the broad limits of a black folk tradition. The failure or success of a literary movement cannot be directly related to the acceptance or rejection of a well-defined political ideology as part of its goals. The Renaissance writers were exposed to a wide range of political attitudes reflected in the black press and in changes the black masses were going through. It is another matter that many individual writers of the Harlem Renaissance did not respond as creative artists to such political attitudes and changes.

It is true that the majority of Harlem Renaissance novels did not deal with issues central to the black masses. Considering the rigid color caste in American society during the twenties, it is difficult to argue that the Renaissance novelists, even though of middle-class backgrounds, were unfamiliar with the lives of lower-class blacks. At the same time, we cannot quarrel with these novelists for choosing to deal with themes and characters they knew more intimately. In doing so, however, some provided narrow or peripheral views of black existence, and their light-skinned, middle-class protagonists proved inadequate carriers of the black person's fears, hopes, and aspirations. The middle-class blacks in the North were undoubtedly affected by the experiences of the Southern migrant, but there is no indication of this impact in the Harlem Renaissance novels. The tensions and contrasts that prevailed in the crowded Northern ghettos were not an issue in Renaissance literature, except for a few short stories by Rudolph

Fisher. McKay explored the possible relationship between the positive values of black life and the then popular issue of standardization, but gave little attention to the ordinary workaday black. The only treatment of Marcus Garvey is the ridicule Countee Cullen poured on the "Back to Africa" movement in *One Way to Heaven*. The relationship of World War I to the issues of Afro-American existence scarcely surfaces. George E. Kent places these matters in perspective when he says: "while the Marcus Garvey nationalist movement and the blues were allowed to make injections, they seemed to remain for most Renaissance writers superficial diversions, bastard brothers and sisters, lovable even in certain ways, but not eligible for Sunday company or a real dining room kind of intimacy."[4]

The bourgeois orientation of the Harlem Renaissance is more a reflection of the inability of its participants to respond satisfactorily to the complex black situation in the twenties than of their middle-class backgrounds as such. However, some of the novelists did deal straightforwardly with lower-class characters and themes without romanticizing or stereotyping them. Langston Hughes' feel for common people and his interest in the folk traditions of the blues and spirituals are well-mirrored in his novel, *Not Without Laughter*. Countee Cullen alone attempted a realistic picture of the working-class, churchgoing black in *One Way to Heaven*. Rudolph Fisher's use of dialect and humor and his sharp characterizations of ordinary blacks, and Jean Toomer's lyrical evocation of rural and urban black life in *Cane* are two other examples of sensitivity to the common folk. Claude McKay and Wallace Thurman broke with middle-class values, but neither fully realized his potential; they failed to turn their interests in white radicalism and bohemianism to creative uses. However, by writing of lower-class life with talent and eloquence, these writers stand out in relation to those who did not empathize with the larger issues of black American existence.

The small black middle class seems to have supported the Renaissance. They subscribed in large numbers to *The Crisis* and *Opportunity*; they also provided the only black audience for books by black writers. Many rich black individuals, such as A'Lelia Walker and Casper Holstein,[5] helped the movement and its writers financially. Considering its limitations in American life, the black bourgeoisie provided significant support for the Harlem Renaissance. The patronage of black middle class was, however, as mixed a blessing as the white patronage. The black bourgeoisie tried to impose its narrow aesthetic criteria on black artists in return for its limited support. Many black reviewers and critics reflected black middle-class attitudes. The vigorous controversy over the portrayal of the Negro directed little or no attention to the failure to mirror the important issues facing the black masses. The DuBois-Brawley school of black criticism, for instance, was too busy either promoting positive delineation of black middle class or attacking the appearance of sensual-primitive types in literature to notice the omission. The failure of black critics, with the partial exceptions of Alain Locke, Sterling Brown, and James Weldon Johnson, to rise above the limitations of their middle-class antecedents and ideologies compounds the failure of the writers.

Some of the thematic and aesthetic concerns of the Harlem Renaissance novelists have ceased to be issues today. Miscegenation, never a major issue with black writers, has lost ground even with white writers who were preoccupied with it around the turn of the century. The black writer today is not obsessed with shades of skin. The mulatto heroes and heroines who crowded the pages of black novels and short stories during the twenties seem to have been routed by Richard Wright's *Native Son* (1940) in its powerful projection of the angry and demoralized black from the urban ghetto in the character of Bigger Thomas. Since then, many other types of the black protagonist have appeared. The continuity of Afro-American literature since the twenties might then be defined in terms of the perspective gained on issues relating to race and art, on literature and didacticism. Some of the Harlem Renaissance writers found it difficult to decide whether they were black writers or writers who happened to be black. These issues seem trivial today, because they were thrashed out during the twenties and the thirties. For example, it is reasonable to assume that no worthwhile discussions of black literature today are marred by a false dichotomy between the claims of art and didacticism, and that it is increasingly difficult to discuss the artistic quality of a literary work apart from the cultural milieu that produced it.

The black writer today has other advantages. With a growing black audience, commercial success does not depend entirely on the whims of white readers. But many challenges that confronted black writers in the twenties must still be faced. Class conflict continues to be important in all facets of Afro-American life, and the black writer cannot afford to ignore its serious implications for the nascent group consciousness of black people. There is also the American ethos, which deprives the present of its past, or at best reconstructs the past to justify the present, to be contended with. Among blacks as well as whites, this form of American "innocence" is manifested in an intense preoccupation with the present and a blatant ignorance of the past. Many young black people today believe that "the Black Liberation movement began two or three hours after they joined the issues and that they themselves invented militancy."[6] Closely related to this narrow, anti-intellectual view of history is the provincialism that most black Americans share with their white compatriots, a myopia that prevents them from seeing beyond the walls built by American ideals and institutions. In 1926, DuBois had asked: "Do we simply want to be Americans? Once in a while through all of us there flashes some clairvoyance, some clear idea, of what America really is. We who are dark can see America in the way that white Americans cannot. And seeing our country thus, are we satisfied with its present goals and ideals?"[7] The question is perhaps more pertinent today than it was then, in view of the greater awareness of race and color in social and political issues all over the world.

Will the black American writer today meet these challenges? Will the black novelist write the epic novel that Charles W. Chesnutt and Alain Locke looked forward to in the twenties? Or has such a novel been already written in Richard Wright's *Native Son*, Ralph Ellison's *Invisible Man*, James Baldwin's *Go Tell it on the Mountain*, or Margaret Walker's *Jubilee*?

A REVIEW OF PREVIOUS
RESEARCH AND CRITICISM

With notable exceptions, the critical evaluation of the Harlem Renaissance has just begun in the 1970s.[1] The *Black World* pioneered the current reexamination of the black artists of the twenties by publishing in November 1970 an issue entitled "Harlem Renaissance Revisited." Although some of the essays included in this issue are either sketchy or polemical, the articles by Faith Berry, George E. Kent, Dorothy West, and John Henrik Clarke do suggest new and challenging perspectives. Since then, two full-length books on the subject—*Harlem Renaissance* (1971) by Nathan Irvin Huggins and *Harlem Renaissance Remembered* (1972) edited by Arna Bontemps—have initiated the long overdue process of discovering the significance of the New Negro movement in America's social, political, and literary history. Also, Darwin T. Turner has written valuable biocritical essays on Jean Toomer, Countee Cullen, and Zora Neale Hurston in his *In a Minor Chord* (1971). Four other works of interest are Stephen H. Bronz's *Roots of Negro Racial Consciousness* (1964), with essays on James Weldon Johnson, Claude McKay, and Countee Cullen; Edward Margolies' *Native Sons* (1968), which contains brief but sharp critical comments on a number of Harlem Renaissance writers; George E. Kent's *Blackness and the Adventure of Western Culture* (1972), which has an article each on Claude McKay and Langston Hughes, besides a general essay on the Harlem Renaissance; and James O. Young's *Black Writers of the Thirties* (1973).

Until 1970, the few attempts at critical assessment of the Harlem Renaissance are usually chapters in books devoted to much larger subjects. In addition to the sections in the books by Gloster and Bone discussed below, significant chapters on the subject include "The Urban Scene" and "Contemporary Negro Poetry (1914-1936)" in Sterling A. Brown's *The Negro in American Fiction* (1937) and *Negro Poetry and Drama* (1937) respectively; "Emergence of the New Negro" in Saunders Redding's *To Make a Poet Black* (1939); "Harlem Background—The Rise of Economic

Nationalism and Origins of Cultural Revolution" in Harold Cruse's *The Crisis of the Negro Intellectual* (1967); and "The Sociological Imagination" and "The Renaissance in Literature" in S.P. Fullwinder's *The Mind and Mood of Black America* (1969).

Hugh M. Gloster's *Negro Voices in American Fiction* (1948, reissued 1965) and Robert A. Bone's *The Negro Novel in America* (1959, revised 1965) are two major studies of the Afro-American novel; together they are invaluable sources of information on black American fiction. Although Bone's sharp critical focus is missing from Gloster's book, the latter's "dragnet" approach permits him to at least grant some attention to all Harlem Renaissance novelists and short story writers. Gloster heavily emphasizes plot outlines and surface relationships, and his treatment of the Renaissance novelists under such broad categories as "Van Vechten Vogue" and "West Indian Realism" prevents him from discovering and developing the more significant points of shared interest among these writers. At the same time, Bone's attempt to see all black novelists from William Wells Brown to James Baldwin as alternating "between the magnetic poles of assimilationism and Negro nationalism" leads him to divide the novelists of the Harlem Renaissance artificially into the opposed camps of "Harlem School" and "Old Guard." Thus he cannot account for the ambivalence and contradictions regarding race and art that a majority of Renaissance novelists reflected in their personalities and their works. Bone's critical framework is for the most part both rigid and narrow and his treatment of many Renaissance novelists consequently is flawed or heavy-handed. It is not surprising that in Bone's evaluation, *Cane* was the only "major" fictional work from the period and three others qualified only as "good." Both Gloster and Bone stress scope at the cost of depth; Gloster's book covers almost every extant black novelist and Bone touches on 103 novels in his study.

In contrast to Bone and Gloster, Huggins concentrates on the black artists and writers of the twenties and develops a theoretical framework that explains the Harlem Renaissance as a natural and logical part of the American scene at that time. Given society's black-white symbiosis, it was inevitable that the Harlem Renaissance would get caught in the white American fad of black primitivism and fail to develop into a conscious movement of black American arts. The black American's confusions over identity are uniquely American; "white Americans and white American culture have no more claim to self-confidence than black." Huggins' approach is valuable in that it cuts across the overrated issues surrounding the integrationist-nationalist (assimilationist-separatist, or what have you) polarities of Afro-American thought to underscore the Americanness of the black American's predicament. But as George E. Kent has pointed out, "it is the absoluteness with which Huggins pushes his thesis of an *inevitable* cultural togetherness in the Renaissance that renders his thesis somewhat controversial."[2] Beginning with the bohemian and pessimistic view of Wallace Thurman's *Infants of the Spring* (a book Huggins overrates as much as Bone underrates it), Huggins carries his thesis through an analysis of many Harlem Renaissance writers and their works. The resultant discussion is at times both absorbing and provocative, as in the case of Jean Toomer and Carl Van Vechten, but more often flawed or unpersuasive as in his evaluations of Claude McKay, Rudolph Fisher, and Countee Cullen.

The Harlem Renaissance Remembered (1972), edited by Arna Bontemps, is a welcome addition to the growing literature on the subject, and is a pioneering step toward assessing the significance of many hitherto neglected aspects and figures of the Harlem Renaissance. It includes a well-researched article on Charles S. Johnson as a promoter and entrepreneur of the Harlem Renaissance, even though the absence of an article on Alain Locke's role is to be regretted. Other neglected figures of the Renaissance who are given much-needed attention in Bontemps' critical anthology include Jessie Fauset, Nella Larsen, Wallace Thurman, drama critic Theophilus Lewis, and poet Frank Horne. Arna Bontemps' "The Awakening: A Memoir" is valuable as perhaps the last detailed writing about the period to come from a writer who lived through the excitement of the twenties and has written frequently about it since then. Other articles that deserve special mention are George E. Kent's "Patterns of the Harlem Renaissance" (reprinted from Kent's *Blackness and the Adventure of Western Culture*), Michael B. Stoff's "Claude McKay and the Cult of Primitivism," Mae Gwendolyn Henderson's "Portrait of Wallace Thurman," and Robert Hemenway's "Zora Neale Hurston and the Eatonville Anthropology." Unfortunately, the book is of uneven quality.

My approach to the Harlem Renaissance novels focuses on issues that have received little attention in Nathan Huggins' book. Huggins' thesis is a valuable approach to the issues of black American identity, but reveals little about the tensions and conflicts existing in Afro-American life in relative independence of white America. I say "relative" because ultimately most intraracial black attitudes and institutions are traceable to the colonial, black-white symbiosis in the United States—a relationship in which blacks have always been at the receiving end, at least socially and economically.[3] Although serious problems arise in defining black

America as an internal colony, many facets of Afro-American life parallel the former colonies of European powers in Asia and Africa. The black's self-hatred and the existence of a black middle class that acts as an "intermediary" between the white power structure and the black masses are two instances of such parallels. Viewed thus, the so-called integrationist-separatist polarities of Afro-American thought are placed in proper perspective as inseparable twins of a divided consciousness. Many basic issues of Afro-American existence lie outside of this matrix, and the controversies over integration and separation frequently cloud these issues rather than expose and crystallize them.

Chapter 1: "WHEN THE NEGRO WAS IN VOGUE"

1. Hugh M. Gloster, *Negro Voices in American Fiction* (1948; rpt., New York: Russell & Russell, 1965), p. 110.

2. Robert A. Bone, *The Negro Novel in America*, rev. ed. (1959; New Haven: Yale University Press, 1965), p. 58.

3. Gloster, *Negro Voices*, p. 264.

4. 6 June 1926, p. 1842.

5. For a discussion of David Walker and Frederick Douglass as representing the ideologies of revolution and reform respectively in the black tradition, see Houston A. Baker, Jr., *Long Black Song: Essays in Black American Literature and Culture* (Charlottesville: The University Press of Virginia, 1972), pp. 58-83. Another study of nineteenth-century black figures is Jean Fagan Yellin's *The Intricate Knot* (New York: New York University Press, 1972).

6. Franklin, *From Slavery to Freedom*, 3rd ed. (New York: Knopf, 1967), p. 513; Brown, "The New Negro in Literature, 1925-55," in Rayford Logan, ed., *The New Negro Thirty Years Afterward* (Washington, D.C.: Howard University Press, 1955).

7. Bone, *The Negro Novel*, p. 64. James Owen Young discusses the black writers of the thirties in terms of the polarity that existed between older "race men" and the young radicals. See *Black Writers of the Thirties* (Baton Rouge: Louisiana State University Press, 1973), pp. x-xi, 3-34, 66-76. In the twenties, however, racial attitudes and expression were generally as much a forte of the young writers as of the older writers and leaders.

8. "The New Negro in Literature, 1925-55." Quoted in Kenny J. Williams, *They Also Spoke: An Essay on Negro Literature in America, 1787-1930* (Nashville: Townsend, 1970), p. 276.

9. "Washington and the Negro Renaissance," *The Crisis* 88 (April-May 1971): 79-82.

10. Clare Bloodgood Crane, "Alain Locke and the Negro Renaissance" (Ph.D. diss., University of California, San Diego, 1971), p. 168.

11. "The Black Renaissance of the Twenties," *Black World* 20 (November 1970): 6.

12. "The Negro," in Harold E. Stearns, ed., *America Now* (New York: Literary Guild of America, 1938), p. 497. Saunders Redding has outlined the indifference and hostility to black writing during the early years of this century in "American Negro Literature," *The American Scholar* 18 (Spring 1949).

13. For a brief comment on DuBois' relationship to the Harlem Renaissance, see Van Wyck Brooks, *The Confident Years, 1885-1915* (New York: Dutton, 1952), p. 323. Brooks' chapter, "Eugene O'Neill: Harlem," in *The Confident Years* is a partial exception to the general neglect of the Harlem Renaissance in American literary histories.

14. For an analysis of *Souls of Black Folk* in relation to the black man of culture, see Baker, *Long Black Song*, pp. 96-108.

15. 1903; rpt., New York: Washington Square, 1970, p. 11.

16. *A Long Way from Home: An Autobiography* (1937; rpt., New York: Harcourt Brace & World, 1970), p. 110.

17. Saunders Redding, quoted in Herbert Hill, ed., *Anger and Beyond: The Negro Writer in the United States* (New York: Harper & Row, 1966), p. xvii.

18. *From Slavery to Freedom*, p. 499.

19. 18 (1919): 14.

20. Rubin, "Washington and the Negro Renaissance," p. 79; Franklin, *From Slavery to Freedom*, pp. 471-75.

21. Franklin, ibid., p. 439.

22. James Boylan, ed., The World *and the 20's* (New York: Dial, 1973), p. 61. Rowland Thomas wrote a series of articles based on records smuggled by Henry P. Fry, a disillusioned Kleagle in the Chattanooga branch of the Klan. These articles ran in the New York *World* for twenty-one consecutive days beginning 6 September 1921.

23. Quoted in Kenneth T. Jackson, *The Ku Klux Klan in the City, 1915-1930* (New York: Oxford University Press, 1967), p. xii.

24. Alain Locke, *The New Negro: An Interpretation* (1925; rpt., New York: Atheneum, 1970), p. 6.

25. Crane, "Alain Locke," p. 6.

26. Among the contemporary white journals which highlighted the problems of the black migrant in the North, a special mention must be made of the *Survey Graphic* and the *Survey Midmonthly*, edited by the Kellogg brothers. See Clarke A. Chambers, *Paul U. Kellogg and the* Survey: *Voices for Social Welfare and Social Justice* (Minneapolis: University of Minnesota Press, 1971), pp. 77-117.

27. Rubin, "Washington and the Negro Renaissance," p. 79.

28. P. 301.

29. Gilbert Osofsky, "Harlem: The Making of a Ghetto," in John Henrik Clarke, ed., *Harlem: A Community in Transition* (New York: Citadel, 1964), p. 24.

30. Rubin, "Washington and the Negro Renaissance," p. 79.

31. Quoted in Clarke, *Harlem: A Community in Transition*, p. 3. We should not overlook the importance of parallel sociopolitical challenges faced by black communities in other American cities like Chicago and Detroit, but it is reasonable to suggest that Harlem represented the black's move to an urban culture in a most intense and inclusive fashion.

32. The following summary is based on Franklin, *From Slavery to Freedom*, pp. 447-49, 475, 486-87, 494; Gilbert Osofsky, "Symbols of the Jazz Age: The New Negro and Harlem Discovered," *American Quarterly* 17 (1965): 230.

33. Nathan I. Huggins, *Harlem Renaissance* (New York: Oxford University Press, 1971), p. 46.

34. Ibid., p. 43.

35. See Crane, "Alain Locke," p. 42; Franklin, *From Slavery to Freedom*, p. 491.

36. Locke, *The New Negro*, p. 296.

37. *The Crisis* 21 (1923): 60.

38. "Africa Conscious Harlem," in Clarke, *Harlem: A Community in Transition*, p. 84.

39. Quoted in Roi Ottley, *New World A-Coming* (Boston: Houghton Mifflin, 1943), p. 79.

40. For a detailed discussion of the term "New Negro" and its uses in the Afro-American tradition, see Lawrence W. Levine, "The Concept of the New Negro and the Realities of Black Culture," in Nathan I. Huggins, Martin Kilson, Daniel M. Fox, eds., *Key Issues in the Afro-American Experience*, vol. 2 (New York: Harcourt Brace Jovanovich, 1971), pp. 125-47.

41. Crane, "Alain Locke," p. 36.

42. Claude McKay, however, charged that the black leaders of the twenties ignored developing racial institutions, obsessed as they were with fighting segregation. McKay makes this point repeatedly in *Banjo, A Long Way from Home*, and *Harlem: Negro Metropolis*. Cf. Wayne F. Cooper, ed., *The Passion of Claude McKay: Selected Poetry and Prose, 1912-1948* (New York: Schocken, 1973), p. 37.

43. Bontemps, "The Black Renaissance of the Twenties," p. 7.

44. For a suggestive account of black theater in the twenties and its antecedents, see Huggins, *Harlem Renaissance*, pp. 244-301; see also Theodore Kornweibel, Jr., "Theophilus Lewis and the Theater of the Harlem Renaissance" in Arna Bontemps, ed., *The Harlem Renaissance Remembered* (New York: Dodd, Mead, 1972), pp. 171-89.

45. For a detailed discussion of plays by Garland Anderson and Wallace Thurman, see Doris E. Abramson, *Negro Playwrights in the American Theatre, 1925-1959* (New York: Columbia University Press, 1969), pp. 22-43.

46. New York: Harper and Brothers, 1927, p. xiv. For a brief discussion of Locke's views on black theater, see Samuel A. Hay, "Alain Locke and Black Drama," *Black World* 21 (April 1972): 8-14.

47. Chase, *Afro-American Art and Craft* (New York: Van Nostrand Reinhold, 1971), p. 111.

48. Letter from Charles S. Johnson to Ethel Ray, 24 March 1924. Quoted in Bontemps, *The Harlem Renaissance Remembered*, p. 11.

49. For a comment on the motives that led Kellogg to bring out special numbers of the *Survey Graphic* on the blacks as well as on the Irish, the Mexican peasants, and the Gypsies, see Chambers, *Paul U. Kellogg and the* Survey, pp. 112f.

50. Ibid., p. 113.

51. Foreword, *The New Negro*, p. xv.

52. For a detailed analysis of Locke's views and role in the twenties, see Crane, "Alain Locke"; see also Young, *Black Writers of the Thirties*, pp. 142-49; S.P. Fullwinder, *The Mind and Mood of Black America: Twentieth Century Thought* (Homewood, Ill.: Dorsey, 1969), pp. 115-22; Michael L. Lomax, "Fantasies of Affirmation: The 1920's Novel of Negro Life," *CLA Journal* 16 (December 1972): 234-38; W.D. Wright, "The Cultural Thought and Leadership of Alain Locke," *Freedomways* 14 (1974): 35-50. The stimulating comments made by Nathan I. Huggins, Harold Cruse, Ralph Ellison, and Albert Murray on 1 December 1973 at a Harvard symposium on the significance of Alain Locke are included in *The Harvard Advocate* 107 (1974): 9-28.

53. Hayden, Introduction, *The New Negro*, p. xii.

54. The summary of Locke's views in the following two pages is based primarily on the opening essay in *The New Negro*, pp. 3-16. (The quotations are also from this essay.)

55. For a discussion of the connections between Locke and other literary radicals of the twenties, see Fullwinder, *The Mind and Mood*, pp. 116-22; Crane, "Alain Locke," pp. 59-62; Huggins, *Harlem Renaissance*, pp. 60ff.

56. Hayden, Introduction, *The New Negro*, p. ix.

57. Huggins, *Harlem Renaissance*, p. 48.

58. Crane, "Alain Locke," p. 67.

59. Ibid., p. 112.

60. *The New Negro*, p. 256.

61. Crane, "Alain Locke," pp. 115-16. For a brief discussion of the connection between folk and formal art based on the views of Alain Locke, W.E.B. DuBois, and James Weldon Johnson, see Bernard W. Bell, *The Folk Roots of Contemporary Afro-American Poetry* (Detroit: Broadside, 1974), pp. 20-31.

62. Crane, "Alain Locke," p. 70.

63. Eugene Levy, *James Weldon Johnson: Black Leader, Black Voice* (Chicago: University of Chicago Press, 1973), p. 311; Cooper, *The Passion of Claude McKay*, pp. 32-33.

64. For detailed discussions of the roles that Walter White and V.F. Calverton played in encouraging the Renaissance writers, see Charles F. Cooney, "Walter White and the Harlem Renaissance," *Journal of Negro History* 57 (July 1972): 231-40; Edward E. Waldron, "Walter White and the Harlem Renaissance: Letters from 1924-1927," *CLA Journal* 16 (June 1973): 438-57; Haim Genizi, "V.F. Calverton: A Radical Magazinist for Black Intellectuals, 1920-1940," *Journal of Negro History* 57 (July 1972): 241-53.

65. This summary is based on Fullwinder, *The Mind and the Mood*, pp. 107-14; Patrick J. Gilpin, "Charles S. Johnson: Entrepreneur of the Harlem Renaissance," in Bontemps, *Harlem Renaissance Remembered*, pp. 215-46.

66. Johnson, "An Opportunity for Negro Writers," *Opportunity* 2 (September 1924): 258.

67. New York: Macaulay, 1932, p. 240.

68. Cf. George E. Kent, *Blackness and the Adventure of Western Culture* (Chicago: Third World, 1972), pp. 51-52.

69. *Harlem Renaissance*, p. 84.

70. Bone, *The Negro Novel*, p. 59.

71. Oscar Cargill, *Intellectual America* (New York: Macmillan, 1941), p. 608.

72. Langston Hughes, *The Big Sea* (1940; rpt., New York: Hill & Wang, 1963), pp. 223-32; Frederick J. Hoffman, *The Twenties*, rev. ed. (New York: Free Press, 1962), pp. 306-8.

73. Paul Morand, *New York* (New York: Holt, 1930), p. 270.

74. Ibid., p. 268.

75. Ibid., p. 270.

76. Gloster, *Negro Voices*, p. 107.

77. This brief account of the Southern Renaissance is based on Trudie Engel, "The Harlem Renaissance" (Master's thesis, University of Wisconsin, Madison, 1959), pp. 72-81.

78. *His Eye is on the Sparrow* (New York: Doubleday, 1951), p. 195.

79. Ibid., p. 196.

80. *New Republic*, 29 September 1926, p. 163.

81. 28 August 1926, p. 248.

82. *Survey*, 1 November 1926, p. 160.

83. *New York Times Book Review*, 22 August 1926, p. 2.

84. *The Chicago Defender*, 21 April 1928.

85. "Our Negro Intellectuals," *The Crisis* 35 (August 1928): 269.

86. *The Messenger* 9 (February 1927): 47.

87. *The Crisis* 32 (December 1926): 81.

88. Faith Berry, "Voice for the Jazz Age, Great Migration or Black Bourgeoisie," *Black World* 20 (November 1970): 12.

89. P. 238.

90. Based on Marion L. Starkey, "Jessie Fauset," *Southern Workman* 61 (May 1932): 217-20.

91. Bontemps, *Harlem Renaissance Remembered*, pp. 25-26.

92. Quoted in Donald Ogden Stewart, *Fighting Words* (New York: Harcourt Brace & World, 1940), pp. 58-59.

93. "The Negro in Art: A Symposium," *The Crisis* 32 (August 1926): 194.

94. Based on a newspaper clipping in the Langston Hughes Clipping Folder, Howard University Library. Quoted in Crane, "Alain Locke," p. 149.

95. James Weldon Johnson, "The Dilemma of the Negro Author," *American Mercury* 15 (December 1928): 481.

96. "Our Literary Audience," *Opportunity* 8 (February 1930): 42.

97. "Our Book Shelf," *The Crisis* 31 (January 1926): 141.

98. *The Crisis* 31 (February 1926): 165.

99. "Alain Locke," p. 140.

100. *The Crisis* 33 (November 1926): 28.

101. *The Crisis* 31 (March 1926): 220.

102. *The Crisis* 31 (April 1926): 279.

103. *The Crisis* 32 (June 1926): 72.

104. *The Crisis* 31 (March 1926): 219.

105. Ibid., p. 220.

106. *The Crisis* 33 (November 1926): 29.

107. *Black World* 20 (November 1970): 18.

108. Richard Wright, "Blueprint for Negro Writing," *The New Challenge* 1 (1937): 53; James Thompson, Lennox Raphael, and Steve Canyon, "A Very Stern Discipline: An Interview with Ralph Ellison," *Harpers*, March 1967, p. 79.

109. *Black World* 20 (November 1970): 20-36.

110. Crane, "Alain Locke," pp. 210-12, 222-23.

111. E.U. Essien-Udom, "Black Identity in the International Context," in Huggins, Kilson, and Fox, *Key Issues*, vol. 2, p. 248.

112. Lilyan Kesteloot, *Les Ecrivains noirs de langue Française: naissance d'une littérature* 2me éd. (Bruxelles: Université Libre de Bruxelles, 1965), pp. 63-82. Cited in Huggins, *Harlem Renaissance*, pp. 178, 317.

113. Quoted in Langston Hughes, "The Twenties: Harlem and its Negritude,"

African Forum 1 (Spring 1966): 18.

114. "Elephant's Dance: A Memoir of Wallace Thurman," *Black World* 20 (November 1970): 80.

115. The term "Niggeratti," a corruption of "Negro literati" has been credited to Thurman and Zora Neale Hurston. See Crane, "Alain Locke," p. 188n.; Hughes, *The Big Sea*, p. 238; Bontemps, *Harlem Renaissance Remembered*, p. 194.

116. Wallace Thurman, *Infants of the Spring* (1932; rpt., New York: Books for Libraries, 1972), p. 132. Pagination in the text is from this edition.

117. Renaissance figures are easily identified among those present at this gathering. Cf. Gloster, *Negro Voices*, p. 171; Huggins, *Harlem Renaissance*, p. 193; Crane, "Alain Locke," p. 188; Young, *Black Writers of the Thirties*, pp. 208-9.

118. Thurman distorted Locke's philosophy in attributing to him a return to African roots and atavism. See Locke, "The Legacy of the Ancestral Arts," *The New Negro*, pp. 254-67. Cf. Crane, "Alain Locke," pp. 188f., 207n.; Huggins, *Harlem Renaissance*, pp. 79ff.

119. Thompson, Raphael, and Canyon, "A Very Stern Discipline," p. 79.

120. For a critical review of reactions in the thirties to the Harlem Renaissance from Benjamin Brawley, W.E.B. DuBois, Alain Locke, James Weldon Johnson, Sterling Brown, Richard Wright, and others, see Young, *Black Writers of the Thirties*, pp. 133-65.

121. Cooper, *The Passion of Claude McKay*, p. 36.

122. *The Big Sea*, p. 228.

123. "The Negro-Art Hokum," 16 June 1926, pp. 662-63; "The Negro Artist and the Racial Mountain," 23 June 1926, pp. 692-94. Hughes' article was followed by letters from Schuyler, Dorothy Fox, Headley E. Bailey, and Michael Gold in *Nation*, 14 July 1926, pp. 36-37. Michael Gold implored black intellectuals "to leave the cabarets of the jaded dilettantes and the colleges of the middle-class strivers, and help the mass of their own brothers in the economic fight." Hughes responded to Schuyler's letter in the issue dated 18 August 1926.

Chapter 2: RACE AND SEX

1. McKay's response to D.H. Lawrence sums up his connections with the dominant mood of the period: "I thought D.H. Lawrence was more modern than James Joyce. In . . . Lawrence I found confusion—all of the ferment and turmoil, the hesitation and hate and alarm, the sexual inquietude and incertitude of this age, and the psychic and romantic groping for a way out." McKay, *A Long Way from Home*, p. 247.

2. Sister Mary Conroy, "The Vagabond Motif in the Writings of Claude McKay," *Negro American Literature Forum* 5 (Spring 1971): 16.

3. Claude McKay, *Home to Harlem* (New York: Harper & Bros., 1929), p. 108. All references for quotations from *Home to Harlem*, *Banjo* (New York: Harper and Brothers, 1929), *Banana Bottom* (1933; rpt., Chatham, N.J.: The Chatham Bookseller, 1970), *God Sends Sunday* (1931; rpt., New York: AMS Press, 1972), *Black No More* (New York: Macaulay, 1931), and *Cane* (1923; rpt., New York: University Place Book Shop, 1969) will appear in the text. Pagination will be in parentheses following quotations.

4. Aubrey Bowser, *Amsterdam News*, 21 March 1928. Most of the quotations from early reviews cited in this study are from newspaper clippings contained in folders on different Harlem Renaissance writers in the vertical file at the Schomburg Collection, New York Public Library. Dates for such quotations have been indicated in the text or in corresponding footnotes.

5. Cooper, "Claude McKay and the New Negro of the 1920's," *Phylon* 25 (1964): 304; Stoff, "Claude McKay and the Cult of Primitivism," in Bontemps, *Harlem Renaissance Remembered*, p. 126.

6. "A Negro to His Critics," *New York Herald Tribune Books*, 6 March 1932.

7. *A Long Way from Home*, p. 283.

8. Cf. Stoff, "Claude McKay," p. 130. In a footnote, Stoff refers to a more concise definition of the concept of the intellectual as one who seeks to make public issues of personal problems in Warren I. Sussman's "The Expatriate Image," *Intellectual History in America*, vol. 2, pp. 145-57.

9. See Stoff, "Claude McKay," and Bone, *The Negro Novel*, p. 69.

10. Conroy tries unsuccessfully to reinterpret McKay's work in order to vindicate his conversion to Catholicism toward the end of his life ("Vagabond Motif"); McKay had been a "free-thinker" most of his life and his conversion to Catholicism was an astonishing turnabout. See Cooper, *The Passion of Claude McKay*, p. 40.

11. *Harlem Renaissance*, pp. 173-78, 188.

12. The description is Michael Stoff's.

13. Bone, *The Negro Novel*, p. 69.

14. Stoff, "Claude McKay," p. 139.

15. Ibid., p. 139. For a different view of *Banana Bottom*, see George E. Kent, "Claude McKay's *Banana Bottom* Reappraised," *CLA Journal* 18 (December 1974): 222-34.

16. Stoff, "Claude McKay," p. 140.

17. Bone, *The Negro Novel*, p. 72.

18. According to Cooper, Squire Gensir is a fictionalized version of Walter Jekyll (1849-1929), an Englishman who wrote and published many books on Jamaican life and folklore. See Cooper, *The Passion of Claude McKay*, pp. 318-19, 332.

19. Stoff, "Claude McKay," p. 142.

20. *Harlem Renaissance*, pp. 124-25.

21. *The Crisis of the Negro Intellectual: From its Origins to the Present* (New York: William Morrow, 1967), p. 203.

22. Bone, *The Negro Novel*, p. 73.

23. *Harlem Renaissance*, p. 188.

24. In Bontemps, *Harlem Renaissance Remembered*, pp. 25-26.

25. 1931; rpt., New York: Macmillan, 1971. For a more detailed comment on *Black No More*, see Michael W. Peplow, "George Schuyler, Satirist: Rhetorical Devices in *Black No More*," *CLA Journal* 18 (December 1974): 242-57.

26. "The Negro-Art Hokum," *Nation*, 16 June 1926, p. 662.

27. Around the time he published *Black No More*, Schuyler had been seriously suggesting massive miscegenation as a solution to America's race problems. "The most cordial and profitable race relations are sex relations," he wrote in "Views and Reviews," *Pittsburgh Courier*, 19 September 1931. See also "Views and Reviews," 13 July 1929.

28. Saunders Redding, *To Make a Poet Black* (Chapel Hill: University of North Carolina Press, 1939), p. 107.

29. Based on information given in Starkey, "Jessie Fauset," pp. 217-20.

30. 1931; rpt., New York: Negro Universities Press, 1969, p. ix.

31. Redding, *To Make a Poet Black*, p. 106.

32. Bone, *The Negro Novel*, p. 88.

33. Darwin T. Turner, *In a Minor Chord: Three Afro-American Writers and Their Search for Identity* (Carbondale: Southern Illinois University Press, 1971), pp. 14, 124.

34. Bontemps, *Cane* (1923; rpt., New York: Harper & Row, 1969), p. xii.

35. *Earth-Being: The Autobiography of Jean Toomer*, in *The Black Scholar* 2 (January 1971): 11.

36. My comments on the Fugitives are based on John M. Bradbury, *The Fugitives* (1958; New Haven: College and University Press, 1964). Allen Tate made two unsuccessful attempts, in 1923 and 1924, to meet Toomer in person. See Bontemps, *Cane*, p. xvi.

37. Cf. Bernard W. Bell, "Portrait of the Artist as High Priest of Soul: Jean Toomer's *Cane*," *Black World* 23 (September 1974): 97.

38. Michael Jay Krasny, "Jean Toomer and the Quest for Consciousness" (Ph.D. diss., University of Wisconsin, Madison, 1972), p. 34.

39. Letter from Toomer to McKay, 9 August 1922. Quoted in Bontemps, *Cane*, pp. viii-ix.

40. For a comment on "Natalie Mann," see Turner, *In a Minor Chord*, p. 12.

41. Bell, "Portrait," p. 92.

42. Cf. Bell, "Portrait," p. 97; Bone, *The Negro Novel*, p. 88.

43. "Four Short Fiction Writers of the Harlem Renaissance," *CLA Journal* 11 (September 1967): 61.

44. Bone, *The Negro Novel*, pp. 83-84.

45. Huggins, *Harlem Renaissance*, p. 187.

46. *Essentials: Definitions and Aphorisms* (Chicago: Lakeside [private edition], 1931), p. lvi.

Chapter 3: THE DICTIES AND THE SHINES

1. For a discussion of class in black America, see Gunnar Myrdal, *An American Dilemma*, 2 vols. (New York: Harper & Row, 1944); Allison Davis, Burleigh B. Gardner, and Mary R. Gardner, *Deep South* (Chicago: University of Chicago Press, 1941); August Meier, *Negro Thought in America, 1880-1915* (Ann Arbor: University of Michigan Press, 1963); Allan H. Spear, *Black Chicago: The Making of A Negro Ghetto, 1890-1920* (Chicago: University of Chicago Press, 1967); E. Franklin Frazier, *Black Bourgeoisie: The Rise of a New Middle Class* (New York: Free Press, 1957); David M. Katzman, *Before the Ghetto: Black Detroit in the Nineteenth Century* (Urbana: University of Illinois Press, 1973).

2. Harold R. Isaacs, *The New World of Negro Americans* (New York: Viking, 1963), p. xii.

3. Taking her lead from Christopher Lasch's *The New Radicalism in America* (New York: Vintage, 1967), Clare B. Crane has argued that the vast majority of Renaissance writers belonged to a new class of intellectuals that was characterized by its alienation from bourgeois values generally and by its efforts to identify with lower classes. See Crane, "Alain Locke," p. 11.

4. My use of Frazier's book rather than a more recent study of black middle class is dictated by the closeness of Frazier's data and conclusions to the period of the Harlem Renaissance. Like Frazier, I recognize that the presentday black middle class includes many individuals who do not share the social background of the bourgeoisie Frazier studied—a group that represented "a fusion of the peasant and the gentleman." See Frazier, *Black Bourgeoisie*, Preface to the Collier Edition (1962), p. 12. Although intraracial class is still a pertinent Afro-American issue, I do not think Frazier's analysis can be applied with impunity to the 1970s.

5. Review of *The Chinaberry Tree, Opportunity* 10 (March 1932).

6. "Amber-Tinted Elegance: A Review of *The Chinaberry Tree*," *Nation*, 27 July 1932.

7. Darwin T. Turner, "*The Negro Novel in America*: In Rebuttal," *CLA Journal* 10 (1966): 132.

8. *The Negro Novel*, pp. 101-2.

9. Gloster, *Negro Voices*, p. 133.

10. Ibid., p. 132.

11. *There is Confusion* (New York: Boni & Liveright, 1924), p. 19.

12. 1931; rpt., New York: Negro Universities Press, 1969, p. 261.

13. P. ix.

14. *New York Herald Tribune Books*, 17 January 1932.

15. Frazier, *Black Bourgeoisie* (1957; rpt., Collier, 1962), p. 189.

16. Gloster, *Negro Voices*, p. 138.

17. Blyden Jackson, "An Essay in Criticism," *Phylon* 11 (1950): 341.

18. Alain Locke, "This Year of Grace," *Opportunity* 9 (February 1931): 49.

19. Young, *Black Writers of the Thirties*, pp. 217-18.

20. Blyden Jackson, "A Golden Mean for the Negro Novel," *CLA Journal* 3 (December 1959): 85.

21. *Not Without Laughter* (New York: Knopf, 1930), p. 313. References for subsequent quotations from *Not Without Laughter, One Way to Heaven* (New York: Harper & Bros., 1932), and *The Walls of Jericho* (1928; rpt., New York: Arno and The New York Times, 1969) will appear in the text with the page numbers indicated in parentheses following the quotations.

22. *The Negro Novel*, p. 77.

23. Cf. Turner, "*The Negro Novel*," pp. 130-31.

24. Jackson, "An Essay in Criticism," p. 342.

25. For one account of Afro-American religion in early twentieth century, see Fullwinder, pp. 26-46.

26. Charles R. Larson, "Three Harlem Novels of the Jazz Age," *Critique* 11 (1969): 75.

27. Alain Locke, "Black Truth and Black Beauty," *Opportunity* 11 (January 1933): 16.

28. Robert Cantwell, *New York Sun*, 19 February 1932.

29. Rudolph Fisher, *New York Herald Tribune Books*, 28 February 1932.

30. From a biographical note on the author in the vertical file for Rudolph Fisher at the Schomburg Collection, New York Public Library.

31. Cf. Oliver Louis Henry, "Rudolph Fisher: An Evaluation," *The Crisis* 77 (July 1971): 150. Henry's analysis of Fisher's short stories shows class-consciousness to be "perhaps the single most consistent theme in Fisher's work."

32. *New York World*, 5 August 1928, p. 7.

33. "The Browsing Reader," *The Crisis* 34 (November 1928): 374.

34. *Amsterdam News*, 8 August 1928.

35. Eric Walrond, *New York Herald Tribune Books*, 26 August 1928.

36. *Harlem Renaissance*, p. 199.

37. *New York Herald Tribune Books*, 28 February 1932.

38. *Saturday Review of Literature*, 25 August 1928, p. 250.

39. *Black Bourgeoisie*, p. 107.

40. "Voice for the Jazz Age, Great Migration or Black Bourgeoisie," *Black World* 20 (November 1970): 15.

Chapter 4: "FOOLING OUR WHITE FOLKS"

1. The figure is from Hughes' *Not Without Laughter*, p. 280. For a brief history of the use of a caste framework to describe American black-white relations, see David M. Katzman, *Before the Ghetto: Black Detroit in the Nineteenth Century* (Urbana: University of Illinois Press, 1973), pp. 213-16. Katzman has argued that terms such as "racism" and "race relations" are inadequate in the context, because although racism refers to "an emotional set rather than to the social structure of a community," race relations "covers a wide spectrum of human interaction without conveying any concept of the essential attitudes or structure of the actions involved." On the other hand, the term "caste" connotes "a specific and widely understood image of human relationships and human interactions. More important, it denotes specific characteristics of the structure and behavior of a society or a community."

2. The phrase is Katzman's; *Before the Ghetto*, p. 83.

3. Bone, *The Negro Novel*, p. 23.

4. Gloster, *Negro Voices*, p. 12.

5. From an article by Chesnutt, published in *Boston Transcript*. Quoted in Robert Farnsworth, "Testing the Color Line: Dunbar and Chesnutt" in C.W.E. Bigsby, ed., *The Black American Writer*, vol. 1: *Fiction* (Baltimore: Penguin, 1969), p. 121.

6. Bontemps, *The Autobiography of an Ex-Colored Man* (1912; rpt., New York: Hill & Wang, 1960), p. ix.

7. *Negro Voices*, p. 82.

8. See more on passing in Myrdal, *An American Dilemma*, pp. 683-88.

9. George S. Schuyler's delightful essay on this subject provides the epigraph to this chapter. See Schuyler, "Our Greatest Gift to America," in V.F. Calverton, ed., *Anthology of American Negro Literature* (New York: Random House, 1929), pp. 405-12.

10. *Saturday Review of Literature*, 22 October 1947.

11. Included in Darwin T. Turner, ed., *Black American Literature: Essays* (Columbus, Ohio: Merrill, 1969).

12. "To Market, To Market: A Review of *Plum Bun*," *The Chicago Defender*, 8 June 1929.

13. *Banjo*, p. 321.

14. *Passing* (1929; rpt., Collier, 1971), p. 14.

15. *The Negro Novel*, p. 98.

16. *Passing*, p. 16.

17. *New York Herald Tribune Books*, 11 April 1926, p. 3.

18. "An Essay in Criticism," *Phylon* 11 (1950): 341.

19. "Fall Books," *The Crisis* 29 (November 1924): 25.

20. Freda Kirchwey, *New York Herald Tribune*, 28 September 1924, p. 5.

21. *New York Herald Tribune Books*, 11 April 1926, p. 3.

22. *Plum Bun* (New York: Frederick A. Stokes, 1929), p. 12. References for subsequent quotations from *Plum Bun*, *Passing* (New York: Knopf, 1929), and *Quicksand* (New York: Knopf, 1928) will appear in the text with the page numbers indicated in parentheses following the quotations.

23. Bone, *The Negro Novel*, p. 102.

24. Hiroko Sato, "Under the Harlem Shadow: A Study of Jessie Fauset and Nella Larsen," in Bontemps, *Harlem Renaissance Remembered*, p. 84.

25. Introduction, *Passing*, p. 18.

26. Some of the early reviewers expressed similar views. See W.B. Seabrook, *Saturday Review of Literature*, 18 May 1929, and Esther Hyman, *Bookman*, June 1929. However, in defending *Passing*, Mary Mabel Youman has recently argued that the novel develops the theme of a lost black heritage; the title is ironic since it is Irene who really "passes" and loses the spiritual values of blackness even though she lives among blacks. But Youman's view fails to explain Clare's character satisfactorily. See "Nella Larsen's *Passing*: A Study in Irony," *CLA Journal* 18 (December 1974): 235-41.

27. *The Negro Novel*, p. 97.

28. E. Merrill Root, *The Christian Century*, 18 October 1928.

29. Bone, *The Negro Novel*, pp. 102, 103.

30. Ed., *The Black Novelist* (Columbus, Ohio: Merrill, 1970), p. 146.

31. Miscegenation has never been a favorite theme with blacks or black writers. Reviewing *Quicksand* under the title of "Miscegenation? Bah!" the reviewer in *Amsterdam News* (16 May 1928) commented: "It was rumored recently that a Harlem lady was about to publish a novel on the theme of miscegenation. . . . They need not have been excited, for the subject of miscegenation is not worth colored people's worry. Let white people do the worrying; they are the ones who bring it about."

32. Sterling Brown, "Negro Characters as Seen by White Authors," *Journal of Negro Education* 2 (1933): 194-95.

33. "A Golden Mean for the Negro Novel," *CLA Journal* 3 (December 1959): 84.

Chapter 5: THE BURDEN OF BLACKNESS

1. *The Blacker the Berry* (New York: Macaulay, 1929), p. 19. Page references for subsequent quotations from *The Blacker the Berry*, *Slaves Today* (1931; rpt., College Park, Md.: McGrath, 1969), and *Dark Princess* (New York: Harcourt, Brace, 1929) will appear in the text in parentheses following the quotations.

2. Although many black novelists have touched on this theme, the only black novel, other than Thurman's, that treats it extensively is Chester Himes' *The Third Generation* (1954).

3. Besides satirizing himself and other Renaissance novelists in *Infants of the Spring* (see Chapter 1), Thurman wrote controversial articles on the literary achievements of these novelists, e.g., "Negro Artists and the Negro," *New Republic*, 31 August 1927, pp. 37-39; "Negro Poets and their Poetry," *Bookman* 67 (1928): 555-61; "Nephews of Uncle Remus," *Independent*, 24 September 1927, pp. 291-98; "High, Low, Past and Present," *Harlem* 1 (November 1928): 31.

4. For a brief but illuminating discussion of the "black-white" and "dark-light" symbolism in Western life and literature, see Isaacs, *The New World*, pp. 74-80. In a footnote, Isaacs traces a similar pattern in the customs and conventions of some non-Western cultures too.

5. Vol. 1 (New Haven: Tuttle, 1913), pp. 296-311. Quoted in Isaacs, *The New World*, p. 73.

6. For a contemporary comment on Harlem house-rent parties in the twenties, see Lester A. Walton, "House Rent Parties: Now a Harlem Feature," *The World*, 19 June 1927, reprinted in Boylan, The World *and the 20's*, pp. 244-47.

7. The experiences of a dark-skinned child in a predominantly fair-skinned family from Puerto Rico, or even India, would offer interesting parallels. He is likely to be nicknamed after his dark skin and be treated in some ways like a stepchild.

8. For a different contemporary view of Liberian conditions in 1931, see W.E.B. DuBois, "Postscript," *The Crisis* 38 (March 1931): 101-2; W.E.B. DuBois, Review of *Slaves Today*, *The Crisis* 39 (February 1932): 68-69; Howard W. Oxley, "The Crisis in Liberia," *Crisis* 39 (December 1932): 373-74. John F. Mattheus is another black writer who treated Liberia in his fiction during the twenties. See Matheus' short story, "Nomah," in *Opportunity* 9 (July 1931): 214-17.

9. *Black and Conservative: The Autobiography of George S. Schuyler* (New Rochelle, N.Y.: Arlington, 1966), p. 181.

10. *Black and Conservative*, p. 184.

11. *New York Times*, 27 December 1931, p. 9.

12. *Black and Conservative*, p. 227.

13. "Our Readers Say," *The Crisis* 39 (March 1932): 92.

14. Examples of such behavior can be found among most despised and rejected groups. See Isaacs, *The New World*, p. 73. Isaacs cites Bruno Bettelheim's interpretations of what happened to some Jews in the Nazi concentration camps as an extreme example. See Bettelheim, "Individual and Mass Behavior in Extreme Situations," *Journal of Abnormal and Social Psychology* 38 (October 1943): 417-52.

15. Charles R. Larson, Introduction to *Black No More* (New York: Collier Books, 1971), p. 13. For a brief analysis of Schuyler's ideological shift during the thirties, see Young, *Black Writers of the Thirties*, pp. 84-93.

16. Pp. 341, 346, 350.

17. *Souls of Black Folk* (1903; rpt., New York: Fawcett, 1970), p. 11.

18. In addition to *Dark Princess* and his first novel, *The Quest of the Silver Fleece* (1911), DuBois also wrote a three-volume fictional trilogy: *The Black Flame–The Ordeal of Mansart* (1957), *Mansart Builds a School* (1959), and *Worlds of Color* (1961). One full-length study of DuBois' novels is Carolyn R. Gipson, "Intellectual Dilemmas in the Novels of W.E.B. DuBois," Ph.D. diss., University of Michigan, 1971. See also Richard Kostelanetz, "Fiction for a Negro Politics: Neglected Novels of DuBois," *Xavier University Studies* 7 (1968): 5-39; Elaine M. Newsome, "W.E.B. DuBois's 'Figure in the Carpet': A Cyclical Pattern in the Belletristic Prose," Ph.D. diss., University of North Carolina, 1971; Sidney Finkelstein, "DuBois's Trilogy: A Literary Triumph," *Mainstream* 14 (1961): 6-17.

19. *Springfield Republican*, 28 May 1928, p. 6.

20. *The New World*, p. 216.

21. Ibid.

22. DuBois, "Criteria of Negro Art," *The Crisis* 32 (October 1926): 296.

23. *Souls of Black Folk*, p. 3.

24. Julius Lester, ed., *The Seventh Son: The Thought and Writings of W.E.B. DuBois*, vol. 1 (New York: Vintage, 1971), p. 16.

25. S.P. Fullwinder ignores the strong emphasis on color and colonialism in seeing *Dark Princess* primarily in Marxist terms. See *The Mind and Mood*, p. 64.

26. See the Introduction in Vincent Freimarck and Bernard Rosenthal, eds., *Race and the American Romantics* (New York: Schocken, 1971) for an informed discussion of the nineteenth-century romantics' positions on race and slavery.

27. Isaacs, *The New World*, p. 220.

EPILOGUE

1. Harold Cruse, *The Crisis of the Negro Intellectual*, p. 37.

2. Faith Berry, "Voice for the Jazz Age, Great Migration or Black Bourgeoisie," *Black World* 20 (November 1970): 15.

3. Cruse, *The Crisis of the Negro Intellectual*, p. 38; Frazier, *Black Bourgeoisie*, p. 107.

4. *Blackness and the Adventure of Western Culture* (Chicago: Third World, 1972), p. 34.

5. A'Leila Walker, daughter of the famous Madame C.J. Walker, had made her fortune from the manufacture and sale of hair and skin preparations. Casper Holstein was a West Indian numbers racketeer who spent his money on many worthwhile literary and educational causes in the black Harlem of the twenties. See Cruse, *The Crisis of the Negro Intellectual*, pp. 24-26; Cooper, *The Passion of Claude McKay*, pp. 265-68, 275-76; Bontemps, *Harlem Renaissance Remembered*, pp. 231-34.

6. John O. Killens, "Another Time When Black Was Beautiful," *Black World* 20 (November 1970): 25.

7. "Criteria of Negro Art," *The Crisis* 32 (October 1926): 290.

A REVIEW OF PREVIOUS RESEARCH AND CRITICISM

1. See Abraham Chapman, "The Harlem Renaissance in Literary History," *CLA Journal* 11 (September 1967): 38-58.

2. *New York Times Book Review*, 2 January 1972, p. 4.

3. For a brief summary of the colonial approach to black America, see John H. Bracey, "Introduction," *Black Nationalism in America*, ed. John H. Bracey, August Meier, Elliot Rudwick (New York: Bobbs-Merrill, 1970), pp. lvi-lx.

BIBLIOGRAPHY

The list of secondary materials is not exhaustive, but every effort has been made to make it useful for a reader who might want to pursue his interest in the subject. A few additional entries may be found in the footnotes for different chapters. The reader may consult the bibliography appended to Hugh M. Gloster's *Negro Voices in American Fiction* for a list of contemporary book reviews of the Harlem Renaissance novels which have not been included here. I have also included a few unpublished dissertations that have a direct bearing on the subject of this book. An asterisk (*) following an item indicates its special importance for further study and research.

PRIMARY TEXTS

Bontemps, Arna. *God Sends Sunday*. New York: Harcourt, Brace, 1931. Reprint. New York: AMS Press, 1972.

Cullen, Countee. *One Way to Heaven*. New York and London: Harper and Bros., 1932.

DuBois, W.E. Burghardt. *Dark Princess*. New York: Harcourt, Brace, 1928.

Fauset, Jessie Redmon. *The Chinaberry Tree*. New York: Frederick A. Stokes, 1931. Reprint. New York: Negro Universities Press, 1969.

———. *Comedy: American Style*. New York: Frederick A. Stokes, 1933. Reprint. New York: Negro Universities Press, 1969.

———. *Plum Bun*. New York: Frederick A. Stokes, 1929.

———. *There is Confusion*. New York: Boni & Liveright, 1924.

Fisher, Rudolph. *The Walls of Jericho*. New York: Knopf, 1928. Reprint. New York: Arno Press, 1969.

Hughes, Langston. *Not Without Laughter*. New York: Knopf, 1930.

Larsen, Nella. *Passing*. New York: Knopf, 1929.

———. *Quicksand*. New York: Knopf, 1928.

McKay, Claude. *Banana Bottom*. New York: Harper and Bros., 1933. Reprint. Chatham, N.J.: Chatham Bookseller, 1970.

———. *Banjo*. New York: Harper and Bros., 1929.

———. *Home to Harlem*. New York: Harper and Bros., 1928.

Schuyler, George S. *Black No More*. New York: Macaulay, 1931.

———. *Slaves Today*. New York: Brewer, Warren and Putnam, 1931. Reprint. College Park, Md.: McGrath Publishing, 1969.

Thurman, Wallace. *The Blacker the Berry*. New York: Macaulay, 1929.

————. *Infants of the Spring*. New York: Macaulay, 1932. Reprint. Freeport, N.Y.: Books for Libraries Press, 1972.

Toomer, Jean. *Cane*. New York: Boni & Liveright, 1923. Reprint. New York: University Place Book Shop, 1967.

White, Walter F. *Fire in the Flint*. New York: Knopf, 1924. Reprint. New York: Negro Universities Press, 1969.

————. *Flight*. New York: Knopf, 1926. Reprint. New York: Negro Universities Press, 1969.

SECONDARY SOURCES

Ackley, Donald G. "Theme and Vision in *Cane*." *Studies in Black Literature* 1 (1970): 45-65.

American Negro Writer and His Roots: Selected Papers from the First Conference of Negro Writers, March 1959. New York: American Society of African Culture, 1960.

Anderson, Sherwood. *Dark Laughter*. New York: Boni & Liveright, 1925.

Aptheker, Herbert. *Annotated Bibliography of the Published Writings of W.E.B. DuBois*. Millwood, N.Y.: Kraus-Thomson Organization, 1973.*

————. "DuBois on James Weldon Johnson." *Journal of Negro History* 52 (April 1967): 128-45.

Arndt, Murray Dennis. "The *Crisis* Years of W.E.B. DuBois, 1910-1934." Ph.D. dissertation, Duke University, 1970.

Baker, Houston A., Jr. *Long Black Song: Essays in Black American Literature and Culture*. Charlottesville: The University Press of Virginia, 1972.*

Barksdale, Richard K. "Symbolism and Irony in McKay's *Home to Harlem*." *CLA Journal* 15 (March 1972): 338-44.*

Barton, Rebecca C. *Race Consciousness and American Negro Literature*. Copenhagen: Arnold Busck, 1934.

Bell, Bernard W. "Portrait of the Artist as High Priest of Soul: Jean Toomer's *Cane*." *Black World* 23 (September 1974): 4-19, 92-97.*

————. "Literary Sources of the Early Afro-American Novel." *CLA Journal* 18 (September 1974): 29-43.*

Bigsby, C.W.E., ed. *The Black American Writer*. 2 vols. Baltimore, Md.: Penguin, 1971.*

Black World. Edited by Hoyt W. Fuller. November 1970. (A special number devoted to the Harlem Renaissance)*

Bone, Robert A. *The Negro Novel in America*. Rev. ed. New Haven: Yale University Press, 1965.*

Bontemps, Arna. *Black Thunder, Gabriel's Revolt: Virginia: 1800*. 1936. Reprint. Boston: Beacon, 1970.

————. "The Harlem Renaissance." *Saturday Review*, 22 March 1947, pp. 12-13, 44.

————, ed. *The Harlem Renaissance Remembered*. Dodd, Mead, 1972*

———. "The Negro Renaissance: Jean Toomer and the Harlem Writers of the 1920's." *Anger and Beyond.* Edited by Herbert Hill. New York: Harper and Row, 1966.*

——— and Jack Conroy. *Anyplace but Here.* New York: Hill & Wang, 1966.

Bourne, Randolph. *History of a Literary Radical and Other Essays.* New York: B.W. Huebsch, 1920.

Bracey, John H., August Meier, and Elliot Rudwick, eds. *Black Nationalism in America.* New York: Bobbs-Merrill, 1970.*

Braithwaite, William S. "Alain Locke's Relationship to the Negro in American Literature." *Phylon* 18 (1957): 166-73.

———. "The Novels of Jessie Fauset." *Opportunity* 12 (1934): 24-28.

Brawley, Benjamin. *The Negro Genius.* New York: Dodd, Mead, 1937.

———. "The Negro Literary Renaissance." *Southern Workman* 56 (1927): 177-80.

Broderick, Francis L. *W.E.B. DuBois: Negro Leader in the Time of Crisis.* Stanford: Stanford University Press, 1959.*

Bronz, Stephen H. *Roots of Racial Consciousness: The 1920's: Three Harlem Renaissance Writers.* New York: Libra Publishers, 1964.*

Brooks, Van Wyck. *The Confident Years, 1885-1915.* New York: Dutton, 1952.

Brown, Sterling A. "A Century of Negro Portraiture in American Literature." *Massachusetts Review* 7 (1966): 73-96.*

———. "The Negro Author and His Publisher." *The Quarterly Review of Higher Education Among Negroes* 9 (July 1941): 140-46.*

———. "Negro Character as Seen by White Authors." *Journal of Negro Education* 2 (1933): 179-203.*

———. *Negro Poetry and Drama* and *The Negro in American Fiction.* 1937. Reprint. New York: Atheneum, 1969.*

———. "Our Literary Audience." *Opportunity* 8 (February 1930): 42-46, 61.*

———. *Southern Road.* New York: Harcourt, Brace & World, 1932.

Butcher, Margaret Just. *The Negro in American Culture.* New York: Knopf, 1956.

Calverton, V.F. "The Advance of Negro Literature." *Opportunity* 4 (February 1926): 54-55.

———, ed. *Anthology of Negro Literature.* New York: Random House, 1929.*

———. *The Liberation of American Literature.* New York: Scribner, 1932.

———. "The Negro's New Belligerent Attitude." *Current History* 30 (September 1929): 1081-88.

———. "The New Negro." *Current History* 23 (February 1926): 694-98.

Cancel, Rafael A. "Male and Female Relationship in Toomer's *Cane.*" *Negro American Literature Forum* 5 (Spring 1971): 25-31.

Chamberlain, John. "The Negro as a Writer." *Bookman,* February 1930, pp. 603-11.

Chapman, Abraham. "The Harlem Renaissance in Literary History." *CLA Journal* 11 (September 1967): 38-58.*

Chesnutt, Charles W. *The Marrow of Tradition.* 1901. Reprint. Ann Arbor: University of Michigan Press, 1969.

———. "Post-bellum, Pre-Harlem." *The Crisis* 38 (1931): 193-94.

———. *The Wife of His Youth and other Stories of the Color Line.* 1899. Reprint. Ann Arbor: University of Michigan Press, 1968.

Christian, Barbara. "Spirit Bloom in Harlem: The Search for a Black Aesthetic During the Harlem Renaissance: The Poetry of Claude McKay, Countee Cullen and Jean Toomer." Ph.D. dissertation, Columbia University, 1970.

Clarke, John Henrik, ed. *Harlem: A Community in Transition*. New York: Citadel, 1964.*

———. "The Origin and Growth of Afro-American Literature." *Negro Digest* 18 (1967): 54-67.

Cleaver, Eldridge. *Soul on Ice*. New York: Dell, 1970.

Coleman, Leon D. "The Contribution of Carl Van Vechten to the Negro Renaissance, 1920-30." Ph.D. dissertation, University of Minnesota, 1969.

College Language Association Journal. March 1971 and March 1972 issues contain four articles each on Jean Toomer's *Cane*. Authors include Bernard W. Bell, Patricia Chase, Bowie Duncan, W. Edward Farrison, Catherine I. Innes, Edward Waldron, Patricia Watkins, and Hargis Westerfield. The June 1974 issue of *CLA Journal* is devoted to Jean Toomer and contains ten articles on his life and work.*

Conroy, Sister Mary James. "Claude McKay: Negro Poet and Novelist." Ph.D. dissertation, University of Notre Dame, 1968.

———. "The Vagabond Motif in the Writings of Claude McKay." *Negro American Literature Forum* 5 (Spring 1971): 15-23.

Cooney, Charles F. "Walter White and the Harlem Renaissance." *Journal of Negro History* 57 (July 1972): 231-40.

Cooper, Wayne F. "Claude McKay and the New Negro of the 1920's." *Phylon* 25 (1964): 297-306.

———, ed. *The Passion of Claude McKay: Selected Poetry and Prose, 1912-1948*. New York: Schocken, 1973.*

Corrigan, Robert A. "Bibliography of Afro-American Fiction, 1853-1970." *Studies in Black Literature* 1 (Summer 1970): 51-86.

Cowley, Malcolm. *Exile's Return*. New York: Viking, 1962.

Crane, Clare Bloodgood. "Alain Locke and the Negro Renaissance." Ph.D. dissertation, University of California, San Diego, 1971.*

Cronon, Edmund David. *Black Moses: The Story of Marcus Garvey and the Universal Negro Improvement Association*. Madison: University of Wisconsin Press, 1965.

Cruse, Harold. *The Crisis of the Negro Intellectual: From its Origins to the Present*. New York: Morrow, 1967.*

———. *Rebellion or Revolution*. New York: Morrow, 1969.

Cullen, Countee. *Color*. New York: Harper and Bros., 1925.

———. Introduction to *Caroling Dusk*. New York: Harper and Bros., 1927.*

———. *On These I Stand: An Anthology of the Best Poems of Countee Cullen*. New York: Harper & Row, 1947.

Cummings, E.E. *The Enormous Room*. New York: Boni & Liveright, 1922.

Davis, Charles T. Review of Nathan Huggins' *Harlem Renaissance*. *American Literature* 55 (March 1973).

Daykin, Walter I. "Social Thought in Negro Novels." *Sociology and Social Research* 19 (1935): 247-52.

Dickinson, Donald C. *A Bio-Bibliography of Langston Hughes, 1902-1967*. Hamden, Conn.: Shoe String, 1967.*

Dillard, Mabel. "Jean Toomer: Herald of Negro Renaissance." Ph.D. dissertation, Ohio University, Athens, 1967.

Dorsey, John T. *The Lion of Judah*. Chicago: Fauche, 1924.

Dreer, Herman. *The Immediate Jewel of His Soul*. St. Louis: The St. Louis Argus Publishing Co., 1919.

DuBois, W.E.B. *Autobiography: A Soliloquy*. New York: International, 1968.*

———. "Criteria of Negro Art." *The Crisis* 33 (October 1926): 290-97.*

———. *Dusk of Dawn: An Essay Toward an Autobiography of a Race Concept*. New York: Harcourt, Brace & World, 1940.

———. *The Quest of the Silver Fleece*. Chicago: McClurg, 1911.

———. *Souls of Black Folk*. 1903. Reprint. New York: Fawcett, 1965.*

——— and Alain Locke. "The Younger Literary Movement." *The Crisis* 27 (1924): 161-63.

Dunbar, Paul Laurence. *The Complete Poems of Paul Laurence Dunbar*. New York: Dodd, Mead, 1913.

———. *The Sport of The Gods*. 1902. Reprint. Miami: Menmosyne, 1969.

———. *The Strength of Gideon and Other Stories*. 1900. Reprint. New York: Arno Press, 1969.

Durham, Frank, ed. Cane: *A Casebook*. Columbus, Ohio: Merrill, 1970.*

Ellison, Ralph. *Shadow and Act*. New York: The New American Library, 1964.*

Emanuel, James A. *Langston Hughes*. New York: Twayne, 1967.*

Engel, Trudie. "The Harlem Renaissance." Master's thesis, University of Wisconsin, Madison, 1959.

Fanon, Frantz. *Black Skin, White Masks: The Experiences of a Black Man in a White World*. New York: Grove, 1967.*

———. *The Wretched of the Earth*. New York: Grove, 1968.*

Feeney, Joseph J. "Greek Tragic Pattern in a Black Novel: Jessie Fauset's *The Chinaberry Tree*." *CLA Journal* 18 (December 1974): 211-15.

Ferguson, Blanche E. *Countee Cullen and the Negro Renaissance*. New York: Dodd, Mead, 1966.

Fisher, Rudolph. "The Caucasian Storms Harlem." *American Mercury* 11 (August 1927): 393-400.

———. *The Conjure Man Dies*. New York: Covici-Friede, 1932.

Franklin, John Hope. *From Slavery to Freedom*. Third edition. New York: Knopf, 1967.*

Frazier, E. Franklin. *Black Bourgeoisie*. Glencoe, Ill.: Free Press, 1957.*

———. "The Garvey Movement." *Opportunity* 4 (1926): 346-48.

Fullwinder, S.P. "Jean Toomer, Lost Generation, or Negro Renaissance?" *Phylon* 27 (1966): 396-403.

———. *The Mind and Mood of Black America: Twentieth Century Thought*. Homewood, Ill.: Dorsey, 1969.*

Gayle, Addison, Jr., ed. *The Black Aesthetic*. New York: Doubleday, 1971.*

———, ed. *Black Expression: Essays by and About Black Americans in the Creative Arts*. New York: Weybright and Talley, 1969.

Genizi, Haim. "V.F. Calverton: A Radical Magazinist for Black Intellectuals, 1920-40." *Journal of Negro History* 57 (July 1972): 241-53.

Gipson, Carolyn R. "Intellectual Dilemmas in the Novels of W.E.B. DuBois." Ph.D. dissertation, University of Michigan, 1971.

Gloster, Hugh M. *Negro Voices in American Fiction*. Chapel Hill: University of North Carolina Press, 1948. Reprint. New York: Russell and Russell, 1965.*

Goede, William J. "Jean Toomer's Ralph Kabnis: Portrait of Negro Artist as Young Man." *Phylon* 30 (1969): 73-85.

Grimké, Angelina. *Rachel: A Play in Three Acts*. Boston: Cornhill, 1920.

Gross, Seymour L. and John Edward Hardy, eds. *Images of the Negro in American Literature*. Chicago: University of Chicago Press, 1966.

Harding, Vincent. "W.E.B. DuBois and the Black Messianic Vision." *Freedomways* 9 (1969): 44-58.

Harth, R.L. "The New Negro." *Independent*, 15 January 1921, pp. 59-60.

The Harvard Advocate. 107 (Number Four, 1974). "Special Issue: Black Odyssey; A Search for Home" contains the proceedings of a symposium on Alain Locke with Nathan Huggins, Harold Cruse, Albert Murray, and Ralph Ellison as panelists.

Hawkins, Hugh. *Booker T. Washington and His Critics: The Problem of Negro Leadership*. Boston: Heath, 1962.

Helbling, Mark. "Claude McKay: Art and Politics." *Negro American Literature Forum* 7 (Summer 1973): 49-52.

Hemenway, Robert, ed. *The Black Novelist*. Columbus, Ohio: Merrill, 1970.*

Henry, Oliver Louis. "Rudolph Fisher: An Evaluation." *The Crisis* 77 (July 1971): 149-54.

Herskovits, Melville J. *The American Negro: A Study in Racial Crossing*. Bloomington: Indiana University Press, 1968.

Heyward, DuBose. *Mamba's Daughters*. New York: Doubleday, 1929.

Hicks, Granville. "An Interview with Wallace Thurman." *Churchman*, 20 April 1927.

Hill, Herbert, ed. *Anger, and Beyond: The Negro Writer in the United States*. New York: Harper & Row, 1968.

Hoffman, Frederick J. *The Twenties*. Revised edition. New York: Free Press, 1962.

Holmes, Eugene C. "Alain LeRoy Locke: A Sketch." *Phylon* 20 (1959): 82-89.

———. "Jean Toomer, Apostle of Beauty." *Opportunity* 3 (1925): 252-54, 260.

Huggins, Nathan I. *Harlem Renaissance*. New York: Oxford University Press, 1971.*

Hughes, Langston. *The Big Sea*. 1940. Reprint. New York: Hill & Wang, 1963.*

———. *Fine Clothes to the Jew*. New York: Knopf, 1927.

———. "Harlem Literati in the Twenties." *Saturday Review*, 22 June 1940, pp. 12-14.

———. *I Wonder as I Wander: An Autobiographical Journey*. 1956. Reprint. New York: Hill & Wang, 1964.

———. *Laughing to Keep from Crying*. New York: Holt, 1952.

———. "Negro Artist and the Racial Mountain." *Nation*, 23 June 1926, pp. 692-94.*

———. *Selected Poems of Langston Hughes*. New York: Knopf, 1965.

———. *Tambourines to Glory*. New York: Day, 1958.

———. "The Twenties: Harlem and its Negritude." *African Forum* 1 (Spring 1966): 11-20.*

———. *The Ways of White Folks*. New York: Knopf, 1934.

———. *The Weary Blues*. New York: Knopf, 1926.

——— and Arna Bontemps. *The Book of Negro Folklore*. New York: Dodd, Mead, 1958.

Hurston, Zora Neale. *Dust Tracks on a Road*. Philadelphia: Lippincott, 1942.

———. *Their Eyes Were Watching God*. Philadelphia: Lippincott, 1937.*

———. "What White Publishers Won't Print." *Negro Digest*, April 1950, pp. 85-89.*

Isaacs, Harold R. *The New World of Negro Americans*. New York: Viking, 1963.*

Jackson, Blyden. "An Essay in Criticism." *Phylon* 11 (1950): 338-43.

———. "Faith without Works in Negro Literature." *Phylon* 12 (1951): 378-88.

———. "A Golden Mean for the Negro Novel." *CLA Journal* 3 (December 1959): 81-87.*

———. "The Negro's Negro in Negro Literature." *Michigan Quarterly Review* 9 (1965): 290-95.

Jacques-Garvey, Amy. *Garvey and Garveyism*. Kingston: A. Jacques-Garvey, 1963.

———, ed. *Philosophy and Opinions of Marcus Garvey*. New York: Atheneum, 1969.*

Jahn, Janheinz. *Neo-African Literature: A History of Black Writing*. Translated by Oliver Coburn and Ursula Lehrburger. New York: Grove, 1969.

Johnson, Charles S. *Ebony and Topaz*. New York: National Urban League, 1927.*

Johnson, Fenton. *Tales of Darkest America*. Chicago: The Favorite Magazine, 1920.

Johnson, James Weldon. *Along the Way*. 1933. Reprint. New York: Da Capo Press, 1973.

———. *Black Manhattan*. New York: Knopf, 1930.*

———, ed. *The Book of American Negro Poetry*. New York: Harcourt, Brace & World, 1922. Reissued 1959.*

———. "The Dilemma of the Negro Author." *American Mercury* 15 (December 1928): 477-81.*

———. *God's Trombones*. New York: Viking, 1927.

———. "Race Prejudice and the Negro Artist." *Harper's Magazine*, November 1928, pp. 769-76.

Jones, Henry Joshua, Jr. *By Sanction of Law*. Boston: B.J. Brimmer Co., 1924.

Jones, LeRoi. [Imamu A. Baraka.] *Home*. New York: Morrow, 1966.

Jung, Carl G. "Your Negroid and Indian Behavior." *Forum* 83 (April 1930): 192-99.

Kaiser, Ernest. "The Crisis of the Negro Intellectual." *Freedomways* 9 (1969): 24-41.

Kallen, Horace. "Alain Locke and Cultural Pluralism." *Journal of Philosophy* 54 (28 February 1957): 119-26.

Kellner, Bruce. *Carl Van Vechten and the Irreverent Decades*. Norman: Oklahoma University Press, 1968.

Kent, George E. *Blackness and the Adventure of Western Culture*. Chicago: Third World, 1972.*

———. "Claude McKay's *Banana Bottom* Reappraised." *CLA Journal* 18 (December 1974): 222-34.*

Kerlin, Robert T. "A Decade of Negro Literature." *Southern Workman* 59 (May 1930): 227-29.

Killens, John O. *Black Man's Burden*. New York: Trident, 1965.

Kornweibel, Theodore, Jr. *No Crystal Stair: Black Life and the "Messenger," 1917-1928*. Westport, Conn.: Greenwood Press, 1975.

Kostelanetz, Richard. "Fiction for a Negro Politics: The Neglected Novels of W.E.B. DuBois." *Xavier University Studies* 7 (1968): 5-39.

Kraft, James. "Jean Toomer's *Cane*." *The Markham Review* 2 (October 1970): 61-63.

Krasney, Michael Jay. "Jean Toomer and the Quest for Consciousness." Ph.D. dissertation, University of Wisconsin, Madison, 1972.

Larson, Charles R. "Three Harlem Novels of the Jazz Age." *Critique* 11 (1969): 66-78.

Lawrence, D.H. *Phoenix: The Posthumous Papers of D.H. Lawrence*. New York: Viking, 1926.

Lester, Julius, ed. *The Seventh Son: The Thought and Writings of W.E.B. DuBois*. 2 vols. New York: Vintage, 1971.*

Levy, Eugene. *James Weldon Johnson: Black Leader, Black Voice*. Chicago: University of Chicago Press, 1973.*

Lieber, Todd. "Design and Movement in *Cane*." *CLA Journal* 13 (September 1969): 35-50.

Liscomb, Harry F. *The Prince of Washington Square: an Up-to-the-Minute Story*. New York: Frederick A. Stokes, 1925.

Locke, Alain. "American Literary Tradition and the Negro." *Modern Quarterly* 3 (1926): 215-22.*

––––––. "Apropos of Africa." *Opportunity* 2 (February 1924): 37-40, 58.

––––––. "Art or Propaganda?" *Harlem* 1 (November 1928): 12.

––––––, ed. *Four Negro Poets*. New York: Simon and Schuster, 1927.

––––––. "The Negro's Contribution to American Art and Literature." *Annals of the American Academy of Political & Social Science* 145 (1928): 234-37.*

––––––, ed. *The New Negro: An Interpretation*. New York: Albert & Charles Boni, 1925. Reprint. New York: Atheneum, 1970.*

–––––– and Montogomery Gregory, eds. *Plays of Negro Life*. New York: Harper & Bros., 1927.

Logan, Rayford, ed. *The New Negro Thirty Years Afterward*. Washington, D.C.: Howard University Press, 1955.*

Loggins, Vernon. *The Negro Author: His Development in America*. New York: Columbia University Press, 1931.

Lomax, Michael L. "Fantasies of Affirmation: the 1920's Novel of Negro Life." *CLA Journal* 16 (December 1972): 232-46.*

Lueders, Edward. *Carl Van Vechten*. New York: Twayne, 1964.

McKay, Claude. *Gingertown*. New York: Harper & Bros., 1932.

––––––. *Harlem: Negro Metropolis*. New York: Dutton, 1940.*

––––––. *Harlem Shadows*. New York: Harcourt, Brace & World, 1922.

––––––. *A Long Way from Home: An Autobiography*. New York: Furman, 1937. Reprint. New York: Harcourt, 1970.*

––––––. "A Negro to His Critics." *New York Herald Tribune Books*, 6 March 1932.*

––––––. "On Becoming a Roman Catholic." *The Epistle* 11 (1945): 21-22.

McPherson, James M., et al. *Blacks in America: Bibliographical Essays*. New York: Doubleday, 1971.*

Malcolm X. *The Autobiography of Malcolm X*. New York: Grove, 1965.*

Margolies, Edward. "The Image of the Primitive in Black Letters." *Midcontinent American Studies Journal* 11 (Fall 1971): 67-77.

———. *Native Sons: A Critical Study of Twentieth Century Negro Authors*. Philadelphia: Lippincott, 1968.*

Meier, August. *Negro Thought in America, 1880-1915: Racial Ideologies in the Age of Booker T. Washington*. Ann Arbor: University of Michigan Press, 1963.*

———. "Some Reflections on the Negro Novel." *CLA Journal* 2 (1959): 168-77.

——— and Elliott M. Rudwick, eds. *From Plantation to Ghetto: An Interpretive History of American Negroes*. New York: Hill & Wang, 1966.

———. *The Making of Black America*. 2 vols. New York: Atheneum, 1969.

Morand, Paul. *New York*. New York: Holt, 1930.

Morris, Lloyd. "The Negro 'Renaissance.'" *Southern Workman* 59 (February 1930): 82-86.

Mulder, Arnold. "Wanted: A Negro Novelist." *Independent* (1924): 341-42.

Munson, Gorham. "The Significance of Jean Toomer." *Opportunity* 3 (1925): 262-63.

Muraskin, William. "An Alienated Elite: Short Stories in *The Crisis*, 1910-1950." *Journal of Black Studies* 1 (1971): 282-305.

O'Daniel, Therman B., ed. *Langston Hughes, Black Genius: A Critical Evaluation*. New York: Morrow, 1971.*

Olsson, Martin. *A Selected Bibliography of Black Literature: The Harlem Renaissance*. Exeter, England: University of Exeter, 1973.

O'Neill, Eugene. *All God's Chillun Got Wings*. New York: Boni & Liveright, 1924.

———. *Emperor Jones*. New York: Boni & Liveright, 1921.

Osofsky, Gilbert. *The Burden of Race: A Documentary History of Negro-White Relations in America*. New York: Harper & Row, 1967.

———. *Harlem: The Making of a Ghetto: Negro New York, 1890-1930*. New York: Harper & Row, 1966.

———. "Symbols of the Jazz Age: The New Negro and Harlem Discovered." *American Quarterly* 17 (1965): 229-36.

Paynter, John H. *Fugitives of the Pearl*. Washington, D.C.: The Associated Publishers, 1930.

Pearson, Ralph L. "Charles S. Johnson: The Urban League Years—A Study of Race Leadership." Ph.D. dissertation, Johns Hopkins University, 1970.

Perry, Margaret. *A Bio-Bibliography of Countee P. Cullen*. Westport, Conn.: Greenwood Press, 1971.

Pickens, William. *The Vengeance of the Gods and Three Other Stories of Real American Color Line*. Philadelphia: A.M.E. Book Concern, 1922.

Redding, Saunders. "The Problems of the Negro Writer." *Massachusetts Review* 6 (1964-65): 57-70.

———. *They Came in Chains: Americans from Africa*. Philadelphia: Lippincott, 1950.

———. *To Make a Poet Black*. Chapel Hill: University of North Carolina Press, 1939.*

Redkey, Edwin S. *Black Exodus: Black Nationalist and Back-to-Africa Movements, 1890-1910*. New Haven: Yale University Press, 1969.

Reimherr, Beulah. "Countee Cullen: A Biographical and Critical Study." Master's thesis, University of Maryland, 1960.

Richardson, Willis, ed. *Plays and Pageants from the Life of the Negro*. Washington, D.C.: Associated Publishers, 1930.

Rive, Richard. "Taos in Harlem: An Interview with Langston Hughes." *Contrast* 14 (1967): 33-39.

Robinson, Anna T. "Race Consciousness and Survival Techniques Depicted in Harlem Renaissance Fiction." Ph.D. dissertation, The Pennsylvania State University, 1973.

Robinson, Armstead L., Craig C. Foster, and Donald H. Ogilvie, eds. *Black Studies in the University: A Symposium*. New Haven: Yale University Press, 1969.

Rosenfeld, Paul. "Jean Toomer" in *Men Seen*. New York: Dial, 1925.

Rubin, Lawrence. "The Castaways: A Story of Three Poets of the Negro Renaissance." Ph.D. dissertation, Columbia University, 1971.

————. "Washington and the Negro Renaissance." *The Crisis* 78 (1971): 79-82.*

Rudwick, Elliot M. *W.E.B. DuBois: A Study in Minority Group Leadership*. Philadelphia: University of Pennsylvania Press, 1961.

Scheiner, Seth M. *Negro Mecca: A History of the Negro in New York City, 1865-1920*. New York: New York University Press, 1965.

Schmuhl, Robert. "Treating The Harlem Human Condition." *Negro History Bulletin* 37 (January 1974): 196-97.

Schuyler, George S. *Black and Conservative: The Autobiography of George S. Schuyler*. New Rochelle, N.Y.: Arlington, 1966.

————. "The Negro-Art Hokum." *Nation*, June 1926, pp. 662-63.*

————. "The Van Vechten Revolution." *Phylon* 11 (1950): 362-68.

Singh, Amritjit. "Misdirected Responses to Bigger Thomas." *Studies in Black Literature* 5 (Summer 1974): 5-8.

Sochen, June, ed. *The Black Man and the American Dream: Negro Aspirations in America, 1900-1930*. Chicago: Quadrangle, 1971.

Spencer, Mary Etta. *The Resentment*. Philadelphia: A.M.E. Book Concern, 1921.

Starkey, Marion L. "Jessie Fauset." *Southern Workman* 61 (May 1932): 217-20.*

Stearns, Harold E., ed. *America Now*. New York: Literary Guild of America, 1938.

Stein, Gertrude. *Three Lives*. New York: Random House, 1936.

Stowe, Harriet Beecher. *Uncle Tom's Cabin*. 1852. Reprint. New York: Harper & Row, 1965.

Thornton, Hortense E. "Sexism as Quagmire: Nella Larsen's *Quicksand*." *CLA Journal* 16 (March 1973): 285-301.*

Thurman, Wallace. "Negro Artists and the Negro." *New Republic*, 31 August 1927, pp. 37-39.

————. "Nephews of Uncle Remus." *Independent*, September 1927, pp. 296-98.

———— and A.L. Furman. *The Interne*. New York: Macauley, 1932.

Toomer, Jean. "Chapters from *Earth Being*." *The Black Scholar* 2 (January 1971): 3-14.

————. *Essentials: Definitions and Aphorisons*. Chicago: Lakeside [private edition], 1931.

———. "Mr. Costyve Duditch." *Dial* 85 (December 1928): 460-76.

———. *The Wayward and the Seeking: A Miscellany of Writings*. Washington, D.C.: Howard University Press, 1975.*

Turner, Darwin T. *Bibliography for Afro-American Writers*. New York: Meredith, 1970. (Goldentree Bibliographies)*

———. *In A Minor Chord: Three Afro-American Writers and Their Search for Identity*. Carbondale: Southern Illinois University Press, 1971.*

———. *"The Negro Novel in America*: In Rebuttal." *CLA Journal* 10 (1966): 122-34.*

Turpin, Waters E. "Four Short Fiction Writers of the Harlem Renaissance." *CLA Journal* 11 (1967): 59-72.

Van Doren, Carl. "The Younger Generation of Negro Writers." *Opportunity* 2 (May 1924): 144-45.

———. "Negro Renaissance." *Century* 111 (March 1926): 635-37.

Van Vechten, Carl. Interview for the Columbia University. *Columbia Oral History*. New York: Columbia University, 1960.

———. *Nigger Heaven*. New York: Knopf, 1926.*

Wade, Melvin and Margaret Wade. "The Black Aesthetic in the Black Novel." *Journal of Black Studies* 2 (June 1972): 391-408.

Wagner, Jean. *Black Poets of the United States: From Paul Laurence Dunbar to Langston Hughes*. Translated by Kenneth Douglas. Urbana: University of Illinois Press, 1973.*

Waldron, Edward E. "Walter White and the Harlem Renaissance: Letters from 1924-1927." *CLA Journal* 16 (June 1973): 438-57.*

Walker, Jim. "Hale Woodruff has Paid His Dues: An Interview." *Black Creation* 3 (Spring 1972): 43-45.

Walrond, Eric. "The New Negro Faces America." *Current History* 17 (February 1923): 786-88.

———. *Tropic Death*. New York: Boni & Liveright, 1926.*

Washington, Booker T. *Up From Slavery*. New York: Doubleday, 1902.

Waters, Ethel. *His Eye is on the Sparrow*. New York: Doubleday, 1951.

Weinberg, Meyer, ed. *W.E.B. DuBois: A Reader*. New York: Harper & Row, 1970.

West, Dorothy. "Elephant's Dance: A Memoir of Wallace Thurman." *Black World* 20 (November 1970): 77-85.*

White, Walter. "Negro Literature." *American Writers on American Literature*. Edited by John Macy. New York: Liveright, 1931, pp. 442-51.

———. *A Man Called White*. New York: Viking, 1948.

Whiteman, Maxwell. *A Century of Fiction by American Negroes, 1853-1952*. Philadelphia: Jacobs, 1955.*

Whitlow, Roger, "The Harlem Renaissance and After: A Checklist of Black Literature of the Twenties and Thirties." *Negro American Literature Forum* 7 (Winter 1973): 143-46.

Williams, Kenny J. *They Also Spoke: An Essay on Negro Literature in America, 1787-1930*. Nashville: Townsend, 1970.

Woodruff, Hale. "My Meeting with Henry O. Tanner." *The Crisis* 77 (January 1970): 7-12.

Wright, Richard. "Blueprint for Negro Writing." *New Challenge* 1 (Fall 1937). A revised version reprinted in John A. Williams and Charles F. Harris, eds., *Amistad 2* (New York: Vintage, 1971), pp. 1-20.*

————. *White Man, Listen!* New York: Doubleday, 1957.

Yellin, Jean Fagan. "An Index of Literary Materials in *The Crisis*, 1910-1934: Articles, Belles Letters and Book Reviews." *CLA Journal* 14 (June 1971): 452-65; and 15 (December 1971): 197-234.*

Young, James Owen. *Black Writers of the Thirties*. Baton Rouge: Louisiana State University Press, 1973.*